SUMMER BASEBALL NATION

SUMMER
BASEBALL
NATION

Nine Days in the Wood Bat Leagues

WILL GEOGHEGAN

University of Nebraska Press | Lincoln

Library of Congress Cataloging-in-Publication Data
Names: Geoghegan, Will author.
Title: Summer baseball nation: nine days in the
wood bat leagues / by Will Geoghegan.
Other titles: Nine days in the wood bat leagues
Description: Lincoln: University of Nebraska Press, 2020
Identifiers: LCCN 2019019162
ISBN 9781496213990 (cloth: alk. paper)
ISBN 9781496219763 (epub)
ISBN 9781496219770 (mobi)
ISBN 9781496219787 (pdf)
Subjects: LCSH: Baseball—
United States.
Classification: LCC GV875.A1 G455 2020 |
DDC 796.357/640973—dc23
LC record available at https://lccn.loc.gov
/2019019162

Set in Scala by Laura Ebbeka.

For Mom and Dad

CONTENTS

PREFACE

The umpire would put both hands up. The batter would step out of the box. The pitcher would turn. The center fielder might wave. And the plea from the press box would come over the speakers. "Would the car in center field please turn off its lights?"

It happened almost every time the Chatham A's played a home game at Veterans Field. At the top of the hill that borders the outfield fence, cars used to be able to pull right up, the baseball vista fitting neatly into the windshield's frame. It was perfect except for the headlights shining right into the eyes of the batter. Longtime Chatham fans knew to flick the lights off when they turned into the makeshift parking lot, but newcomers needed the nudge. If it took them a while to get the hint or if they couldn't find the knob on the rental car, mock cheers would go up when the lights finally flickered out.

My family always found it very funny. Here was a high-level baseball game stopped momentarily by tourists in a Toyota. And nobody was particularly mad about it. Can you imagine a Major Leaguer's reaction? These batters just stepped out, waited, maybe shared a chuckle with the umpire when it took a while. Can you picture the howls about pitch clocks and baseball games being too long? Here, it was just another piece of charm.

As the summers went by and I went from playing pickle beyond the outfield fence to writing about sports for a living, the headlight delays carved out a spot in my baseball memory bank. They seemed so fitting for the Cape Cod Baseball League. The batter stepping out might have been a few years away from big-league at bats. The pitcher could have been throwing in the mid-90s. But the next pitch had to wait—big-time baseball on pause because of its setting. The fans are close enough to pull up a car in center field, the towns small enough to embrace their teams and fill that parking lot every night, everyone so content to play and watch baseball on a long summer night that they share a laugh.

It was the spirit of summer baseball in a pair of headlights.

I've always been taken by that spirit. I grew up in Louisville, Kentucky, but my parents were Boston natives. Every summer they packed up my sister and me, filled every inch of a Chevy Astro van, and road-tripped to Cape Cod. My dad, a baseball diehard, always made sure to grab a Chatham A's schedule from the grocery store. My first game at Veterans Field likely came when I was six months old.

In the early days my sister and I enjoyed the nearby playground and the annual Twinkie Night more than the baseball. Eventually, I watched more pitches than I threw in pickle games. I loved how the fog would roll in, hovering in right field. And when the names I remembered began popping up on Major League rosters, I was hooked.

After graduating from college and moving to Rhode Island, I started a website called RightFieldFog.com that chronicled each summer in the Cape League. It was a labor of love, and I relished every quick drive to catch a game. My now wife joined me on many of the trips. She loved Cape Cod and would grow to love Cape League games, provided I let her keep score.

Around the same time, a good friend and I started to become regulars at Newport Gulls games in Rhode Island. It wasn't quite the Cape League, but the baseball was good and the atmosphere was great. My imagination was captured again. A few years later I got a job at a different newspaper and began covering the Ocean State Waves, the Gulls' New England Collegiate Baseball League

(NECBL) neighbor. Summers in the press box at Old Mountain Field became my favorite part of the sports calendar.

In my Cape League writing and my NECBL coverage, I gradually became more aware of other summer baseball hotbeds. I already knew about the Alaska League and was fascinated by the Midnight Sun Game. There was a team in California that dominated every year. The Northwoods and Coastal Plain Leagues drew enormous crowds.

There was a whole big summer baseball nation out there.

I had long dreamed of writing a book about the Cape League, but a host of great stories about the league had already been told in books and documentaries. Hollywood even got in on the act with *Summer Catch*.

But a book about summer baseball around the country? Nobody had done that. The idea stuck in my head and never left. In 2016, with some vacation time saved up and enough money for flights and a few nights at cheap hotels, I took the plunge. I reached out to teams and was greeted with open arms. Turns out people in summer baseball love summer baseball, too.

I went to Cape Cod and Newport, then flew cross-country to Alaska and California. I went to the shores of Lake Michigan, the nation's capital, and the steamy Virginia peninsula. At every stop I found great stories, surrounded by the same trappings that had always seemed so perfect. Big dreams. Small towns. Warm nights. Through the lens of nine days, a summer picture emerged.

It was a summer I'll always remember, and I was fortunate to have the opportunity to write it all down in these pages.

Soak up a summer night—or pine for one if it's cold—and settle in to the stories of summer baseball nation. If you happen to be in a center field somewhere, don't forget to turn off your headlights.

ACKNOWLEDGMENTS

I must begin by thanking my wife, Meg. She made all of this possible with her faith in a crazy thought, her encouragement, her support, her ideas, her planning skills, her ability to find gluten-free restaurants in every city I went to, and her willingness to pick me up at airports and train stations at all hours. Also, we bought a house and moved at the same time as I traipsed across the country, and you were cool with that. Thank you, babe. I love you.

Thanks also to a furry member of our family. Banjo the cat was by my side while many of these chapters were written. And to Molly—you were just an idea in 2016, but you've been a very snuggly coeditor in 2019.

To my parents, thanks for the constant support and for all the Cape Cod vacations. Without them, there would be no summer baseball fascination. And thanks to my sister, Julie, for not protesting too much when another vacation night was filled with a baseball game. To Julie, John, and Jolie, thanks for letting me sleep on your couch during my travels.

Thanks to Uncle Bill and Auntie Anne for being there and encouraging a young writer. And thanks to the Fraser family—Bob, Heather, Kelley, Mike, and Lilly—for your excitement about the project.

To my friends, especially Dave and Ed, thanks for checking in throughout the process. Dave, your name is first here because of alphabetical order; don't brag about it. Thanks to my then boss Liz

Boardman, whose support of her staff extended to allowing me to juggle my schedule in the summer of 2016.

The project might never have truly gotten off the ground without my agent, Rob Wilson. I'm glad I found an agent who loves baseball. Thank you for taking a chance on an unpublished author and finding a home for *Summer Baseball Nation*. Thanks also to Rob Taylor at the University of Nebraska Press for taking the same chance. And to copyeditor Annette Wenda and Ann Baker, Haley Mendlik, Courtney Ochsner, Anna Weir, and the team at the University of Nebraska Press. I am privileged to join UNP's deep baseball catalog.

I learned a lot from summer baseball writers who have come before me. Christopher Price's *Baseball by the Beach* provided invaluable information about the Cape League, Lew Freedman's *Diamonds in the Rough* did the same on the subject of baseball in Alaska, and Jim Collins's *The Last Best League* has long been an inspiration.

I'm grateful to have had the opportunity to tell the stories of *Summer Baseball Nation*, and grateful to the people who allowed me to tell them. Here was a writer most of them had never met, sending them an email or calling in the middle of winter, proposing an idea out of left field. They responded and welcomed me with open arms: Joe Cavanaugh, Bruce Sherman, Mike Roberts, and Chuck Sturtevant in Cape Cod; Chuck Paiva and Matt Finlayson in Rhode Island; John Lohrke, Don Dennis, and Todd Dennis in Alaska; Bill Pintard, Steve Schuck, Tony Cougoule, and Skyler Ellis in Santa Barbara; Steve Schmitt, Conor Caloia, Rich Marks, Vern Stenman, and Dick Radatz Jr. in the Northwoods League; Mike Barbera, Barry Direnfeld, Antonio Scott, Chris Spera, and Reggie Terry in Washington; and Henry Morgan, Hank Morgan, and Jeffrey Scott in Hampton.

Their players knew even less of the book idea but were more than willing to share their stories. Thanks especially to Cotuit Kettleers Ross Achter, Patrick Dorrian, David Gerics, and Colton Hock.

The world of summer baseball is defined by the people who make it happen, and I'm lucky to have met some of the best.

1 / CAPE COD

JUNE 2, 2016

Ross Achter's first pitch of the summer floats and flutters toward home plate. It almost has the look of a knuckleball, the kind of pitch that dances past flailing hitters and confounds lunging catchers.

The pop of the bat sends the wobbling pitch flying back out like a rocket, whistling over Achter's head, through the infield and into the outfield. Nine of the best college baseball players in the country chase after it. They skid across the damp grass in socks, their spikes left behind by the foul line. Hagen Owenby sprints out of the batter's box, drifts around first base, and belly-flop slides into second, drawing laughter from his teammates that echoes over the makeshift diamond in the right-field corner of Lowell Park.

It's the first day of summer practice, and the Cotuit Kettleers—sixteen-time champions of the famed Cape Cod Baseball League—are playing Wiffle ball.

Every summer in Cotuit starts just like this. It's by design, a plan hatched in the baseball mind of longtime manager Mike Roberts. Before his Kettleers touch the seams of a baseball or squeeze the handle of a wood bat, they grip the familiar perforated white plastic of backyard games and the thin yellow bat of neighborhood home run derbies. The Wiffle-ball game is part icebreaker, part tone setter, part reminder that the game that has brought the best players in college baseball to this place is supposed to be fun. When the fans pack the bleachers and the scouts dust off the radar guns, the guys in uniform may just need that reminder.

Roberts and two of his assistant coaches watch from the edge of the field. It's sixty-two degrees with a blanket of low clouds hovering, a cool day even for Cape Cod, where baseball fans trade beach-day swimsuits for game-night hooded sweatshirts. For players who basked in California sunshine or sweated in Florida humidity on college diamonds all spring, it will take some getting used to.

Whether the players believe it or not amid today's chill, warmer days will be here before they know it. The forecast says it's supposed to be seventy-seven and sunny by the weekend. The sudden arrival of summer will be fitting for a baseball league where the days come as quickly as the radar gun–tracked pitches. Roberts knows the rhythms as well as anyone by now. It feels early for a good long while, until it suddenly feels late. There's almost no middle to a season in the Cape Cod Baseball League, just a beginning and an end.

This season will be Roberts's thirteenth in Cotuit. It starts in eight days. It will be over in sixty-two.

For the players embarking on their season in America's top summer collegiate baseball league, those sixty-two days will be memorable and fleeting, pressure packed and fun, humbling and affirming all at once.

Cape Cod juts into the Atlantic Ocean south of Boston, an idyllic spit of sand that welcomes thousands of tourists to its shores every summer. Baseball players make the same pilgrimage, but their destinations sit just a little ways inland from the scenic beaches.

The Cape Cod Baseball League was once a local circuit like any other, where players hooked on with their hometown teams. The advent of summer collegiate baseball, the league's visionary leaders, a switch to wood bats, and natural geographical advantages— ten franchises within an hour's drive—turned it into the mecca for college baseball players that it is today. Everyone who spends his spring on college diamonds knows the best place to play for the summer. One in seven Major League Baseball players took a step on their journeys here. The ever-growing alumni list includes current big-league stars Kris Bryant, Aaron Judge, and Chris Sale. Before them the fields were home to Craig Biggio and Frank Thomas, who would claim plaques in the Baseball Hall of Fame in Cooperstown thirty years later.

The Cape League is the standard-bearer for a brand of baseball that has put down deep roots in the sprawling landscape of America's pastime. Summer ball evolved from amateur and semipro leagues, as teams tapped into college players as a new source of talent. The now defunct Basin League in South Dakota may have been the forerunner, as it recruited college players to pair with a few rising pros in the 1950s. In the 1960s the Cape League and the Alaska Goldpanners hooked into the college blueprint, and a perfect marriage for players and teams was born.

College baseball was growing, but it was by necessity a spring sport due to the school-year calendar, and the players needed a place to hone their talents in the summer. Amateur leagues back home didn't cut it. The players were often too good, the competition too uneven. Summer leagues could provide a level playing field, and they welcomed the influx of high-level players. Better baseball meant more fans.

Wood bats added a degree of difficulty—college baseball uses aluminum bats and their larger sweet spot—and created a draw for pro scouts, who suddenly had a new lens through which to evaluate players. As big-league organizations expanded their scouting and player-development operations, summer leagues held on to their niche as a proving ground. Major League Baseball began chipping in funding to many of the nonprofit leagues and still does.

The Cape League, which counts 1963 as the beginning of its college-centric modern era, began attracting top talent like Charlie Hough, Carlton Fisk, and Thurman Munson. Twenty-two years later the league embraced wood bats, and the boom really began. In Alaska the Fairbanks-based Goldpanners were founded in 1960 and welcomed Tom Seaver and Dave Winfield in their early years.

The National Collegiate Baseball Federation was founded in 1963, as summer leagues began to spring up across the country and the National Collegiate Athletic Association (NCAA) certified the best of them. The leagues varied in size, talent, infrastructure, and fan support, but the foundations were the same—quality baseball, family fun, a chance to catch a future star, and a stamp on the communities that became home.

Leagues have come and gone, but the model has taken hold, with popularity soaring in the past twenty years. The Northwoods League in the upper Midwest—a pioneer of a new for-profit model—drew a million fans to its ballparks in 2014. With promotions and contests that would make a carnival barker proud, the league's attendance leader in Madison averaged 6,358 fans in 2015.

In the shadow of Cape Cod—as close as seventeen miles in the case of the Wareham Gatemen and the New Bedford Bay Sox—the New England Collegiate Baseball League has grown from a small league in Connecticut to a thirteen-team circuit with a host of franchises across the region that have become institutions in their towns. The Newport Gulls play at historic Cardines Field and draw more than 2,000 fans per game. Every Major League Baseball organization will have a scout watching when the Gulls host the NECBL All-Star Game in July.

There is summer ball in California, where the Santa Barbara Foresters have built an unmatched tradition. Near the nation's capital, the Cal Ripken Collegiate League welcomes top young talent, and its DC Grays are making an impact off the field, too. The Coastal Plain League in the Carolinas and southern Virginia follows the for-profit model and has seen many of its teams fill a void. In Hampton, Virginia, forty years of professional baseball in a charming ballpark built by legendary Dodgers executive Branch Rickey faded into seven years without high-level baseball when its last affiliated Minor League club left town. The Peninsula Pilots brought the game back in 2000. They now welcome in more than 2,000 fans per game and have won two league championships.

In all forty-one leagues across the country will play summer collegiate ball this year. On a given night roughly five hundred teams will be in action. Hundreds of thousands of fans will be watching.

Most college players have taken swings in summer baseball nation—staying with host families, signing autographs, killing time on long bus rides, playing every day. It can be a grind. It's not glamorous. But it's a chance to play the game on long summer nights, with dreams still out there for the taking.

The eighteen players on Cotuit's Wiffle-ball diamond will do it again this summer, in a place where a lot of dreams have already started to come true.

◆ ◆ ◆

"Summer in Cotuit is the Kettleers," Mike Roberts says.

The newest crop lines the dugout bench. With his back to the field, Roberts points to the wooden bleachers that will be packed for every home game. The franchise has won more championships than any team in the Cape Cod Baseball League, and Cotuit—a small village in the town of Barnstable—loves its baseball. The league doesn't charge admission, but the regulars in Cotuit may as well be season-ticket holders. Lawn chairs and seat cushions will be set up in the same spots, game after game. Kettleer baseball has long been woven into the fabric of summertime here. There's the beach and there's baseball.

The unique name of Cotuit's club comes from the village's history. Legend has it that the town was part of a land purchase made by Myles Standish of the Plymouth Colony. The price? A large brass kettle and a hoe.

The year-round population of the village is about twenty-six hundred, a number that swells by more than 50 percent in the summer. The villages of Mashpee, Marstons Mills, and Osterville border Cotuit, and baseball-fan residents there would consider the Kettleers their home team.

The road to Cotuit Center from the Mid-Cape Highway is lined by weathered-shingle cottages, peeks of salt ponds, even a cranberry bog to complete the picture. The quaint village houses a market, a library, a post office, a few shops, and the Kettle Ho Restaurant, where baseball championships are celebrated.

Tucked nearby, less than a mile from the water, is Elizabeth Lowell Park. Like most fields in the Cape League, it's home to high school teams and local clubs outside of the summer months. The Cotuit Athletic Association—the nonprofit group that runs the Kettleers—has made significant upgrades over the years, so much so that even a casual passerby would realize it's not the average high school field.

The recently built press-box building is redbrick mixed with the shingles that are a signature of Cape Cod cottages. Surrounding the press box is a walkway of bricks engraved with the names of supporters and former players. Metal bleachers hug the first base side and the visitors' dugout. The home bleachers were replaced a few years ago by a sturdy wooden grandstand, with its first row perched above the home dugout. Behind the grandstand are bathrooms, a concession stand, and a small courtyard, all designed in the same rustic style. There are no lights. Cotuit plays its games at 5:00 p.m., along with three other Cape League teams. The rest play later in the evenings. Scouts like the schedule, since it gives them the chance to catch two games a night.

In every corner the field is bordered by green, Cotuit's all-natural answer to the green walls and seats that dot Major League ballparks. The outfield seems cut out of the woods, like the cornstalks in Hollywood's *Field of Dreams*. The trees are so essential to the Lowell Park identity that the Cotuit Athletic Association teamed with the Barnstable Land Trust in 2015 to raise $1.8 million for the purchase of nineteen acres in and around the property, a move designed to prevent future development.

The green of the outfield grass is as vibrant as the fully leafed trees. The infield dirt is perfectly manicured. The dugouts are wide and comfortable. It's nothing like the old Minor League stadiums or college facilities that other summer leagues can boast, but inside the chain-link fences—green, of course—Lowell Park and its Cape Cod counterparts are first class. Aerial views of Cotuit serve as a perfect postcard for baseball on Cape Cod. Sailboats dot the shimmering blue water of Cotuit Bay less than a mile south of the first base line.

The setting is reason enough for Cotuit to love its baseball, but the baseball has also been very good. Legendary Kettleers general manager Arnold Mycock—who died at ninety-two in the spring—built his baseball team into a powerhouse as the Cape League entered its modern era. Another Cape team based in Sagamore had started the wave of college talent, and the rest of the teams began to do the same to keep up. Mycock's Kettleers perfected the art of recruiting, going national and bringing in some of the Cape's first stars. Again, other teams fought to keep pace, and the league's status as summer ball's best has its origins in that arms race. Mycock also pushed hard for the switch to wood bats, another milestone in the league's development.

Cotuit won four consecutive championships in the 1960s and matched that feat in the '70s. No franchise in the league has won more titles than the Kettleers' sixteen. They've never gone more than ten years without a championship, sustaining success even as faces change and the league evolves. When they win it all they raise a trophy that's named after their former general manager.

The 2013 club was the most recent to add to the trophy case. Top Indians prospect Bradley Zimmer was one of the team's stars. Cotuit also won in 2010, with Vanderbilt's Michael Yastrzemski—Carl's grandson—in the outfield.

Hundreds of Major Leaguers have called Lowell Park home. Will Clark was a Kettleer in 1983. Joe Girardi and Greg Vaughn played on the 1984 team. Chase Utley patrolled the infield in 1999. Charlie Blackmon and Josh Harrison came through more recently.

Of the future big leaguers who spent summers here, some were players whose star had already risen. The high school ranks provide roughly half the draft pool in a given year, so talent is identified quickly in scouting circles. With the advent of showcases, base-ball's prospect-making machine seems to start humming earlier and earlier every year. Once they reach college ball, stars in turn get funneled to the Cape League.

Others who might have been pigeonholed a level below use a summer on Cape Cod to bump themselves to the top tier. Or they scuffle against the challenge but turn it into a springboard and deliver a big subsequent season for their college club.

For some a summer in Cotuit means everything. In the dugout Roberts tells his newest players about Nick Tropeano, who starred for Cotuit's 2010 championship team. A right-hander from Stony Brook University on Long Island—a place that's a bit off the beaten scouting path—he started the first game of the season and closed out the last game. In between his career got its jump start. He was a fifth-round pick of the Houston Astros the next year and now pitches for the Los Angeles Angels.

Roberts has seen every path at this point. He's a baseball lifer, and he has made Cotuit his summer home since 2004. Before that he was the longtime head coach at the University of North Carolina. He's also an instructor with the Chicago Cubs and a sports man-agement professor at Asbury University. His son, Brian, played in the Cape League for Chatham and went on to be a Major League All-Star with the Baltimore Orioles.

In the dugout Roberts says he and his coaches are here to open doors. The eighteen players in front of him, wearing maroon Ket-tleers gear, with stray colors from hats bearing their college logos, hope it's their turn to step through.

◆ ◆ ◆

David Gerics got pulled over almost as soon as he found out he had a roster spot with the Kettleers. It happened a few days ago in his home state of Connecticut, which has hands-free laws for cell phone conversations while driving. The call came in, and, well, he couldn't exactly decline it. He didn't mind too much when the flashing lights appeared in his rearview mirror, even when the cop wasn't swayed by the story.

This is his chance.

Gerics is here from Pomona College, a small school in Claremont, California, that teams with Pitzer College to form a Division III baseball program. DIII pitchers are not frequent visitors to the Cape Cod Baseball League, but his temporary contract has opened the door just a crack.

College teammate Tanner Nishioka—a native of Hawaii—also signed a temp contract and is in town, five thousand miles from home. He and Gerics were the first to arrive for today's practice. Nishioka walked to home plate on the empty field, wood bat on his shoulder, and stared out at all the green.

Gerics wants to play professional baseball. He stands five-foot-eleven, which doesn't help. But he owns a fastball that touches the low 90s, and that's enough to get a look. He's been successful for Pomona-Pitzer, too. He was 7-0 in the spring and struck out a team-best sixty-three batters.

He felt he was underrecruited out of high school. He couldn't find the right match between baseball program and academic profile and ended up in DIII as a result. It's a chip on his shoulder, one he'll carry all summer if he can hook on and stick around that long.

It's not an easy task. Cape League rosters for one summer are sketched out as soon as the previous summer ends. As with the NCAA system, there's no compensation for players in summer ball, but they sign contracts that serve as commitments to one team and one league. Players inked to full contracts are guaranteed a spot and cannot sign with another Cape League team unless they're released from the contract.

With the NCAA postseason still ongoing, injuries constantly cropping up, and college programs keeping a tight leash on talented young players, much can change from the time a roster is penciled in to the first day of practice. That's where temporary contracts come in. Of the eighteen players in Cotuit today, only seven are on full contracts. The other eleven are here for a chance.

Patrick Dorrian will be trying to stick around, too. He's a junior-college player—another somewhat rare sight in the Cape League—but his path there was unusual. Dorrian was a twelfth-round pick of the Atlanta Braves out of high school in 2015 but ended up not signing.

The dry-erase board at the home-plate end of the dugout is an accidental monument to the possibilities. The lineup from last year's final game endured mostly intact through the cold winter, save for a few smudges. It was from a playoff loss to Hyannis. On the list of available pitchers that day was Justin Dunn, a righty from Boston College who had caught the eyes of scouts in a breakout summer. Seven days from now he'll likely get selected in the first round of the Major League Baseball Draft.

As Roberts runs through the week's schedule, he tells pitchers when they need to arrive and notes that they're welcome to get there early. Dunn did that, he says, and so did Nick Tropeano. Talent matters, of course, but guys who understand how to practice, Roberts says, are the ones who make the big leagues.

Roberts keeps in touch with many of his former players. One Minor League pitcher was in Cotuit just ten days a few summers ago, but he texts Roberts from time to time and has said that his brief stay with the Kettleers was a big part of getting to where he is. To the temp players hearing that now, it's an encouraging message.

Ever curious about the ingredients for success, Roberts has asked former players what he should tell the incoming Kettleers. The key, they've told him, is buying in. Roberts uses Tropeano and Dunn as examples of players who seized the moment, who put the work in and started making their big-league dreams come true. And he could go on. Thirty-six of his former Cotuit players spent time in the Majors last year. Dozens more have been there. Hundreds more have played pro ball.

Ross Achter sits at the far end of the dugout, listening to the names and stories and hearing a familiar one. His cousin A.J. came to Cotuit on a temporary contract, not knowing how long he'd stay or if he'd get bumped.

Temp success stories are well known on the Cape and common enough to provide a spark for each year's crop of underdogs. Perhaps the most famous tale belongs to Charlie Furbush, who came to a Cape League tryout from St. Joseph's College, a Division III school in a small town in Maine. He struck out three batters on nine pitches in the tryout and was immediately signed by the Cape League's Hyannis Mets. Two months later—after he had struck out fifty-five batters in just fifty innings—he was a star. That summer changed everything. Furbush would later transfer to college baseball powerhouse Louisiana State. Later, he was selected in the fourth round of the Major League Baseball Draft. He's now a mainstay in the Seattle Mariners' bullpen.

A. J. Achter arrived in Cotuit from Michigan State in the summer of 2010. He'd been selected late in that year's draft by the Twins, in the forty-sixth round out of fifty, and he came to the Cape to prove he was better than that. With a 1.42 earned run average (ERA) and an all-star nod, he accomplished that mission and signed at the end of the summer. He won a championship with the Kettleers to boot. Four years later he made his Major League debut. He's now in the Angels system, bouncing between Triple A and the big-league club.

Ross hopes that maybe he'll follow in those footsteps. He's on a temporary contract, too, taking it one day at a time, not expecting to be here all summer but relishing the chance to be in town now. He'd always wanted to play in the league, particularly in Cotuit. His cousin isn't the only family connection to the Kettleers. His dad, Roger, played for Cotuit in the 1980s. The legendary general manager Arnold Mycock was his host dad.

Roger remembers his time on the Cape fondly. He and Ross drove to Cotuit together this week, a literal trip down memory lane. Roger watches part of the first practice from the bleachers on the third base side.

Ross is getting his chance after a solid season at the University of Toledo. The six-foot-four left-hander had a 3.10 earned run average, best among the team's starting pitchers, and he led the squad in innings pitched. He's been at Toledo four years already and has his degree, but a medical redshirt in 2013 means he has one more year of baseball eligibility. He'll do graduate work while he finishes out his collegiate career next season.

Achter and his teammates introduce themselves, going down the line from one end of the dugout to the other—name, school, hometown, college, major. Roberts jots it all down on a legal pad. They will go through introductions again, a few at a time, as more players arrive over the next few days.

For now, these are the Cotuit Kettleers.

◆ ◆ ◆

On Route 28, the main street for a half-dozen Cape Cod towns, a small sign points the way down a side street to Kettleers baseball. Stay straight on Route 28, and you'll come within a few long home runs of four more Cape League parks. They're all starting to hum to life this time of year, armies of volunteers and interns prepping them for twenty-two home games apiece.

The ballparks offer picture-perfect scenes and legends that go back decades. At Eldredge Park in Orleans, the only thing resembling a grandstand is a wide grass berm on the first base line, which stretches all the way to the fence. For big games beach chairs and blankets will cover most of the grass—and they'll be there by ten in the morning, as locals claim their favorite spots.

The left-field line hugs Route 28. The outfield runs to a point in center field, where the sign says it's 434 feet from home plate. As the story goes, Frank Thomas blasted a home run right over the sign when he played for Orleans.

Eight miles back on Route 28, past picturesque Pleasant Bay, you'll hit Main Street in Chatham. The lights of Veterans Field—home of the Anglers—loom close behind the shops and restaurants, uplighting the fog for which Chatham is famous. With the town at the elbow of the Cape's arm-shaped peninsula, surrounded by water on two sides, the fog rolls in thick on game nights a few times every year. It infamously ended a historic pitching performance in 2004, when future Major Leaguer Andrew Miller struck out twelve batters in the first four innings of a July game, every out by way of strike three. The fog was getting thicker, though, and umpires called the game before the five innings needed to make it official could be completed. It lives on in Cape League lore, if not in record books.

Harwich's Whitehouse Field sits a few miles west, tucked into the woods like Lowell Park. Brewster's Stony Brook Field—one of the league's newer home parks—shares land with an elementary school.

At McKeon Park in Hyannis, you can hear the ferries blowing their horns as they depart for Nantucket and Martha's Vineyard. Falmouth's Arnie Allen Diamond occupies part of Guv Fuller Field, which hosts Falmouth High School football games in the fall. Former Major Leaguer Darin Erstad—who was also a kicker for the University of Nebraska—used to practice field goals in the afternoons before his games with the Commodores. The Wareham Gatemen play at the same kind of facility at Clem Spillane Field, where goalposts rise above the fence in right-center field. From the Bourne Bridge, the gateway to the Cape that spans the Cape Cod Canal, the lights of the Bourne Braves' Doran Park illuminate the sky like a beacon.

In Yarmouth Red Wilson Field is the Cape League's bandbox. The fence is unmarked by distance signs, but everyone knows it isn't very far. In the decisive game of the league championship series in 2012—a season in which a difference in baseballs at the manufacturer level fostered historic home run totals—the host Yarmouth-Dennis (Y-D) Red Sox and the Wareham Gatemen combined for eight home runs, several that cleared the fence and the trees, landing in the backyards that border the field. Current Chicago Cubs outfielder Kyle Schwarber hit two of them.

Wareham won that slugfest to take the championship. It was a rare finals loss for the Red Sox, who in recent years have put themselves in the company of the Cotuit teams of the 1960s and '70s. Y-D won the 2004 championship and took back-to-back titles in 2006 and 2007, with teams that included future San Francisco Giants All-Star Buster Posey. They lost in the championship series in 2010 and 2012, but have won the last two, both as the No. 3 seed from the league's East Division. Eight of ten teams now make the playoffs—a recent shift in the postseason structure—and Y-D has trademarked the playoff peak, somehow building a dynasty despite new rosters each year, in a league essentially made up of all-star teams.

The 2016 Red Sox will be looking for a three-peat. Cotuit's 2013 squad was the last to win the title before Y-D's current reign. Wareham and Harwich have been champions in recent years. Hyannis and Falmouth have been contenders, both looking to snap long title droughts. Falmouth was right there in 2014, riding the exploits of two-time league batting champ and future first-round pick Kevin Newman to a finals date with Y-D. The Red Sox swept the title series, though, keeping Falmouth from ending the league's longest championship dry spell. It's been since 1980.

The ever-changing cast of players means streaks and droughts aren't well known in dugouts, but a funny thing happens when competitive kids form a bond with their teammates and their fans. The championship dog piles tell the story. The legends of the Cape's ballparks grow by the year.

Hundreds of players are on Cape Cod fields these days, ready to wow scouts and chase a title. After a few days at home when their spring seasons ended, they hit the road, driving in with college teammates from down south or out west. Others flew into the nearby Boston or Providence airports, getting rides from team volunteers over the bridge, arriving in their baseball paradise.

Summer is almost here.

• • •

In Newport, Rhode Island, seventy miles west of Cape Cod, summer hasn't popped. Kids are still in school. Traffic in town and on the Claiborne Pell Bridge isn't bad. The beaches are quiet, and tours of the city's Gilded Age mansions aren't booked up yet.

The New England Collegiate Baseball League's Newport Gulls often mirror the city's summer awakening. With the best tradition in the league—six championships—the Gulls recruit from power-houses like Vanderbilt, Louisville, Stanford, and Oklahoma State. Sometimes, as the college postseason marches on, it takes a while for all the talent to arrive in Newport.

Full roster or not, the team's summer traditions are already in motion this year. In a few days, before they even start the season, the Gulls will dispatch players to local schools as part of the team's "FANatic about Reading" program. The mascot, Gully, sometimes makes an appearance with them. Players read a story or two and encourage kids to do their own reading over the summer. Before they've even taken a swing, they've been introduced to the community.

The reading program started almost a decade ago, another in a long line of steps that have made the Gulls a fixture in the City by the Sea. Newport claims a unique sports scene. The Gulls' home field sits next to America's Cup Avenue, named for the sailing mega-event that's been held here a dozen times. The International Tennis Hall of Fame is close by, with its annual grass-court tournament drawing some of the world's best. Baseball, though, has found a home. The Gulls are often the top story in summer sports pages of the *Newport Daily News*.

Cardines Field is a destination in itself, a tiny park from the same era as Wrigley Field and Fenway Park hemmed into a city block. Its spot in downtown Newport, a short walk from shops, restaurants, and the waterfront, made Gulls games an easy sell, but the team's front-office leaders did a lot of selling all the same.

The outreach efforts—from camp scholarships to fifty-fifty raffles that support community organizations—are mutually beneficial. They've helped the Gulls become part of the city's fabric, and the impact on residents has been real.

The DC Grays don't yet have the following of the Gulls, but a similar community push is a fundamental part of the franchise's mission. Amid a full slate of games in the Cal Ripken Collegiate League, the Grays host clinics and lead the city's chapter of Major League Baseball's RBI program. The acronym stands for Reviving Baseball in Inner Cities, and the Grays are doing their part. Many RBI programs are sponsored by Major League teams. With the Washington Nationals making their own community effort at the Nationals Youth Baseball Academy—a facility the Grays share— the summer-league squad took on the RBI program. The Grays also sponsor the baseball team at a nearby middle school, again seeing a need and stepping up. The middle schoolers represented the Grays in the spring. Their older counterparts are arriving in the nation's capital now, their summer season opening up in five days.

The starting line is quickly approaching in Fairbanks, Alaska, too, but it always feels a little further away. The temperature is in the midfifties today, pretty typical for this time of year. The solace, of course, is that the sky is bright. The sun sets just after midnight these days and rises a few hours later, lending a celebratory mood to the summer months in Fairbanks. Why not run a 5K that starts when the clock strikes 12:00? The Midnight Sun Festival features concerts and vendors and draws thousands to downtown Fairbanks.

The Alaska Goldpanners—the old summer baseball pioneers— have gotten in on the act for a half century. On the summer solstice, the Goldpanners host the Midnight Sun Game. First pitch is at 10:30. Action continues past midnight and through the sunset into twilight. The lights never go on.

It's a new era for the Goldpanners this summer. John Lohrke is taking over as president and general manager, and the team will play a barnstorming schedule outside of the Alaska Baseball

League's usual summer slate. It's part of an effort to make a run at the National Baseball Congress World Series, an August destination for summer collegiate teams and semipro clubs. The Goldpanners have won six World Series championships, more than any other franchise. In the push to go back, they're embracing their roots.

If the Goldpanners make it to the World Series, they'll likely run into another West Coast summer-ball powerhouse. The Santa Barbara Foresters, who play in the California Collegiate League, have won five national championships, just shy of the Goldpanners' total.

This time of year longtime manager Bill Pintard always wonders how his team will look come World Series time. It's not easy to make a forecast. When the Foresters open the season two days from now in San Diego, they'll have four of their projected regulars on the field. Pintard likes some of the players who are in town on temporary contracts, but the team as he drew it up has pieces bound for NCAA regional tournaments from Texas to Oregon. Many of the Foresters' league mates won't have the same problem, but they also won't be able to keep up when Santa Barbara gets to full strength.

It's expected to be another fun summer for the Foresters, with several veteran players returning and waves of new talent lined up. There's also a big opportunity on tap. The Foresters will face Team USA—a summer team featuring the best of the best in college baseball—in an exhibition game at Dodger Stadium in Los Angeles. The next night the Foresters get the all-star squad on their own home field in Santa Barbara.

In the Midwest the Northwoods League season is already in full swing. The league will cram seventy-two games into the summer for each team, significantly more than the forty-four of the Cape League and the NECBL. The league prides itself on providing preparation for professional baseball and all its demands, while offering its teams a wealth of home dates. Off days are limited, and bus rides are long. On opening night the Mankato Moondogs made a four-hundred-mile trip to face the Thunder Bay Border Cats, the league's Canadian franchise.

When they get to the Minors, Northwoods League alumni will be accustomed to the promotions, too. In Kenosha, Wisconsin, halfway between Chicago and Milwaukee, the Kingfish have already staged a stadium-blanket giveaway and an Elvis Bobble-head Night. In a few weeks it'll be the ever-popular Bratwurst Appreciation Night.

The Kingfish are run by Big Top Baseball, a group that owns four Northwoods League franchises in Wisconsin, including league attendance leader Madison. Founder Steve Schmitt considers a home date one part baseball game, another part circus, hence the company name. Teams constantly try new promotions.

July will bring the newest and biggest yet. The Kingfish play their home games at Simmons Field, a mile from Lake Michigan, and they will host the Northwoods League All-Star Game. The night before, they'll take the league's home run–hitting contest to the lake for the Home Run Derby at the Harbor. Players will stand on a pier and launch long balls into the water. The Big Top crew expects a huge crowd.

Creative promotions and big crowds are a staple in the Coastal Plain League, too. In Hampton, Virginia, the Peninsula Pilots just busted out new uniforms, orange pinstripes with a *P* on the chest. They're a nod to old uniforms worn by the Philadelphia Phillies, a franchise whose Carolina League team once called Hampton home. They were one of seven Major League franchises with roots there. War Memorial Stadium saw the likes of Satchel Paige, Johnny Bench, and Bret Boone.

The players who call it home these days are a little further from the bigs, but fans love the baseball all the same. When the franchise was founded, owners held a contest to name it. That approach has yielded scores of odd names for Minor League teams, but the people of Hampton went with an old standby. The Pilots were one of the names that graced the Minor League clubs of the past.

The 2016 Pilots had their season opener rained out last night, summer delayed by a day. They'll try again tonight.

◆ ◆ ◆

The dusty parking lot at Lowell Park offers a sure sign that the home team is back in town. There's a Volvo with New Jersey plates, a Ford Focus from Indiana, a jeep from Virginia. Bumper stickers and window decals tout the baseball teams from Virginia Tech, East Tennessee State, Connecticut. Fans driving by and sneaking a peek know it's that time of year.

The Kettleers have trotted out to left field, where Roberts is showing them a running and stretching routine that he built for his instructional work with the Chicago Cubs. He also talks up the fitness routine he watched Cubs ace Jake Arrieta doing in spring training. He says it in passing, but the name drop doesn't go unnoticed. It's another example of what it takes to get there and another sign that Roberts knows the route.

Behind home plate a crew is setting up a radar-gun system and getting set to calibrate it once practice ends. When the fastballs start popping the mitt next week, the velocity numbers will flash on the scoreboard, giving fans a glimpse of the game that scouts are seeing from their perch behind home plate.

For all the charm wrapped into baseball on Cape Cod, the beach chairs and the no-frills diamonds are only part of what brings in the crowds. The baseball is good, and the talent waves keep coming year after year. The league's slogan is "Where the stars of tomorrow shine tonight." When the 95s and 96s pop up on the radar-gun readings, when sluggers somehow crank those pitches out of the park, stars are born—and remembered.

The job of picking out those stars before they shine in the Cape League falls to general managers and field managers. They lean on years' worth of baseball connections to construct their rosters, building trust with college coaches along the way. Cotuit always seems to bring in a Vanderbilt star or two. North Carolina's aces often spend a summer in Chatham. Falmouth got in on the ground floor as Oregon State became a college baseball powerhouse.

Every franchise on the Cape will welcome in a talented team. That's the baseline. Molding it into a winner is the harder job. It requires an emphasis on player development, with a competitive streak baked in. It requires adjustments on the fly as players come and go. And it takes plenty of luck. The best player in college baseball could hit a slump for a few weeks. That might add up to half a season in the forty-four-game Cape League schedule. A few slumps at the same time can short-circuit a team's summer.

There's no shame in a tough year. Winning is only one piece of a successful summer; sending improved players back to school is at least an equal part of the mission. Winning sure is nice, though. Roberts tells his newest group that the players on the 2010 and 2013 Cotuit championship teams realized they had something special going. They bonded, and amid all the pulls and tugs of home at the end of the summer, they decided that they wanted to stick around and make a run at the championship. The 2013 team even had Bradley Zimmer come back to Cotuit for the final push after he spent most of the summer with Team USA. Winning was important. In summer baseball that's as close as it gets to a magic formula.

For the Kettleers this season the picture has only just begun to come into focus. General manager Bruce Sherman is part travel agent this time of year, arranging airport pickups and shoring up living arrangements with host-family coordinator Terry Moran. He's also scoreboard watching, with future Kettleers dotting NCAA Tournament rosters. Regionals begin this weekend.

Colton Hock should be here soon, and that's good news for the Kettleer pitching staff. His Stanford team didn't qualify for the NCAA Tournament, finishing 31-23 and 15-15 in the Pac-12 Conference.

Hock did his part. A tall and powerfully built right-hander, he excelled at the back end of the bullpen, putting up a 2.15 earned run average in twenty-five games and finishing second on the team with sixty-one strikeouts. He saved four games. It was a major step forward after Hock finished his freshman year with a 5.25 ERA.

Hock hails from Bloomburg, Pennsylvania, and he was back east last summer, too, pitching for the Newport Gulls in the NECBL. He logged innings as a starter and finished with a 3.85 ERA, flashing his potential every time he took the mound.

This summer will be an important one. After another spring in the bullpen, Hock will pitch as a starter for Cotuit, and scouts will be watching closely. There's no question the fastball is big—up to 93 or 94 miles per hour in the spring—but the starting role in the Cape League will offer the chance to showcase secondary pitches and give scouts a look at how well he can maintain his velocity deep into starts. If he profiles as a starter, his stock could soar.

Scouts making their way to Cotuit will also want to see Jeren Kendall, but they'll have to look quickly. A budding star with the Kettleers last summer, the Vanderbilt outfielder had a huge sophomore season—.332 batting average, nine home runs, twenty-eight stolen bases—and was chosen for USA Baseball's collegiate national team. He plans to spend about a week in Cotuit before joining Team USA.

The Kettleers are also waiting on Kendall's Vanderbilt teammate Alonzo Jones Jr., a highly touted freshman. Standouts from Mississippi State, Coastal Carolina, and the University of California (UC) at Santa Barbara are still with their college teams, too, but remain ticketed for Cotuit. A few others on the original roster won't be here.

The juggling of the roster is not easy for the front office and the coaches. For players on temporary contracts, it can be even more nerve-racking. Final rosters are due July 3. Additions and subtractions can still happen, but at that point temps have to be signed to full contracts or released. With dozens of players still on the way and a roster limit, it's a tricky numbers game.

Stretching in left field, David Gerics, Ross Achter, Patrick Dorrian, and their teammates are just happy to have a shot.

"Whether you're with us a day, a week, a month, the whole summer," Roberts says, "I want you to have a good experience here."

◆ ◆ ◆

Ross Achter doesn't actually want to work his way out of this jam. In Kettleers Wiffle ball, you pitch to your own team. Hagen Owenby's first-inning double goes for naught anyway. The next two batters pop out. A line-drive single sets up a play at the plate, and Owenby gets tagged out between third and home.

Pitchers throwing to their own team, like Roberts explained to the players beforehand, makes it a hustle game, and the Kettleers are buying in. The third out is barely made before the team in the field sprints to the plate and a pitcher races to the mound. They want to get a ball in play before the defense is ready.

Roberts likes hustle games. In his book everything is a hustle game. A lifetime in the game has given Roberts a finely tuned set of baseball philosophies. To his Kettleers, he preaches "Backyard Baseball." They play aggressive; they steal bases; they chip in at multiple positions. He wants them to be baseball players, not pitchers or second basemen or outfielders. The philosophy was literally written on the wall of the home dugout at Lowell Park last season, white block letters painted on the green cinder blocks: "Backyard Baseball is a passionate, instinctive, fun game."

Wiffle ball fits right in. The action also gives Roberts hints of how his players move, shows him the kind of athletes he's looking at. He's seen too many players in this generation who are at their best in a batting-cage session or a sixty-yard dash at a showcase. He believes what they really need are the instincts that the backyard game fosters.

To the park today Roberts carried a duffel bag stuffed with the trappings of his particular brand of baseball—small infield training gloves that might not fit a Little Leaguer, a ball that's half black and half white for honing pitch rotation, two books he published about stealing bases, even an old metal cup that he bangs on the dugout railing for emphasis. You can play hard with a cup like that, he says.

Bowlegged with a hitch in his gait, Roberts is a coil of energy in workouts. Up until a few years ago, Wiffle ball wasn't the only tradition for the inaugural summer practice. Roberts would stand at home plate and tell his players to mimic what he was about to do. He would then sprint down the first base line, round the bag, and slide headfirst into second base. One by one the Kettleers would follow, plenty doing it faster, but few sliding quite so perfectly. He could probably still do it today, but he has left that ritual in the past.

Roberts cherishes his place in the Cape League's coaching fraternity. It's a group that doesn't often have openings, and why would it? These are dream jobs. The men who fill them have spent decades in the game. Chatham's John Schiffner became the league's all-time winningest manager last summer. A high school coach in Connecticut in the spring, he fits so perfectly in baseball central casting that the movie *Summer Catch*—a fictionalized account of a summer with the Chatham A's—used his real name. Brian Dennehy played the role.

Bourne's Harvey Shapiro has managed in Falmouth and coached in Wareham and Yarmouth-Dennis. He isn't too far behind Schiffner's career-wins pace. Jeff Trundy has managed Falmouth for more than twenty years.

Scott Pickler is the architect of Y-D's dynasty. He spends the rest of his baseball days in California, where he built Cypress College into a junior-college powerhouse. Orleans manager Kelly Nicholson was a star pitcher and later a coach at Loyola Marymount. His Firebirds have led the league in earned run average in more than half his seasons at the helm.

Steve Englert has managed the Harwich Mariners since 2003, while coaching in the spring with Boston College and Northeastern. Hyannis's Chad Gassman and Brewster's Jamie Shevchik are the next generation, younger coaches from small colleges who get their fill of the big time every summer.

The newest coach in the league isn't exactly a newbie. Jerry Weinstein is in his first summer with the Wareham Gatemen. His most recent stop before that was with the Colorado Rockies organization. In 1992 he was a coach on the U.S. Olympic Team.

Roberts first came to Cape Cod in 1984, when he managed Wareham to a runner-up finish. After his time with the University of North Carolina came to an end, Roberts returned to Wareham in 2000. Four years later he took over in Cotuit.

His coaching style may not be too different from what his players are used to, but his philosophies and eccentricities make his presence unique. Before he sent the players to left field for their stretching session, he pulled out his phone and a wireless speaker and played a song called "Hey, Hey, Cotuit"—a song he wrote himself.

"I do different things for fun," he explains.

He had the song professionally recorded by a local musician. It has the feel of "Go Cubs Go," the anthem that blasts after Cubs wins at Wrigley Field. A few heads bobbed and foots tapped as the song played. At the line "Dock your skiff and take a walk," Roberts yelled, "The water's right there!"

"No comments," he said after the final note. "We love it, whether you do or not."

It might be a little corny, but the song reflects Roberts's love for the summer baseball home he's found in Cotuit. His trip back is especially welcome this year. In February his wife, Nancy, passed away suddenly. They used to spend the summers here together, roots firmly in the community.

As he reconnects with the town, hugs have been frequent. Roberts touches on it briefly with his players, saying he's still trying to find his usual passion. He might be a little quieter this summer, but he promises he'll give the team everything he has. The rhythms of baseball will be a good thing.

◆ ◆ ◆

The Kettleers were supposed to play six innings of Wiffle ball today. They get to nine before someone asks what inning it is. They figure it's the eighth, maybe the seventh—and keep playing. They've loosened up. Baseball chatter has crept in. They finally call it a day when Ross Achter scoops a ground ball and dives to get a force out at second.

Mike Roberts gathers his players together and explains the method to his madness. That's the way they grew up playing the game, he says, and unorganized play can improve instincts. It's also a nudge toward simply enjoying the game, something that can easily get lost as a baseball career blossoms and as a summer of baseball dreams begins.

"It's a kid's game," Roberts says. "And that never changes."

Eighteen of the best college baseball players in the country, still shoeless, are listening.

2 / NEWPORT

Mark Powell hears his name crackle through the speakers at Cardines Field and bounces out of the dugout. He heads for shortstop, two Little Leaguers trailing in his footsteps. They stop when they reach the infield dirt, and Powell gives them fist bumps. The three of them set up side by side as the rest of the lineup is introduced, each player accompanied by a Little Leaguer or two. The team photographer snaps photos of the trios and duos. Powell's charges chat with him and then stand at attention for the national anthem, watching the flag and stealing a glance or two at the player they're shoulder to hip with.

He is not thinking about it now—not with first pitch looming, not with the season in full swing—but Powell is tracing footsteps, too. He used to be a Little Leaguer who filled his summer nights with baseball in Newport, Rhode Island, watching heroes who weren't that much older than him but who seemed it, chasing foul balls, loading up on snacks at the concession stand. He grew up in neighboring Middletown, and his family hosted players from the New England Collegiate Baseball League's Newport Gulls when he was growing up.

The memories from all those years spin together into one picture, one long summer night like this one—fading sun, a sea breeze making it a tad bit chilly, good baseball on the field. When the national anthem concludes, Powell sends his Little Leaguers back toward the stands, where they'll make their own set of memories, and gets in position to field warm-up ground balls at shortstop. He scrapes the ground with his spikes in between tosses, smoothing out the dirt on a field that has always felt like home. His white uniform gleams. He has become his baseball role models—a Newport Gull for the summer.

In the spring Powell finished his junior year at Bucknell University, playing well enough for the Division I Bison to earn a temporary contract with his hometown team. Though he's close with president and general manager Chuck Paiva—his former coach in Little League and at Middletown High School—the gig with the Gulls isn't just some gift. He has started at shortstop every game so far, and he believes he can earn his keep. He had two hits on opening night.   .

"We try to put a local kid on the team if we can," Paiva says. "But what we won't do is put a local kid on the team who can't compete on this level."

That Powell dreamed of being a Gull is a testament to the minor baseball miracle that's happened here. For kids to imagine and dream from the stands, to picture themselves in the players they seek autographs from, there has to be a little magic to capture the imagination.

Fifteen years ago the Gulls started to create it.

◆ ◆ ◆

When Mark Powell was born the stage for so many of his baseball memories was just an old field with a long history and the hint of an uncertain future. A high-quality amateur league—the historic Sunset League, known as the oldest amateur circuit in the country— called Cardines Field home and still does, but amateur leagues are a different animal when it comes to fan support, when it comes to sparking the imagination. The Gulls, at the time, did not exist. And with tourism on the rise in Newport, proposals to turn the historic field into a much-needed parking lot had been floated.

When Powell was picking up a bat and making his way onto a T-ball field, the team he would grow up cheering for was founded as the Rhode Island Gulls in Cranston, a suburb of eighty thousand situated just south of Providence and thirty miles north of Newport. Home was Cranston Stadium, a nice-enough park, but not a draw in and of itself. Nestled in a neighborhood, and stocked with a full schedule of Babe Ruth, high school, legion, and amateur ball, the stadium is not a place that inspires baseball curiosity—people don't drive by and wonder who's playing. Like a number of teams in the early days of the New England Collegiate Baseball League, the Rhode Island Gulls barely registered a blip on their local sports radar.

Down Interstate 95 and Rhode Island Route 4, across the Jamestown Verrazzano Bridge and the Claiborne Pell Bridge, there was baseball potential, something like a raw power hitter who just needed a chance to get to the plate. The owner of the Cranston-based Gulls saw the possibilities and approached the city of Newport about moving south. The mayor was interested and told him to talk to Chuck Paiva.

At the time Paiva was the president of the Sunset League and was well known in the community as a baseball guy. He got together with the owner and the commissioner of the NECBL for lunch in November 2000, and he sketched out the area's baseball landscape for them. They wasted little time asking him if he'd be interested in serving as the general manager.

"Originally, I thought, 'Oh, this'll be interesting,'" Paiva recalls. "'It's only a two- or three-month gig. It's not too big of a commitment. This will be fun.' I decided to try it."

It was a perfect match, and the two- or three-month gig soon turned into much more. A new owner took over after the team's first season in Newport, in 2001. He asked Paiva to stay on as general manager. Paiva agreed on the condition that he would then get the chance to take over ownership.

The next year Paiva and friends Chris Patsos, Ron Westmoreland, Mark Horan, and Greg Fater teamed up to form an ownership

group and purchased the team. They were baseball people—former
players, coaches, league presidents. Patsos spent a summer playing
for the Wareham Gatemen of the Cape Cod Baseball League in the
1980s. Westmoreland's son Ryan would go on to be a fifth-round
draft pick of the Boston Red Sox.

They were local baseball people, too, with roots in the community and a desire to sow a baseball team's seeds in the same ground.

◆ ◆ ◆

The Gulls were a winner immediately in Newport, bringing home
the franchise's first NECBL title in 2001, their first year in town.
They made it back-to-back crowns in 2002 and have won four
more championships since. As the NECBL has expanded and raised
its profile, the Gulls have kept themselves a step ahead of their
league mates, attracting top talent by building trust with big-time
programs and selling the chance for players to spend a summer in
Newport. This year's team features players from powerhouses like
the University of California at Los Angeles (UCLA), Oklahoma State,
Clemson, and Louisville, the same types of programs that populate
Cape Cod Baseball League rosters.

The list of Newport alumni who have played professional baseball
gets longer by the year. The total is up around two hundred now.
There are pipelines from Stanford and Vanderbilt, with young stars
from those schools often getting a ticket to Newport for their first
taste of summer collegiate ball. The Cardinal's Mark Appel came
to Cardines Field after his freshman year in 2010 and pitched to a
1.87 ERA with the Gulls. Three years later he was the No. 1 overall
pick in the Major League Baseball Draft.

Success on the field has been accompanied by success in the
stands. The Gulls annually lead the league in attendance, with
better than 2,000 fans a night filling every nook and cranny of the
cozy ballpark. Last season 46,290 people watched the Gulls over
the course of the summer.

"We introduced baseball to Newport again," Paiva says. "Our attendance started out lower in our first year, but by the end of the season, we had a pretty good crowd at our championship series. We created the excitement around having a team in Newport."

The fans come for the baseball and the place and the fun, but they also come because the Gulls are theirs. Newport and its neighboring towns on Aquidneck Island are places with a strong sense of themselves. Before the Newport Bridge was completed in 1969, Aquidneck Island was cut off from most of the Rhode Island mainland despite close proximity to it. Access is easier now, but the island mentality remains. And the Gulls have become the island's team.

It didn't happen overnight, but the steady outreach efforts put the name, the players, and the product into the area's consciousness. Tonight is Tiverton Little League Night at the park. The town lies just off Aquidneck Island to the east, bordering Massachusetts, and dozens of players and parents have made the trek to the field. Announcements between innings will include information on fall-ball signups, and volunteers from the league will sell fifty-fifty raffle tickets during the game. A portion of the raffle proceeds will go to the league. In the coming weeks other organizations and community groups will be part of the same routine, from local churches to the YMCA.

"Our goal, our focus, from the beginning was being a community-based team—contributing back to the community," Paiva says. "We've contributed over a million dollars back to the local community with scholarships, donations, raffles, tickets. We've supported people who might need help, people with cancer, ALS [amyotrophic lateral sclerosis]. We use the team as a vehicle to help this community and give back."

Each group that's welcomed to a game brings a new set of fans. They find spots among the regulars and the host families and the tourists. Some years there's even a boisterous contingent of Irish fans stationed high in the third-base stands. A group of them started attending Gulls games while working in the hospitality industry for the summer, and their ranks grew to resemble a soccer fan club back home. They called themselves the Newport Gulls Irish Army.

The Gulls are such a model that they have an imitator across the bridge. The team in town for tonight's game at Cardines Field is the Ocean State Waves. Founded in 2013, their home is in Wakefield, a village in southern Rhode Island tucked between the beaches of Narragansett and the campus of the University of Rhode Island. It's a short drive to Newport—across the mouth of Narragansett Bay, with two bridges and a stop in Jamestown in between. The teams play one another six times in the regular season, with their budding rivalry dubbed the Pell Bridge Series, in honor of the span that connects them.

Off the field it's a friendly rivalry. Matt Finlayson, the president and general manager of the Waves, stops by Chuck Paiva's office a few times a month, bearing coffee and summer baseball conversation. This year the teams are honoring each other's season ticket passes for the rivalry games.

Finlayson hopes the Waves can someday build the following of the Gulls, but it's a high bar. These days a summer in Newport wouldn't be the quite the same without its baseball team.

◆ ◆ ◆

The newest Gull arrives forty minutes before game time. He's permitted to be a little tardy since he's coming straight from the airport, off a long flight from his home in California. Jake Brodt, a first baseman from Santa Clara, carries a duffel bag and a wood bat into Cardines Field, the luggage of a baseball player. Teammates and coaches introduce themselves in the dugout, Chuck Paiva the last in the receiving line. He shows Brodt to a room underneath the stands where he can change into uniform.

Brodt won't start tonight's game—it was a long journey—but he might play. The roster is a little thin, as it often is for the Gulls this time of year. For the season opener four days ago, they had only three pitchers in town. Like Brodt, catcher Ben Breazeale from Wake Forest just got here today. Others are on the way, delayed by long seasons and tournament runs by their college squads.

It can make for an uneven start. The Gulls dropped their season opener to the Ocean State Waves by a 6–4 score. The Schooners from nearby Mystic, Connecticut, beat them 12–11 in game two. Newport moved into the win column yesterday, returning the favor to the Schooners with an 8–1 win.

Scuffling starts rarely last. From a 2-2 record last year, the Gulls reeled off eight wins in a row. Talent influxes help, but there's also an identity at work. Success has set a high standard that trickles down from Paiva to the coaching staff and then catches on with the players, even though they're just learning of it.

When the Gulls last won the league championship in 2014, they finished six games out of first place and needed the full three games to win their first two playoff series. It all clicked in the finals, and they swept to the title.

The Gulls have won at least twenty-five games for fifteen years running—every year they've called Newport home—leaving them on the positive side of the forty-plus game ledger each season. The Cardines Field faithful might not know what to do with a losing team.

To get to sixteen straight years and chase banner number seven, the Gulls will lean on their usual mix of young talent from power conference schools and veterans from midmajors. Stephen Scott is in town from Vanderbilt and champing at the bit after starting just one game for the Commodores this spring. Devin Mann, who hit .310 as a freshman for a top-five Louisville team, is due to arrive soon. Adam Wolf is coming from Louisville, too, where he pitched out of the bullpen and flashed potential with his big left arm and six-foot-six frame. Southpaw Kris Bubic had a 3.26 earned run average as a freshman at Stanford.

Though only a year older than the likes of Scott, Mann, Wolf, and Bubic, players like Jake Brodt and Wright State's Gabe Snyder amount to veterans for the purposes of summer ball. Soon-to-be juniors are eligible for the Major League Draft a year from now. If they get chosen or sign a free-agent deal, their next summer will be spent in the Minor Leagues.

The Gulls also have a true veteran in Hunter Schryver, a Villanova left-handed pitcher who's set for his third summer in the league. He pitched for the Waves after his freshman year before heading across the bridge to join the Gulls last year. He'll make his 2016 debut in a few days.

On the mound tonight is Andrew Gist, a lefty from the University of Georgia. He's coming off his first year with the Bulldogs after transferring in from a junior college.

Mark Powell is batting in the sixth spot and manning shortstop. He's 5-for-12 on the young season, making an early bid for a full-time gig even when more talent arrives.

Newport was shut out for four innings when it played the Waves a few days ago on opening night and never quite got back into the game. No matter the standards, off nights happen, especially when the roster remains a work in progress.

The NECBL's top franchise will keep pushing.

◆ ◆ ◆

At 6:38 p.m., three minutes after Andrew Gist fires in a strike on the game's first pitch, Chuck Paiva finally sits down.

He's been at Cardines Field for most of the afternoon, making the rounds with his coaches, watching batting practice swings, chatting with players. He made sure everyone got their blue and orange batting gloves so they'll fit in with the Gulls' color scheme. He checked in with Matt Finlayson of the Waves and talked high school ball with Waves coaches Jim Sauro and Pete Clays, who pull double duty this time of year while their South Kingstown High School team is still alive in the playoffs.

Paiva steered the batting cage to its spot in the bullpen, greeted Tiverton Little League parents, and caught up with some of his current high school players, checking in about legion ball and summer schedules. One of them, Mark Powell's brother, is lined up to be the Gulls' bullpen catcher.

When game time approached Paiva hopped on the mic and played emcee for ceremonial first pitches, saluting the Tiverton Little League outgoing president for her years of service. He shared a hug with former Gull Pat Light, now a pitcher with the Boston Red Sox who's in town for the night.

In the first row of the stands behind home plate, Paiva settles into his usual spot, leather briefcase bag beside him on the dark-green wooden bench. Before the clock ticks to 6:39, he's back up, leaning a few rows behind him to mention something to his sound guy. Then he's saying hello to fans passing by his spot.

This is baseball season for Paiva. He's in constant motion, shepherding every part of the Gulls experience along. Around the country, it's people like him who have made summer ball.

"You need a Chuck," Finlayson says.

Paiva has spent many a summer at Cardines Field. The diamond is what brought him to town in the first place.

He grew up in Naugatuck, Connecticut, north of New Haven. He was a pitcher for Naugatuck High School, the driving force in a storybook run to the state championship in the late 1970s. College ball took Paiva to the warm and sunny fields of Florida, where he starred for Eckerd College in St. Petersburg, a perennial powerhouse in the NCAA Division II ranks.

In the summer of 1980, after his junior season at Eckerd, Paiva returned to New England to get some innings in amateur ball before returning to school. His destination? The Sunset League in Newport.

The city became a piece of his baseball journey, and it would soon become home. When his playing career ended Paiva joined his alma mater's staff as the pitching coach. He returned to Newport in 1986 to become the pitching coach for the baseball team at Salve Regina University. He stayed in the post for several years, but being a Division III assistant coach was a heavy lift financially.

Paiva left Salve Regina but not Newport, settling on Aquidneck Island with his young family. He ended up working in the commercial bait industry and is now president of Newport-based International Marine Industries.

Along the way he kept a hand in the game, running a baseball school for local kids and returning to the Sunset League as a coach and later as the league president. Those baseball side jobs ultimately led him to become the man the Gulls needed to talk to when they wanted to make their move.

He and his partners have run the team ever since taking over in 2003. It's their baby. Chris Patsos is the vice president. Greg Fater is a vice president for legal, Mark Horan a vice president for sponsorships. Ron Westmoreland is the treasurer.

They have built a well-oiled machine. The team wins year in and year out. The fans fill the ballpark. The front office has grown to include a director of baseball operations, a director of broadcasting, and an army of interns and volunteers.

"I saw the potential in the first year," Paiva says. "In the second year, it got better. And then once we took over, every year got better and better with our attendance, with how we ran the team and all the little details that are involved in running a baseball team. We kept improving the way we did things."

It's a labor of love, but the work never ends.

At 6:43, five minutes after he sat down, Paiva hears feedback on a wireless mic used for promotions on the field. He heads down to check it out.

♦ ♦ ♦

In the same way designers of the new generation of Major League Baseball stadiums drew inspiration from the game's old cathedrals like Wrigley Field and Fenway Park, an architect tasked with drafting blueprints for the perfect summer collegiate league ballpark would probably start at Bernardo Cardines Field.

According to the history books, they've been playing baseball here since the late 1800s, when employees of a local railroad turned a muddy basin that previously supplied water for steam locomotives into the beginnings of a diamond. The George S. Donnelly Sunset League began play in 1919. The city bought the field in 1936, and the Works Progress Administration fashioned the grandstands that turned the diamond into a ballpark.

The third base line hugs America's Cup Avenue, the main route into downtown Newport. A stone building with bathrooms and storage closets doubles as the base of one grandstand. Farther down the line, bordering left field, sits a wooden grandstand painted dark green, with arches on the street-side facade and a picket-fence line on the top row.

The same green adorns the roofed grandstand behind home plate and the bleachers down the first base line, bordering Marlborough Street. One more set of wooden stands farther down is angled toward home plate.

The Gulls utilize every inch, finding unique ways to house the machinery of their baseball operation. There isn't enough space on the third base side of the field for anything but foul territory, so the tiny home and visitor dugouts sit side by side on the first base line. Coaches camp out on folding chairs outside the dugouts rather than taking up space on the ten-foot benches.

The cameras that film for live webcasts are situated on top of the dugouts, with the interns manning them, climbing a ladder to get up and ducking behind batting-practice screens for protection. The top two rows of the home-plate bleachers double as a press box.

The field's borders are defined by a city block, but not even a full one. Beyond the outfield fences the park shares the block with houses, backyards, a playground, and a parking lot. A warehouse—with the field's scoreboard on its facade—forms part of the right-field foul line, and a bar nudges into foul ground. At the Mudville Pub you can grab a table and watch the action from a fenced-off porch built onto the edge of the grass. The apartment above the pub has a deck overlooking the field, à la Wrigley Field's rooftops.

The hemming of the field into the neighborhood created odd angles in the outfield. The high chain-link fence takes a normal-enough path in left and left-center. On its turn to right-center, it hits a detour, jutting out for twenty feet and then straight back in toward the right-field line. It comes to a point—perfect for shallow home runs—before returning to the usual route in right field.

The quirks add to the character. No two baseball fields are the same, and Cardines is more one of a kind than most. Like Wrigley Field and Fenway Park, it's a draw for fans in its own right. And even a perfect replica couldn't match its spot in Newport. Sailboat masts are visible from the top row of the bleachers, the waters of Newport Harbor less than a mile away. It's a short walk to the restaurants and shops of Thames Street and the waterfront views of Bannister's Wharf. The Gilded Age mansions on Bellevue Avenue that once made Newport "America's First Resort" and the Cliff Walk with its stunning views of the Atlantic are just a few miles away.

The city buzzes on summer nights, traffic backed up on the bridge and parking hard to come by. On twenty-two of those nights every summer, the Gulls play at home, with a banner touting "Game Tonight" draped off the home-plate grandstand. You can't miss it. At the ticket window a sign reads, "Come in. Relax. Enjoy the game." Each of those twenty-two nights, thousands of people do.

◆ ◆ ◆

The Ocean State Waves may be the little brother in their rivalry with the Gulls, but they're getting the upper hand again tonight, just as they did in the first meeting between the teams. After a scoreless first inning, Ocean State's Ryan Blanton leads off the second inning by lifting a home run just over the towering fence. The quirks of Cardines Field often give to the home team in the form of a well-played carom or a favorite gap target for a lefty power hitter, but sometimes they take away. Blanton's home run went out over the shallow part of center field, where the fence cuts in. A walk and three singles plate two more runs to give the Waves a 3–0 lead.

Jordan Fulbright, the Waves' starter from North Carolina–Asheville, makes quick work of the Gulls after getting staked to the early lead. With two outs in the bottom of the second, Mark Powell digs into the left-handed batter's box, aiming to take a chunk out of Fulbright's momentum. He gets ahead in the count two balls and no strikes and whips his smooth swing through the zone on the next pitch. His line drive is the hardest hit ball of the night so far, but it goes straight to the right fielder and the inning comes to an end.

Gulls staffers descend on the field in the half-inning break and bring two young fans with them. They'll play a game called laundry toss, where they hoist bags of clothes into baskets manned by mascots Gully and Gully Jr. Contests and promotions like this one fill every spare minute. The race around the bases is always a hit. The giant doughnut-eating contest gets the crowd going, too. Every kid in the place takes advantage of the chance to run across left field and high-five Gully in center during one of the late-inning breaks. And a night at Cardines Field isn't complete without the sound effect of glass shattering anytime a foul ball leaves the yard and the announcer quickly chiming in, "Better call Newport Glass."

The laundry starts flying on the field, but Chuck Paiva isn't in on the fun this time. From his spot behind home plate, his eyes are trained on the dugout, where Gulls catcher Charlie Carpenter is being tended to on the bench. The six-foot-six 230-pounder from South Carolina Upstate tweaked a muscle in his leg while running out a ground ball in the bottom of the second inning. Now, with the top of the third about to start, he's not coming out. Ben Breazeale— one of the players who just arrived today—will have to slide from designated hitter to the catcher's spot.

A move by the designated hitter into the field also means the pitcher has to hit, but Paiva is more worried about the long-term complications than any impact on tonight's game. An inning later Paiva makes his way to the field and checks in with Carpenter, the coaches, and the training staff. The early impression is that it's a hamstring issue. Like any injury requiring significant rest, it's a tricky one for summer ball and its short seasons. If it looks like the injury is going to take a month to heal, a player will often head home. There's little incentive to rush back in summer ball, and watchful college coaches want their players back healthy.

Carpenter's prognosis won't be clear for a day or two, but with only one catcher on the roster, Paiva can't be overly patient. Back in his seat in the grandstand behind home plate, he pulls his cell phone out of his pocket. Earlier today he had a college coach from a major program texting him, looking to find a spot for a young catcher. He also got a call from a St. John's University player who had taken it upon himself to check in with the Gulls and see if there were any opportunities. Now it looks like there might be.

It's a fact of life in summer ball that teams are always adjusting on the fly. Injuries or pitch-count limits create openings. And there are always players looking for a place to play, whether it's a case of other plans falling through, an injury forcing some time off after the spring, or summer school classes keeping a player on campus for a few weeks. Ever year a host of players who start on temporary contracts in the Cape Cod Baseball League end up spending most of their summers in the NECBL, with teams like Newport and Ocean State. Often, they make the trip back to where they started if their NECBL teams don't make the playoffs and a Cape League squad is in need of reinforcements.

Paiva navigates to the college team websites for his potential new recruits and quickly scrolls through statistics. The young catcher received only six at bats in the spring season, buried on the depth chart behind veteran players. He has a good pedigree and probably a lot of talent, but learning on the job isn't easy in this league, especially for hitters. Most years the league leaderboards in batting average, home runs, and runs batted in (RBI) are packed with players heading into their junior or senior season.

Paiva sees something different in the St. John's box scores. Troy Dixon just completed his third season with the Red Storm and handled the bulk of the catching duties. He started fifty games in the spring and earned all-conference honors for the second year in a row after batting .253 and ranking third on the team in RBI. As a junior he was draft eligible, but forty rounds went by without his name popping up.

The Gulls have had players from St. John's before. They're usually a tough breed and a good fit in Newport.

Paiva closes out the stats page and calls Dixon. "We might need a catcher," Paiva says. "Can you get here quick?"

The answer is yes. Paiva tells Dixon to hold tight. He'll call later tonight and let him know for sure.

◆ ◆ ◆

With Charlie Carpenter sidelined for the rest of the game, pitcher Andrew Gist digs into the batter's box to lead off the fifth inning. He puts a decent swing on the first pitch he sees but grounds out. Two pitches later Shane Matheny flies out to left field. Mark Powell shows a little more patience, working the count to three balls and a strike, but he grounds out, too. Jordan Fulbright is cruising, perfect through five innings.

Waves president Matt Finlayson watches the dominant start from the edge of the visitors' dugout. In the tight spaces of Cardines Field, he's right on top of the action. At home games Finlayson typically bounces around like Paiva, from the field to the concession stand to the press box, chatting with fans and sponsors. On the road he gets a chance to watch a little more baseball.

This is year four for the Ocean State franchise. Finlayson has been around since the beginning. He grew up in Higganum, Connecticut, and played baseball not far from Cardines Field at Salve Regina University, where Chuck Paiva once coached.

Chasing a career in sports, Finlayson was working as the director of baseball operations at the University of Rhode Island when plans were drawn up to create the Waves. Tabbed as the general manager for the team's first summer, Finlayson worked closely with founder Jeff Sweenor as the foundation was laid. When Sweenor, a local builder, stepped away after two seasons, ownership was transferred to Finlayson, who was more than happy to embrace the challenge. Working largely as a one-man show in his first year at the helm, Finlayson recruited players, sold advertising space at the field, and focused on building community relationships. One day last winter he even fixed a leaky pipe in the office space the franchise rented.

Finlayson has leaned on Paiva throughout. That was kind of the plan, after all. When initial talks were underway about getting the Waves off the ground, the franchise leadership team was eyeing a spot in the Futures League, a new entry into the summer base-ball ranks with the same New England footprint as the NECBL. A meeting with Paiva made it clear that the Gulls would welcome an in-state foe in the NECBL. In fact, Paiva loved the idea, believing there was plenty of room for two Rhode Island teams and that it could even be mutually beneficial. At one time in the early 2000s there had been two teams from Rhode Island in the league, with the Riverpoint Royals in West Warwick playing alongside the Gulls. The league agreed that another foray into Rhode Island made sense, and the course was charted.

The relationship between the two franchise leaders grew from there. Finlayson tries to follow the Gulls' blueprint for community outreach. Waves players read at elementary schools, too. Baseball camps fill the summer calendar. This year the franchise is sponsoring an Amateur Athletic Union (AAU) tournament for youth teams from around the region. A youth travel program shares the Waves name.

As with the Gulls—and every NECBL team—building a following takes time. And the Waves don't have the infrastructure that helped set the stage for the Gulls' success. Tourists flock to Newport every night of the week. In South County, the Waves' home base, beaches are a big draw, but nighttime foot traffic is quiet. And while Car-dines Field is a postcard for the idyllic charm of summer baseball, the Waves play at Old Mountain Field, a municipal diamond in the village of Wakefield. The franchise has made a significant investment there—building a scoreboard and press box—and has a good relationship with the town, which maintains the facility and playing surface. Open space means kids can chase foul balls to their heart's content, but seating is limited to one set of bleachers behind home plate and the lawn chairs that fans carry in.

The product has been good, with the Waves making the playoffs in each of their first three years in the league. Two days ago one of last summer's stars, slugging first baseman Tim Lynch, went to the New York Yankees in the ninth round of the Major League Baseball Draft. In the next round pitcher Mitchell Jordan was picked by the Oakland Athletics. Jordan was on the mound at Old Mountain Field in 2014 and then dominated the Cape Cod League with the Orleans Firebirds the next year, tying a league record for earned run average.

Attendance numbers have grown amid the success, though not to the range the Gulls typically reach. The Waves are not alone in that shortfall—last summer Newport averaged nine hundred more fans per game than any other team in the league.

There are challengers to the throne, though. The Valley Blue Sox have begun to make a mark in Holyoke, Massachusetts. The Keene Swamp Bats are a fixture in New Hampshire, their stands almost always full. The league is as healthy as it's ever been, talent on the rise and fans enjoying every bit of it.

The Waves have their talent on display tonight. Finlayson congratulates Fulbright after the fifth inning. His night is done. Nick DiEva from Stony Brook University comes on for the sixth inning and picks up where the starter left off. Ben Breazeale works a two-out walk to end the Waves' perfect-game bid, but DiEva strikes out the next batter. Six innings in, the Gulls are getting no-hit.

◆　◆　◆

If nothing else—and there isn't much else on the wrong side of a no-hitter—Gulls fans have their postcard for the evening. The sun peeks out from behind a bank of clouds just in time for a spectacular sunset. Phones are pulled out of pockets and purses for photos. The team photographers turn their big lenses away from the action for a moment, too. Even rambunctious Little Leaguers in the stands take notice as the whole sky seems to turn yellow. It goes to pink and then to an orange glow that tints everything for a few fleeting moments.

In the dugout Al Leyva may not have noticed the sunset, but he appreciates these Newport nights all the same. Leyva is in his first year as the Gulls manager after spending the last five seasons as the team's hitting coach. When Mike Coombs—the man at the helm for every Gulls championship and the league's winningest manager—departed after last season, Leyva was the natural choice to take the reins. In addition to his time with the Gulls, he has managed two other NECBL teams and has coached in the Minor Leagues. His brother, Nick, is a longtime coach at the Major League level. Al lives in California but makes the cross-country trek to Newport every summer.

The switch to the head job has been smooth. "The difference for me is I've got to do the paperwork now," Leyva says. "Everything else is status quo—coaching third, working with the hitters."

Leyva expects to pick up where Coombs left off and keep the Gulls humming. While it's not easy to win baseball games every night, it's easy to set the bar, given the franchise's history. With each summer's new crop of Gulls come players who know nothing of the team or the league. But they learn quickly that they're about to be part of something special. "It's one of the things we talk about when they first get here—our history," Paiva says. "A commitment to our tradition, just playing the game hard, the right way, competing while they're wearing this uniform. Those are things we talk about with the players."

Living up to the standards requires the right work ethic and the right approach. That point is hammered home, too, and Paiva always reminds the players that they aren't doing it just to have a strong

season this summer. "For us, it's why they're here. They're prepar-
ing for professional baseball," Paiva says. "If somebody doesn't play
the game the right way over a forty-four-game season, it's going to
be awfully difficult when they get to the pros."

At least for tonight, playing the right way means hanging tough.
In the seventh inning, still stuck on the low side of a 4–0 score,
the Gulls finally break the spell. Chris Chatfield, an outfielder from
South Florida, leads off the inning and falls behind in the count one
ball and two strikes. But he smacks the next pitch into the outfield
and races into second base with a double, the first hit of the night
for the home team.

Gabe Snyder follows with a walk, giving the Gulls their first scoring chance of the night, but Chatfield gets picked off second base.
Two strikeouts end the threat as quickly as it began. Mark Powell
is left in the on-deck circle.

The push is nice to see, fitting in with what Leyva and Paiva
expect, but it's starting to look like it won't yield much tonight.

◆ ◆ ◆

Ocean State's Ryan Blanton leads off second base in the top of the
eighth inning. Behind him Mark Powell bounces from one foot to
the other and then darts behind the runner, miming a pickoff, and
dances back to his spot.

His movements remind Chuck Paiva of someone, the same player
Powell has always reminded him of. It's no accident. When his
family was hosting players, one of the Gulls who came through
was a shortstop from East Carolina named Jack Reinheimer. It was
2011, with Powell's own baseball career blossoming. And here was
a blueprint—same position, similar body types.

Reinheimer batted .259 and shined defensively in his summer
with the Gulls, earning an all-star nod. He played for the Bourne
Braves of the Cape Cod League the next summer and was even
better, a springboard to a fifth-round selection in the 2014 Major
League Draft. He's in Triple A this year.

Powell is wearing the same No. 2 that Reinheimer wore as a Gull, and he's covering the same ground at shortstop. Five years in a baseball life can take you places, even when the destination feels like home.

After the missed opportunity in the seventh inning, Powell leads off the bottom of the eighth for the Gulls and works a four-pitch walk. He's now reached base in four consecutive games.

Another walk puts Stephen Scott on base and sends Powell to second. Both move up on a wild pitch, and a walk to Ben Breazeale loads the bases. But again the rally goes for naught. Waves reliever Tyler Barss from the nearby University of Rhode Island strikes out the next two batters.

The Gulls make one last push in the ninth. Late arrival Jake Brodt gets his first at bat and strikes out, but Powell draws another walk and then steals a base. Soon the bases are loaded again, and this time Cole Fabio from Rhode Island's Bryant University singles to bring in a run.

It's 4–1, but that will end up being the final score. With the bases still loaded, another Waves reliever notches a strikeout to end the game.

♦ ♦ ♦

It was a long game—just a shade over three hours—and with school still in session, the crowd thinned out. A few remaining kids crowd onto the field for autographs, waiting by the backstop while the team finishes up a postgame chat.

Jake Brodt and Ben Breazeale, the new arrivals, played a game before they met their host families. They get the chance now, their first night in a new bed just a few hours away.

Chuck Paiva and Matt Finlayson share a few words outside the Waves dugout. Another coffee meeting is set for later this week.

Mark Powell catches up with his family. If Powell can stick with the Gulls, they'll be at Cardines Field a lot this summer, like usual, but with a new rooting interest. He's doing everything he can to make it happen, running with the chance, remembering what got him here. "It's been great to play in front of my hometown crowd," Powell said. "I always came to games when I was younger. Now that I'm actually playing for them, it's kind of a big accomplishment I owe to a lot of people—my parents, coaches. I couldn't have done it without them."

As interns put the field to bed for the night, the players slowly make their way to the picnic area outside the first base bleachers. A postgame buffet awaits.

Paiva checks in with the players, makes sure everybody has enough to eat. Soon, he'll pull out his phone. He still needs a catcher.

3 / FAIRBANKS

At 10:34 p.m. Joe Fernandez toes the rubber of the mud-caked pitching mound, takes a small step back with his right foot, and winds up for the first pitch of the game. It's a high-and-tight fastball, and it sails on him. The leadoff batter ducks out of the way. The catcher stretches out his arm as the ball screams past his mitt. It keeps on flying, smacking into the backstop with a thump.

Maybe Fernandez is a little too amped up for this. Or maybe he can't actually see his catcher too well. At the Midnight Sun Game, you never know.

Hype and anticipation build for it. The biggest crowd of the season squeezes into Growden Park, filling the bleachers and jockeying for a view in standing-room-only spots. For the players on the turf field, adrenaline flows with a little more power than usual. At the very least they know they're part of something unique. The more reflective among them can appreciate being part of history. There's a big-game feel.

Also, it's a little bit dim. Something like the ninth inning of a long American Legion game on a field with no lights—it's not too dark to call it quits, but the umpires are urging players to hustle in and out of the dugout between innings. Here there is no need to hustle. Dim is kind of the idea. It's a twilight that seems to last forever, the darkness never quite closing in.

In Fairbanks, Alaska, the sun sets forty-eight minutes after midnight on the summer solstice, the longest day of the year. It dips slowly toward the horizon at the slightest angle, casting the familiar golden glow of a sunset for an unfamiliar hour or two. When it finally disappears, the persistent twilight keeps darkness at bay. It never gets pitch-black. An hour later the sky starts to brighten. Two hours and ten minutes after it sets, the sun is back up again.

It's a simple fact of living almost on top of the world, but the easy explanation takes little away from the wonder of it. For someone from outside—Alaskans' term for pretty much everywhere else—it's jarring, a strange experience that toys with the sense of time. Even for native Alaskans it may not be novel, but it's embraced and appreciated. You'll find energy you didn't know you had, they say. Who needs sleep? The reward for single-digit temperatures in the fall, four-hour days in the winter, mountains of snow, and a thaw that comes sometime in mid-May are these endless summer nights.

Baseball and summer nights are a natural fit, of course, and the sport's pioneers in Alaska realized years ago what their long nights could allow them to create on the diamond. According to historic accounts, teams of locals representing two area bars—the Eagles Club and the California Bar—gathered for the first Midnight Sun Game in 1906. Legend has it they played to settle a bet. The California Bar won. Their efforts were led by Eddie Stroecker, who's considered the father of the Midnight Sun Game.

Even then, people realized it was unique. The headline in the *Fairbanks Daily Times* read, "Crowd Present at Ball Game." The writer urged people who had witnessed the game to carry around the box score as proof that they saw baseball played at midnight. And many saw it. According to the article, "Fully 1,500 people were present and there has never been such hooting at a local game."

Various amateur teams from Fairbanks and barnstorming squads from outside played the game through 1959. In 1960 the fledgling Alaska Goldpanners summer-ball team made the game its own and have hosted it ever since.

If it began as a novelty and caught on as a curiosity, it has lately become legendary. ESPN cameras have filmed it. Countless magazine stories have waxed poetic on it. A documentary has captured it. Baseball fans have tacked it onto bucket lists. Local fans have kept filling the stands.

The Goldpanners' pitcher for tonight's edition—the 111th Midnight Sun Game—watched it from the dugout last summer. He's back with the team this year. On the mound now, the adrenaline still pumping, Fernandez fires two more pitches out of the strike zone to the leadoff batter, works the count to three balls and a strike, and then loses him to a walk. Five batters later, with the bases loaded, he gets a ground ball to end the inning, his wild first pitch a distant memory.

It's a good start for the home team. The cheers echo.

It hasn't gotten any darker.

♦ ♦ ♦

Six hours ago stubborn rain clouds lingered around Fairbanks, obscuring the dark-green hills to the north. It poured for a while, then drizzled. Pockets of green dotted the radar all day. Water pooled on the tarp at Growden Park.

The timing couldn't have been worse. The weather is usually perfect this time of year—seventy-degree temperatures, sunny, low humidity. It makes the endless summer nights even better, the perfect backdrop for a baseball tradition. This night, of all nights, might not be so picture-perfect.

John Lohrke walked around Growden Park in the mist. Droplets of rain beaded on his bright-red Goldpanners jacket, the vintage kind that the team has worn since its early days. He checked on ticket sales and dispatched interns to sweep pools of water off the bleachers, stealing glances at the wet field. He had checked the weather forecast a half-dozen times by then. He gave everybody he ran into the same report. "It's supposed to get better and better," he said.

That would probably be his prediction with or without the Weather Channel. Accepting Fairbanks weather and looking on the bright side of it comes with the territory. The Midnight Sun Game will go on.

Lohrke is a veteran of baseball in Alaska's frontier, but he's in uncharted territory tonight. He took over as the Goldpanners' president and interim general manager just a few months ago and stepped into big shoes. The franchise has had only four presidents in its long and storied history, and the general manager position had been in one family for decades. Don Dennis, one of the team's founding fathers and a legend in summer collegiate baseball circles, stepped away from day-to-day involvement a few years ago. He and his wife, Ann, will keep tabs on tonight's game from their new home in California. Their son, Todd, grew up around the team and had his own stint as general manager before stepping down in the spring. From the third generation, Todd's son, Tom, takes photos and helps run the show on game days.

This will be Lohrke's first Midnight Sun Game at the helm of the team. He'll enjoy it, but he'll also take a deep breath when it's over. The year has been tough on the franchise. In addition to the personnel changes, a dispute with the borough of Fairbanks left Growden Park's future uncertain. The borough leases the park to the team, and the lease requires certain maintenance benchmarks. The first base bleachers had recently been deemed unsafe, and the borough issued a notice to vacate the stadium in March. Lohrke and the board of directors worked with borough leadership to agree on a new lease. The borough chipped in funding to remove the old bleachers and bring in portable sets for the coming season.

Lohrke is optimistic about the relationship with the borough and the future of the park. For now it's a work in progress. Last-minute improvements are still ongoing as the Midnight Sun first pitch approaches, from advertising banners going up above the concession stand to the finishing touches on a set of wooden stairs up to a terrace level.

Lohrke points out other changes. There's a fresh coat of blue paint on the part of the stadium that fronts the main gate and dozens of potted flowers that line the steps up to the concourse. Posters of Goldpanners legends hang on the wall by the concession stand. Walking through an old weight room that has fallen into disrepair and locker rooms that have seen better days, Lohrke sees what still needs to be done. He envisions more improvements that could turn the park into a state-of-the-art facility.

That the franchise is playing catch-up is emblematic of the challenges that have cropped up for baseball teams here. The Alaska Baseball League—once on the same pedestal as the Cape League—doesn't draw the same level of talent that it used to. Plenty of good players, particularly from the West Coast, still make the trek, but these are not the days of Barry Bonds, Dave Winfield, and Tom Seaver.

"I remember what it was like here in the seventies," Lohrke says. "What about the last five years? What can we do to make it better?"

The growth of other summer leagues around the country has cut into the Alaska League's status. The Cape League faces competition, too, but so far top talent continues to arrive every summer. Whether it's the long distance or scouts having other options, Alaska hasn't been as lucky.

The league has never had a central office. Teams operate on their own, perhaps a product of the state's frontier spirit. This season the league will play with five teams. The Goldpanners' board of directors decided to step back from the league slate and play an independent barnstorming schedule. The goal is to reinvigorate the team and the town's old quest for the National Baseball Congress World Series, where the Goldpanners are royalty. The Alaska League schedule overlaps with the NBC slate, and it has kept the Goldpanners from playing in the tournament several times, including last year. Lohrke says the community likes to see the team on the national stage. They'll be there this summer. As Lohrke says, given their history in the tournament, all they have to do is call Wichita and say they're coming.

Whatever the makeup of the league, whatever path the Gold-panners pursue next, Lohrke believes summer collegiate baseball in Alaska will hold on to a niche. And he's a firm believer that it should. For prospective players, it's an adventure. "If you're going to play a couple of summers, this has to be one of them," Lohrke says. "It's an experience for all these guys—just being here, seeing the sights. I hope all of them get to put a line in the water."

Lohrke knows about baseball adventures here. He grew up in California, the son of former Major Leaguer Jack Lohrke, who played seven seasons in the bigs. His older brother, Kurt, starred at Santa Clara University and spent time in the Minor Leagues. Lohrke followed him to Santa Clara but admits he didn't have the same baseball talent. The game still captured his imagination, though. When one of his coaches at school signed up to head north and lead a brand-new team in the Alaska League, he encouraged Lohrke to go with him. Lohrke was twenty-three years old, and he took the leap of faith. Thrust into the general manager role, he was a jack-of-all-trades. "I had a ball," he says.

He never left and soon planted roots in the state. He's been with a local Ford dealership for thirty-four years. He and his wife, Rhonda, have raised a family here. Through it all baseball remained a constant. Lohrke was general manager of the Alaska League's Kenai Peninsula Oilers for several years. His son plays high school and American Legion ball. Rhonda works as the host-family coordinator for the Goldpanners.

The return to the Goldpanners franchise has taken Lohrke back in time. The history of the team and the league and baseball in Alaska is important to him. And as crazy as things have been since he took over, the crack of the bat can still get him dreaming.

Of his new team, he says, "I think we've got some talent."

♦ ♦ ♦

Trappings of Alaska surround Growden Park. Beyond the left-field fence and Second Avenue sits the Fairbanks Curling Club. The Chena River—a hot spot for fishing and kayaking—snakes nearby. There's a convention center that doubles as a hockey rink for the University of Alaska–Fairbanks Nanooks. Hills loom to the north, with the promise of mountains behind them.

Then there are the baseball diamonds. Eleven of them fan out in all directions surrounding the Goldpanners' home field. There are two full-size diamonds by the river. Two with a big infield but smaller outfield expanses sit beyond Growden Park's right-field foul pole. Four diamonds for youth baseball are situated across the street. Three fields with dirt infields suitable for softball back up to a nearby elementary school.

For much of the year they're covered by snow, making the sport seem like an odd fit here. Their home plates are about 198 miles from the Arctic Circle, after all. There's a town close by called North Pole. Hockey and curling make sense. Fishing. Hunting. But on summer nights like this that almost literally last forever, America's pastime makes its home, too.

American Legion ball is big for Alaska's high school ballplayers. In many places around the country, the circuit has lost some steam, as AAU and other travel options have caught up. Here the state has seventeen teams. Clubs from around the country converge for the annual Alaska Airlines Series.

Alaska has no college baseball teams—a spring season would be nearly impossible without a domed stadium—but collegiate summer ball has been a fixture since the Goldpanners came on the scene.

They were founded in 1960 by Red Boucher, a New Englander by birth who made his way to the frontier and started a sporting-goods outfit. With local players—and, tellingly for the future, several players from the University of Arizona—Boucher introduced the Pan Alaska Goldpanners, named for his company. He was a one-man band, managing, promoting, and organizing the schedule for the club.

Boucher was a larger-than-life character, a salesman by trade who later became mayor of Fairbanks and Alaska's lieutenant governor. His life story has a Forrest Gump quality to it—legend has it that Franklin Delano Roosevelt gave him the nickname Red when Boucher, with a shock of red hair, was a kid. His family was attending Roosevelt's inauguration parade in Washington DC. Roosevelt saw him and asked his name. He replied with his very formal full name—Henry Aristide Boucher—and Roosevelt said they ought to call him Red. After a stint in the navy, Boucher went back home to Fall River, Massachusetts, where he helped a junior senator named John Kennedy get reelected. It was Kennedy who told him Alaska was going to become a state and that it would be a good place to go for someone with a pioneer spirit.

The birth of the Goldpanners happened partially by accident, when a local Fairbanks team folded, leaving its sporting-goods supplier—Boucher's company—with a whole lot of brand-new gear. Instead of swallowing the loss, Boucher reached out to baseball people he knew from his time in the navy, from former Boston Red Sox player Bobby Doerr to Abe Chanin, the founder of the *Collegiate Baseball Newspaper*. Chanin connected Boucher with University of Arizona coach Frank Sancet. Six of his players were soon on a plane to Alaska, and the Goldpanners were born.

They were a ragtag outfit. The town didn't know who they were, just that Boucher was always scrounging around for donations. As the story goes, Boucher first ran for public office in Fairbanks because the city council wouldn't give him the grass seed he needed for the Goldpanners' home field.

Boucher dreamed big and quickly talked his way into the NBC World Series. The Goldpanners were the tournament runner-up in just their third year of existence. When they came back to a victory celebration in Fairbanks, Alaska baseball had its spark.

◆ ◆ ◆

It was 1964 when Red Boucher got a call from legendary University of Southern California (usc) coach Rod Dedeaux. The Trojans' head man was recruiting a pitcher from Fresno City College and wanted to send him north to see if he could prove himself worthy of a scholarship. His name was Tom Seaver.

He was, in fact, worthy of a scholarship. In Seaver—who went on to win three Major League Baseball Cy Young Awards with the New York Mets—the Goldpanners had their first star. And with Dedeaux, they had their first pipeline. The talent began arriving from usc in droves.

As Boucher expanded the operation, he also recruited help for the front office in the form of Don Dennis. Then a newspaper sports editor in Grand Junction, Colorado, Dennis became aware of the Goldpanners when he read an article about the 1963 Midnight Sun Game. He figured the Goldpanners might be coming through Grand Junction on their way to the NBC World Series, and, in his moonlighting role as the business manager for a summer club called the Grand Junction Eagles, he reached out about organizing a game. Dennis and Boucher hit it off, and for the next four years—amid trips to the Midnight Sun Game for the Eagles and meetings at the NBC World Series—Boucher poked and prodded Dennis about coming to Alaska and running operations for the Goldpanners. The recruiting pitch eventually worked, though there might have been some moments of doubt during those first cold months. Fairbanks has supermarkets and big-box stores now. In those days it was still very much the frontier. "After four or five months of dead winter, you begin to learn how to live up there," Dennis says.

The early years were busy. Dennis worked for a new daily newspaper until it folded and then hooked on with the more established *Fairbanks Daily News-Miner*. The University of Alaska–Fairbanks didn't have a sports-information director for its athletic department, so Dennis took on that job, too. Baseball filled the summer nights—and plenty of other nights, too. "The opportunities were everywhere," Dennis recalls. "My wife used to say, every time the phone rang, it was another opportunity."

As the Goldpanners became a fixture in Fairbanks and in the summer baseball world, the operation grew. A board of directors was formed. Dennis took on business and publicity responsibilities. Boucher hired Lyle Olson, the coach at San Diego State, to lead the team on the field.

The 1960s were good and the '70s even better, as the Goldpanners made six consecutive NBC championship-game appearances and won four of them. A supportive community grew around them, led by local banker Bill Stroecker, the son of the original Midnight Sun Game pioneer. Bill became team president, a position he held for forty-seven years. Another San Diego State coach, Jim Dietz, took over as the manager and would become an Alaska legend. He led many of the Goldpanners' best teams, in addition to the twelve hundred games he won with the Aztecs.

Baseball soon carved out a place in the collective consciousness of summer in Alaska. The Goldpanners won big, playing mostly against barnstorming teams that made the trek to Fairbanks. A team in Anchorage—the Bucs—was getting off the ground, and Anchorage resident Joe Keenan teamed with Dennis to organize an Alaska state championship series. More than three thousand people jammed into the stands. The next year fans were chartering planes to get to the away games in the series.

There was never a vision for forming a true Alaska league, just year-by-year growth and a general aim of expanding the game while turning a profit. Teams popped up in Kenai and Palmer. Even a team from Hawaii came up for parts of the summer and joined the association, a team from America's fiftieth state somehow part of the forty-ninth state's league.

The circuit, loosely organized though it was, began to gain a reputation in college baseball circles. West Coast talent poured in every summer—Dave Winfield, Barry Bonds, Mark McGwire—and winning followed. The Goldpanners were an NBC World Series powerhouse. They often had to turn players away more than they had to recruit.

Over the years change was a constant for Alaska baseball. Some teams wanted to put a greater emphasis on the national tournament in Wichita, so they would switch to a barnstorming schedule one year. The Anchorage Pilots formed their own league for a time. The North Pole Nicks came and went. The Goldpanners-led association teamed up with the Pilots' league to form the Alaska Federation. At one point local newspapers ran three sets of standings that included some of the same teams. More recently, the Goldpanners fielded two teams, one as an entry into the Alaska League and the other for barnstorming. "It was pretty difficult because of the different visions," Dennis said. "People generally have referred to Alaska. They've never known about a central league or a federation. There was always a lot happening behind the scenes."

On the field, though, the baseball was good, and Fairbanks loved its team. Dennis remembers someone doing the math once—if the New York Yankees sold as many tickets per capita for the Big Apple's population as the Alaska Goldpanners did in Fairbanks, they'd need a stadium for a million people.

♦ ♦ ♦

First pitch is still four hours away, but the grill is hot. Jim Dixon, Trent Fieldson, and Howard Maxwell sit on lawn chairs in the patch of grass outside the baseball field's gates, down the right-field line, sidled up to picnic tables and park-style grills. They figure they've been gathering like this since 1999 or so. They're regulars at Goldpanners games all summer, and before the Midnight Sun Game they tailgate. Bratwursts and hot links are cooking now.

Dixon wears a red Goldpanners hat. He's been on the franchise's board of directors in the past and is serving as a vice president this season. When he's not studying volcanoes and seismic activity as part of his job at the U.S. Geological Survey, baseball fills his free time. In particular, it's baseball off the beaten path that has caught his imagination. Beyond helping out with the Goldpanners, he started a website in 1995 that covers Division III college baseball. Today it's a hub for the sport at that level, with more than thirteen thousand followers on Twitter.

Fieldson is retired from the U.S. Air Force. He got sucked into the game years ago by a Minor League club in Louisiana, where he was stationed. Maxwell teaches and coaches soccer. Baseball brings them—and dozens of others—together. By the time first pitch arrives, their tailgate party will be hopping.

The trio trade stories about the team and the game, some of them tales from before their time. There was the year it was thirty-eight degrees, and the game, of course, went extra innings. One year the Panners hosted a team from Japan. The visiting manager wanted to call the game when it started getting dark. It seemed he didn't quite understand the concept. They have their kazoos ready for a Growden Park tradition, when the speakers blare the song "Happy Boy" and a chorus of kazoos accompanies.

The players in town now aren't the stars of the good old days, they say, when legend has it that Dave Winfield was hitting home runs onto the roof of the curling club. Terry Francona was here. All the Boones—Bob, Bret, Aaron. Jason Giambi. There's nostalgia for those days, but with a tailgate going and the sun still high in the sky and baseball players warming up, it doesn't feel like much is missing.

Dixon makes his way into the stadium around a quarter past seven to rope off a section of the bleachers for his tailgating crew. When the wind kicks up a few minutes later, they carry their food-stocked picnic table to a covered gazebo thirty feet away, and the party goes on. This is Alaska, where you make things work.

Inside the park Samuel Bell snaps photos with his phone. He has arrived early for tonight's game, but this trip was a long time coming. Growing up in the 1980s, he was a bat boy for the Seattle Mariners. Several of the big leaguers had played in Alaska and talked with reverence about the Midnight Sun Game. It lodged in Bell's memory.

He'd been meaning to come up year after year. Now an employee of Horizon Air Lines, an affiliate of Alaska Airlines, he can make the trip easily. In a blue Dodgers hat, he pulled in around seven, ready to stake out a general admission spot. He got an upgrade to a reserved seat on the third base side when he stopped in at the ticket booth. On his way to it he bought a red Goldpanners T-shirt and started the photo documentation of his trip. "Thirty-one years later, here I am," Bell said.

The weather might keep some fans away tonight. The game's attendance record was set in 1967, when fifty-two hundred people watched future Major Leaguer Bill "Spaceman" Lee pitch against a team from Japan. Lee came back forty-one years later, in 2008, and pitched in the Midnight Sun Game again. Somehow, at sixty-one years old, he went six innings and got the win. The stands were filled again, with an announced crowd of forty-nine hundred.

Fans here for tonight's game start streaming through the gates around eight o'clock. Many wear the gear of Major League teams—Cardinals, Red Sox, Giants, A's, Yankees—a sign of the diehards that the game attracts. Some of them make a stop at the merchandise stand to add Goldpanners red to their collections.

As they find their seats there isn't much to see on the field yet. For the players the late start means there's more time to kill than usual. Six Goldpanners are playing fungo golf, trying to hit the ball closest to an outfield-wall advertisement or an infield base. Four of their teammates are in the batting cage down the left-field line, taking swings off tees.

Billy Sample watches from the edge of the dugout. A former Major Leaguer with the New York Yankees, Texas Rangers, and Atlanta Braves, he's been a broadcaster and columnist in the years since and wrote the screenplay for a baseball movie called *Reunion 108*. In the summer he helps out the Goldpanners as an assistant coach, adding Alaska to his eclectic baseball résumé. When he's not doing battle with mosquitoes in the first base coach's box, he tries to be a resource for the players. He sees some talent this summer.

Starting right fielder Isaiah Aluko has tools, he says. The six-foot-three 215-pounder from Valdosta State certainly looks the part. "I'd have been a Hall of Famer with that size," Sample says with a laugh.

The presence of people like Sample and field manager Tim Kelly—a scout for three decades—reflects how much Alaska is part of baseball's fabric. These are baseball people, and they can find a home here in the long summer nights.

The general admission seats down the left-field line are starting to fill up. On the East Coast it's 1:30 a.m. Summer ball in the rest of the country has gone to bed for the night.

Here, Joe Fernandez is just starting to get loose.

◆ ◆ ◆

Wearing a gray Compton Baseball sweatshirt, Fernandez sits on the bench in the Goldpanner dugout, the team's logo in peeling paint on the wall behind him. On the field just in front of the dugout rail, performers from Fairbanks Fire and Flow are twirling flaming torches as part of the pregame entertainment.

Like Minor Leaguers watching kids and mascots race, Fernandez and his teammates chuckle at the sight. When baseball takes you places, you see a lot. Fernandez hails from Southern California and played junior-college ball at El Camino–Compton Center. His next stop was Georgetown College, a National Association of Intercollegiate Athletes (NAIA) program in Kentucky, just north of Lexington, where he just finished his junior season with a 3.66 earned run average and a team-best ninety strikeouts. In his final start of the spring, he pitched a complete game with fourteen strikeouts but took the loss in a conference playoff game.

Last summer Fernandez was the Goldpanners' most consistent starter, posting a 2.66 ERA and leading the team with forty-five strikeouts. He didn't pitch in the Midnight Sun Game, when the Panners won 7–4 over the Seattle Studs. Two days later he went eight shutout innings in his second start of the summer and continued to pitch well from there.

He's nervous for this one. His last start with Georgetown was more than a month ago. He's pitched twice this summer but is still getting up to speed. The crowd adds something, too. He didn't think much about the fact of pitching in the Midnight Sun Game before today. It's hitting him now.

Fernandez and his Goldpanners teammates are 6-5 so far this season. The Kenai Peninsula Oilers—their opponents tonight—are an Alaska League team based south of Anchorage, about a nine-hour drive away from Fairbanks. They've been a familiar foe already this season, hosting two games and now in town for a five-game set that includes the Midnight Sun event. The Oilers won the last two games, 10–7 and 6–4.

Several Panners are off to fast starts, led by Isaiah Aluko. The tools Billy Sample spotted have been on full display. He's currently riding a seven-game hitting streak and batting .483 with a home run. Like Fernandez, Aluko has been on a winding baseball road. He started his collegiate career at Columbia State Community College and played this past season at Valdosta State University.

As winding roads go, teammate Alex Mascarenas has Fernandez, Aluko, and everybody else beat. He's twenty-five years old, for starters. His collegiate career started at UCLA—on a football field. He played defensive back for three seasons for the Bruins, starting two games in 2011 before concussions forced him to give up the sport. A baseball standout in high school, he decided to return to the sport at Santa Ana Junior College, where he played the 2014 and 2015 seasons. The dream of playing pro ball persists, and it has brought him north this summer. Mascarenas is playing second base for the Goldpanners tonight.

The Panners' roster blends players like Mascarenas, Aluko, and Fernandez with others from more established programs. Outfielder Kevin Connolly is in town from Creighton, where he hit .301 in his junior season. Cole Krzmarzick batted .368 at Nevada. Two players are due in from Arizona once the Wildcats finish their run in the College World Series.

The performances have been up and down so far, but the big goals of this season remain front and center. When Lohrke takes the microphone for pregame ceremonies on the field, he reminds the crowd that the Goldpanners have won six national championships. "We're always trying to win another," he says.

◆ ◆ ◆

It's fifty-seven degrees with the gray clouds still hovering and the bleachers full. Wearing old-school red stirrups under white pants and a red uniform top, Fernandez is on the mound, trying to find his way out of the first inning. After his wild first toss and the walk to the leadoff batter, he gets the second hitter to fly out to Isaiah Aluko in right field.

A typical game here with a 7:00 p.m. start would be over by now, or in the ninth inning at least. This is different, and the crowd's buzz matches it. When the next Oiler batter checks his swing on a two-strike count, the crowd boos. He ends up knocking a single, and the fans boo again.

Fernandez doesn't look rattled. His fastball feels good, lively. Other than that first backstop-bound pitch, his command is on. With runners on first and second, he strikes out the third-place batter for the second out. He's still not out of the woods, though. The cleanup hitter gets hit by a pitch to load the bases.

Tim Kelly, the manager, jogs to the mound for a chat. Brody Wofford, from Louisiana State University, is due up next in his Alaska debut. The Tigers just lost in an NCAA Super Regional to Coastal Carolina. The matchup tonight is NAIA versus NCAA baseball powerhouse, but Fernandez wins it. A ground ball bounces to shortstop, where Tanner Negrette fields it and flips to second base for the final out of the inning.

Alex Mascarenas steps to the plate to lead off the bottom of the first inning and quickly gives the big crowd something to cheer about when he smacks a double over the head of the Oilers' left fielder. Oilers starting pitcher Zack Hamilton, a righty from

Louisiana Tech, comes back with a strikeout and a flyout. He leaves Mascarenas stranded on second when he fans Aluko.

But the leadoff double was a good sign for the Panners. Fernandez works a one-two-three top of the second inning, and they're back at it quickly on a hit-by-pitch and a base hit by Kevin Connolly. Cole Krzmarzick—Nevada's hot hitter—lines a base hit to bring home the first run of the game.

It's just the beginning. Mascarenas singles in his second at bat and drives in another run. Keaton Smith and Justin Harrer follow suit, and when the dust settles Hamilton is watching from the dugout and the Goldpanners are up 5–0.

It's no surprise. They own this game, leading the all-time series 46–11. Maybe they're used to the twilight.

♦ ♦ ♦

As the Goldpanners trot out to the field for the top of the third inning, the sun begins to poke out from under a bank of clouds, where it's been stuck all night. The night's gray hue suddenly gives way to a golden glow over Growden Park. The photos that will be printed in newspapers and posted online tomorrow have their setting. It was more the Midnight Clouds Game for much of the night, but the slowly setting sun made an appearance just in time.

The sunlight might make the pitches a little easier to see, but it doesn't matter to Joe Fernandez. The top of the third inning is his best effort of the evening. Facing the top of the Kenai batting order for the second time, he strikes out the side. After Kenai's threat in the top of the first inning, Fernandez has now retired seven batters in a row, five of them by strikeout. They announced him as "Smokin' Joe Fernandez" in pregame introductions, and the nickname fits tonight.

Tanner Negrette singles with two outs in the bottom of the third inning, and Alex Mascarenas reaches on an error before the threat ends with a flyout. The Panners' lead stays at 5–0.

Between innings, at 11:53 p.m., one of the annual game's signature traditions takes center stage. At the inning break closest to midnight, the crowd stands for the singing of "Alaska's Flag," which is the state's official song.

The duo that sang the national anthem in the pregame festivities returns to home plate to lead the chorus. The crowd rises. Some fans join in the singing. Others soak it in or take cell phone videos. "Eight stars of gold on a field of blue," the song begins. "Alaska's flag, may it mean to you." Behind the singers, Growden Park's center-field fence is a mirror of the flag, with eight gold stars on the navy-blue wall.

Everybody in the crowd joins in for the final lines: "Alaska's flag to Alaskans dear. The simple flag of a last frontier."

Like a sunset on pause, the sky still radiates gold. As the fourth inning begins and midnight approaches, fans check watches or peer at the timestamp on their phones. You want to remind yourself that it's midnight, that you're watching baseball, that the sun is still above the horizon. You have seen the pictures. You know this is the deal. In person, with the sun hanging low in the sky over left field and the glow seeming like it will last forever, it still gets you.

◆ ◆ ◆

The "Alaska's Flag" song is all pomp and circumstance. At the next break between innings, the press box blares "Sunglasses at Night" over the speakers. The clock has ticked past midnight, and it's time to embrace the fun of the witching hour.

The Goldpanners want in on the party. A base hit by Kevin Connolly in the fourth inning brings home a run, and an error lets another one cross the plate. Cole Krzmarzick singles in Connolly to make it 8–0. In their sixth game of the season against the Oilers, the Panners are finally making some headway at the plate. It's one of their best showings of the season.

Joe Fernandez has retired ten batters in a row when the leadoff batter reaches in the fifth inning. The sun sits halfway below the horizon, and the golden sky has given way to a steel gray. The leadoff single kicked through the infield, and shortstop Tanner Negrette might have gotten a late break on the ball. Was it because of the darkness? Maybe. It's certainly darker than it's been all night.

Fernandez keeps firing, striking out the next batter and getting a pop-out to second base for another out. A base hit—with another possible late break at third base—keeps the inning alive, but a fly-out ends it.

The night is done for Fernandez, and it was a dominant one—five innings, no runs, three hits, eight strikeouts. "After the first inning, it was easy," he says.

As the Goldpanners come to the plate for the bottom of the fifth, general manager John Lohrke settles into a seat in the grandstand behind home plate. He hasn't been in one place for more than five minutes yet, buzzing from the ticket window to the concession stand, doing television interviews and checking in with season-ticket holders.

Five innings in, he can take his first deep breath. The prevailing emotion for now is relief. Pulling everything together for the Midnight Sun Game is never an easy feat. It comes just four games into the home slate. There's no warm-up before the club has to orchestrate its biggest game of the year. "We were ready," Lohrke says.

He's been impressed—but not surprised—by the team's performance, saying the Panners were due to play well. Fernandez was a perfect match for the twilight, a hard thrower with swing-and-miss stuff. The offense came around at a good time.

Alex Torson, a native of Vancouver who pitches in the junior-college ranks at Lower Columbia College, relieves Fernandez and works around a double for a scoreless top of the sixth inning.

Before the bottom of the sixth, umpires and the managers of each team chat at home plate. It's darker still, the kind of twilight that your eyes adjust to outside, as it creeps in. Inside, with a look back through the window, it might surprise you how dark it is.

The show goes on with a quick bottom half of the sixth inning. It's 12:58 when the Panners jog out to warm up for the bottom of the seventh. The sun is officially down and will be for two more hours. The low clouds that have persisted all day damper what's left of the twilight. It's always a little dark at this point in the game, but not typically this dark. After another home-plate conference, the umpires send the players off the field.

Lohrke heads down to the turf to check on the situation, his sigh of relief quickly abandoned. Behind home plate, a chant of "Let's play ball" gets going, and the whole of the crowd picks it up soon after. At 1:02 a.m. the Panners jog back onto the field, but the inning doesn't start. They're pulled back off a few minutes later as umpires announce a thirty-minute delay.

The public address announcer comforts the antsy crowd. "Get a beer; get something to eat," he says. "We're finishing this game. We're Fairbanks!"

◆ ◆ ◆

Earlier in the night, as the sunset moved so slowly, the sky didn't seem to be getting any darker. Now, it's not getting any brighter. The low shelf of clouds remains. The sun won't stay down for long, but it will for longer than the thirty minutes allotted for the delay.

Players are signing autographs at the edge of the stands. The fungo golf game is back on. At 1:27 a.m. the umpires and managers convene at home plate. The crowd has thinned, but the diehards pick up the "Play ball" chant again.

It's not happening. For the second time in its history, the Midnight Sun Game is getting suspended due to darkness. The "Play ball" chant gives way to boos as the announcement comes over the speakers. They'll finish the game tomorrow—or later today, since it already is tomorrow.

It's an anticlimactic ending. In 2011—the other suspension—the game was in extra innings when it was called early, and rain was a factor. This time, it was the thick clouds making it darker than it should have been. Too dark? That's up for debate.

A columnist in the *Alaska Dispatch News* laments the break with tradition the next day, writing, "Let the record show, it was dim, not dark." An Associated Press story hammers home the irony: "A summertime sports tradition in the land of the midnight sun was foiled early Wednesday morning by an unlikely foe: darkness."

The teams shake hands at home plate to a few more scattered boos. The Goldpanners pack up their gear and head for the parking lot. Unlike the keepers of tradition, they don't seem too upset. It was a little shorter than it should have been, but they've had their moment in the midnight sun.

♦ ♦ ♦

June 22 is a more typical Fairbanks summer day—bright-blue skies, warm sun, low humidity, a pleasant breeze. The Goldpanners and the Midnight Sun Game missed the good weather by a day.

Back at Growden Park, they play an originally scheduled game at 7:00 p.m., switching it from nine innings to seven. After some discussions about marking the suspended Midnight Sun Game as a final without completing it, the teams settled on finishing the last three innings after the 7:00 game.

The Goldpanners win the first game 3–1. Armed with the 8–0 lead in the resumption of the Midnight Sun Game, they cruise to the finish line for a 9–2 victory. Joe Fernandez, watching from the dugout, gets credit for the win. Daniel Ferrell, from Lindsey Wilson College, pitches all three innings of the resumed game and gets the save.

The day after the summer solstice is fourteen seconds shorter. When the game ends around 10:30, the sky is cloudless. There's plenty of sunshine left.

4 / SANTA BARBARA

Even the McDonald's a few miles from campus in Goleta has gotten in on Santa Barbara's historic baseball spring. The sign under the Golden Arches that's typically reserved for value-meal deals and seasonal specials instead salutes the baseball team from the University of California, Santa Barbara.

The Gauchos delighted their hometown with the best NCAA Tournament showing in the program's growing history. There was the regional title on the home field of perennial powerhouse Vanderbilt, the stunningly dramatic walk-off grand slam in the Super Regionals that knocked out Louisville, and the program's first trip to the College World Series in Omaha. It was a groundbreaking spring, even when the clock struck midnight on the Cinderella ride.

Back in Santa Barbara, the team that shares Caesar Uyesaka Stadium with the Gauchos watched from afar as it prepared to dig into its own season, eager for its own postseason run as spring turns to summer.

It may be special. It may be memorable. It will not exactly be groundbreaking.

The Santa Barbara Foresters are California's summer baseball powerhouse. Gaucho blue and gold dominates the decor of the on-campus home turf, but the small patch of signage hanging in the bleachers behind home plate reveals the tradition of UC Santa Barbara's roommate. The banner lists the years—all five—of the

Foresters' National Baseball Congress World Series championships. Every summer there's a chance they'll be needing a bigger
banner soon.

The man who built the powerhouse and stewards it every summer
backs his gray pickup truck into a spot just outside the park. The
California license plate is bordered by a New York Yankees frame.
Stuck to the back windshield is a Foresters decal.

As his team sets up for pregame batting practice, Bill Pintard
walks through the stadium gate and heads for the dugout, cell
phone at his ear. He's been on it all day, trying to hammer out the
logistics for a pair of upcoming games against USA Baseball's Collegiate National Team. The squad is coming to Southern California for a training stopover on the way to a tournament in Taiwan.
The Foresters signed on for two games, one at Dodger Stadium a
hundred miles to the south and another here in Santa Barbara.

Team USA may feature the best of the best among college players,
but it will have its hands full with the home team. The Foresters are
perennial contenders in the California Collegiate League. Last year
they lost seven league games all summer. The other eleven teams
in the league—scattered from Long Beach to wine country—have
some talent, too, but the Foresters often seem to have more of it.
When they scuffled early this season, it was because most of their
recruited players were still finishing up with their college clubs,
competing in the NCAA Tournament. Even now the Foresters are
waiting on a few arrivals from Omaha. That's the caliber of player
Santa Barbara welcomes.

While the California league is home, the Foresters have made
their boldest mark on the road, at the NBC World Series in Wichita,
Kansas. The team has become royalty there over the past decade.
Its first World Series crown came in 2006, with four more following close behind. All five of their titles were won in a nine-year
span. No other team captured more than one championship in
that time frame.

It all adds up to a pile of victories. Pintard is believed to be the winningest active coach in summer collegiate baseball. Two seasons ago the franchise commemorated his eight hundredth career victory. There's no master list of national summer collegiate records. The all-time mark is likely held by the late Merl Eberly of the MINK League's Clarinda A's, who won fifteen hundred games over thirty-seven years, but it's a safe bet that Pintard sits atop the current list. The Cape League's all-time winningest manager is Chatham's John Schiffner, who became the first in league history to hit five hundred wins in the summer of 2015. With few leagues seeing coaches stick around like they do on the Cape, Schiffner could well be in second place behind Pintard, more than three hundred wins back.

Pintard was inducted into the NBC World Series Hall of Fame during the same summer that he reached eight hundred wins. He's rapidly approaching nine hundred this summer, but he'd be perfectly fine if the milestone passed without any fanfare. He likes to win and has built a baseball team that does a whole lot of it, but a lifetime in the game of baseball has a way of instilling humility and an appreciation for the present. The victory his team will chase today is the only important one.

With his phone calls done for now, Pintard changes clothes in the dugout, trading jeans and a polo for pinstripe uniform pants and a royal-blue Foresters pullover. As he ties his shoes, he tells assistant coach Tony Cougoule that he's been thinking about the pitchers and catchers. Given the time of year, they need to work on communication. It's summer ball, and they barely know each other.

With a wide smile on his face, he jokes about the ribbing that awaits one of the players in his team's version of baseball's kangaroo-court tradition. Apparently, the kid forgot his jersey today and needs his host mom to bring it.

Pintard catches a player walking by who's gotten off to a slow start and offers a quick nugget of insight. He's overthinking everything, Pintard says, because he's smart.

The coach ambles out of the dugout and fist-bumps players on the way to his spot behind the batting cage. He's been here about ten minutes. The first seeds for another win are already in the ground.

◆ ◆ ◆

The original seeds for summer ball in Santa Barbara were planted back in 1991. Bob Townsend, a Santa Barbara native and a baseball man, provided the push to get the Foresters organization off the ground, resurrecting the name from a former semipro team that had been sponsored by the local Forester lodge. Most of the players hailed from local colleges, and the team played an independent schedule against similar West Coast outfits.

Pintard started with the team as the pitching coach. When Townsend was getting ready to step away from the club in 1995, he asked Pintard to take over. It was a natural fit, but Pintard didn't say yes right away. "I went to a bunch of my friends here in Santa Barbara and said, 'I can't do this myself,'" Pintard said. "I kind of have a little Huck Finn in me. I said, 'Here's the paint. Here's the walls. Let's build something.' And they all bought in. I had a great support group behind me, and we started building it."

The club had already started to solidify itself in the summer collegiate scene, having joined the California Collegiate League and the National Baseball Congress. They were winning locally, but the chance to win at the national level drove Pintard and his crew of supporters to keep building. They believed something special was brewing in their seaside city. "The whole goal was to go to Wichita," Pintard said. "And we said, 'If we're going to go, we might as well win.'"

A veteran of professional scouting, Pintard tapped his connections in the baseball world to expand the team's recruiting base. Longtime University of Southern California coach Mike Gillespie and University of Texas legend Augie Garrido were among the first to sign on, sending some of their top players Pintard's way. At home, fans rallied around the call for host families. In a few years' time, the players from UC Santa Barbara, Westmont College, and Santa Barbara City College were joined by stars from all over the map.

Every summer Pintard molded a winner. His coaching chops found a perfect marriage with a philosophy that's unique to summer ball, one that has become increasingly important over the years. In an era when players grow up in controlled baseball environments—college coaches calling pitches from the dugout and keeping tight leashes on base running, showcase events, and travel ball jamming up schedules—Pintard and his staff realized the magic that could be produced simply by taking the reins off. The product was an aggressive, freewheeling team, and the style persists today.

It's a mix that suits Pintard's personality. He's laid-back but fiercely competitive, perhaps a product of his varied roots. He grew up in New York and learned the game there, playing on city diamonds and watching his beloved Yankees. When he was sixteen his family moved across the country to California. He coached high school ball and became a scout for the Yankees in the 1990s. He has continued to work in scouting throughout his time with the Foresters, spending a decade with the Los Angeles Angels before returning to the Yankees in the past few years.

With the Foresters Pintard leads recruiting efforts and manages in the dugout, pulling the kind of double duty that not many summer-ball franchises employ. It's a small operation, size belying the team's success. But the players keep coming. Who wouldn't want to spend a summer in Santa Barbara? Nestled between the Santa Ynez Mountains and the shimmering blue water of the Pacific Ocean, the city of ninety thousand promotes itself as the American Riviera. It features California weather at its best. No matter where your host family lives, it's not far from the beach.

And given the history, you're going to win some games.

◆ ◆ ◆

Hunter Williams smashes a towering drive toward left-center field at Caesar Uyesaka Stadium. Teammates shagging balls in the outfield stop to watch it soar. The ball clears the fence with room to spare and bounces hard off the pavement of an empty lot by the university's parking services building. A few days ago cars lined the fence. Seems the parking services people have learned where not to park when the Foresters are taking batting practice.

The balls are flying out today, with loud cheers from teammates accompanying the deepest of the deep drives. The real work of batting practice is already done. With some time to spare, the Foresters are having some fun by engaging in a kind of hitting derby. Get a hit and you keep going. Get a long one and everybody cheers.

Bill Pintard and assistant coach Steve Schuck watch from behind home plate, elbows on the batting cage. They laugh and cheer along with the guys, but they're not sure about this little game before the game. If the Foresters keep taking big hacks and hitting pop-ups like they did against real pitching in yesterday's game, they're going to scrap it. For now they let the fun continue.

Williams is in town from Tulane University. A stout 215-pounder from West Monroe, Louisiana, he plays first base and designated hitter for the Green Wave. His spring season was partially derailed by a broken hamate bone, but he made up for lost time when he returned, hitting nine home runs in thirty-nine games and playing his best baseball in the postseason. In an NCAA Regional hosted by Ole Miss, Williams racked up eight hits in four games, half of which went for extra bases. He earned a spot on the All-Regional team.

Williams was a late addition to the Foresters' roster. His Tulane teammate Lex Kaplan played here last summer and is back this year. With the Foresters looking to fill another opening, they went to the Green Wave again. When Williams texted Kaplan that he was coming out, Kaplan replied, "You're going to love it." He's been right so far. Williams homered in his summer debut and has tallied three long balls in just seven games.

Kaplan's bat is scorching hot, too. The outfielder is hitting .630 through six games and has already stolen five bases. He had six steals all season at Tulane. In Santa Barbara the hands-off approach means you get to run. Like many of his teammates, Kaplan loved that style last summer—"It's like going back to when we were little," he says—and he jumped at the chance to head west again.

Tulane has developed into a recent pipeline for the Foresters. The Green Wave's Jeremy Montalbano was one of the heroes of the 2014 NBC World Series championship game and was back for the summer of 2015.

The University of Texas could be called the Foresters' original pipeline. Before retiring in the spring of 2016, Augie Garrido sent three or four of his Longhorns to Santa Barbara every summer. This year infielder Bret Boswell and pitchers Kyle Johnston, Nick Kennedy, and Connor Mayes are here. Even without Garrido in the dugout going forward, the Forester connection is likely to continue. New Texas coach David Pierce is heading to Austin from Kaplan and Williams's Tulane club, where he had been at the helm for two seasons.

Boswell is off to a blistering start with the Foresters. He had a hit in his first nine games before the streak ended two days ago. He's getting the day off today, his .466 average and four home runs in the dugout. His Texas teammates Johnston and Mayes are also off to good starts. Johnston pitched six shutout innings and struck out seven in his last start. He's getting lined up to pitch against Team USA when the Foresters host the all-star squad. Mayes is pitching well, too, riding a streak of thirteen scoreless innings in his last two outings. He'll start when the Foresters play Team USA at Dodger Stadium.

They expect to contend against the national team. They would have confidence regardless, but it helps even more that one of their players is quite literally Team USA material. Keston Hiura, a star at UC Irvine and one of college baseball's top sophomore prospects, is playing a few games with the Foresters on a temporary contract, tuning up after an injury in the spring. Since he's a Team USA trials invite, he'll swap Forester blue for red, white, and blue in the two-game set and try to make the national team.

Though the logistics work forced Pintard to have Team USA on his mind today, he doesn't want his players thinking about it too much. They have a more important task at hand. Yesterday's loss up in San Luis Obispo was the team's second defeat in a row on the heels of an eight-game winning streak, and it was among the shakiest performances of the season. The team's record sits at 11-5.

Pintard is about to issue a challenge, but he lets the batting-practice game wind down first. Williams steps back into the cage with teammates watching. He and Brian Bussey—a catcher from Florida State—are the last two hitters standing. Williams has smashed deep fly balls and home runs, but, on the next pitch, he pops it up, and he's saying, "Oh no," before the ball gets even ten feet into the air. Bussey lines a hit into left field to win the battle.

It's the last swing of batting practice. Pintard tells his players to meet in the dugout. The winningest coach in summer collegiate baseball has something to say.

♦ ♦ ♦

"We lost our way last night," Pintard says. "That's the last time we're going to put up with that."

His team is squeezed onto the dugout bench, listening in silence. The pregame chat started innocently enough, with a rundown of the schedule for the next few days, some information about the Team USA game, what uniforms they'll be wearing when. Then Pintard came to the reason for the meeting, and the dugout grew quiet.

With their roster pretty much at full strength now, the Foresters have the talent to win way more often than they lose. An off day is going to happen, but the coaching staff didn't like what caused it last night. "I'm a firm believer in playing loose and relaxed, enjoying the game," Pintard says. "But you need to be focused."

It's a difficult balance to strike in summer ball, especially with the Foresters using the hands-off philosophy. Players may not be reined in on the field, but today's meeting is a reminder that their approach will be. Hustling isn't running out a ground ball, Pintard says. It's paying attention to everything and being ready. They're not here to make friends, he adds. He wants them to, of course, but they can't get lost in the social part of the summer. Their laid-back California days should also include mental preparation and work in the batting cage. Players are here to get better, and Pintard wants them to seize the opportunity.

Chats like this build the foundation of every season in Santa Barbara. Pintard has a feel for what buttons to push and when to push them. He connects with his players—he's all fist bumps and shared laughs much of the time—but he demands a lot. His deft touch means the players don't question his motives on that front. They know he wants the best for them. And they respond.

Assistant coach Skyler Ellis marveled a few years ago when he heard a story from the host dad of Jeremy Montalbano, the Tulane star. The Foresters had just lost two games in a row. "Jeremy told him, 'I never want to lose for that guy again. I don't want to disappoint him,'" Ellis says. "I don't even know how he does it, but he's able to get guys to play for him at a very hard time of the year. The guys just truly want to win here."

The assistant coaches are drawn to that attitude, too. Ellis grew up in Santa Barbara and played youth-league ball for a former Foresters assistant. After finishing his playing career at Oklahoma Baptist University, he got into coaching and now spends his springs with Rogers State University in Oklahoma. He used the connection with his former coach to hook on with the Foresters for the summer.

Tony Cougoule is the pitching coach at nearby Westmont College and is just starting his first summer with the Foresters. He's well aware of the tradition he's joining. To some extent, he says, the Foresters get more attention than UC Santa Barbara. On the West Coast they're the team everybody knows. Cougoule learned quickly why that is. "Bill holds guys to a high standard but still knows how to connect with them," he says. "He gets them to play their best."

Pintard was scouting at a showcase tournament in Arizona when Steve Schuck showed up with a résumé and cover letter. A high school and summer-ball coach in Arizona, he wanted a chance to help out in Santa Barbara. When he got the job offer he had to change his summer plans on the fly and told Pintard he needed a few hours to sort it out. A half hour later Schuck called back and said yes. He couldn't wait. For people who know summer baseball, an offer with the Foresters isn't something you say no to.

Schuck has owned two businesses, but baseball is his passion. His old-school style fits well with Pintard and the Foresters. "Just hustle, go out and play your best, and that's all we ask," Schuck says.

The Foresters always tend to be receptive to that message. Pintard likes grinders, kids who want to play hard. When he's lining up his roster a year out, those qualities are what he's asking college coaches about, more than bat speed or arm strength. Do they play hard? Do they love it? Do they have that competitive fire? If it goes according to plan, the roster is full of players who want to listen, learn, and win.

The team's tradition pulls it all together. The new Foresters know what they're getting into. They've seen the banner up in the stands, and a quick Google search will fill in the rest. Once they're in uniform the tradition isn't a taboo subject. It's something that's talked about, a standard to be met. "We teach the players that name on your chest really means something," Schuck says. "There's a lot of tradition and a lot of big leaguers who have worn that uniform. You're following the legacy, and they get it. They buy into it."

For the current group, the path for adding their chapter to the legacy has been sketched out for them, and today is a signpost. They can be relaxed. They can enjoy every bit of a summer in Santa Barbara. But the opportunity for a winning summer is more fun than anything. "I have fun every time I come to the yard," Pintard says. "I love this game. Have fun. Be focused. That's all I got."

◆ ◆ ◆

First pitch is set for 5:00, a little over an hour away. The Walnut Creek Crawdads have arrived from the Bay Area and are setting up shop, unpacking their gear, taking their turn in the batting cage and on the field. While their opponent warms up, the Foresters scatter to the dugout, the bullpen, and shady spots in between, hydrating and grabbing snacks. Bill Pintard unwraps a sandwich while he and Steve Schuck sketch out the lineup. With Boswell out, there isn't as much pop as usual, but after a few scratch-outs and fill-ins, they like what they've got.

Pintard joins radio broadcaster John Martony outside the dugout to record a brief pregame interview. He starts it with a look around and a reminder to the listeners that it's a beautiful day at the ballpark. That's nothing new but worth appreciating all the same, and Pintard does. There's not a cloud in the sky. It's sixty-eight degrees, like it is pretty much every day. The palm trees outside the stadium's front gates sway in a gentle breeze. Beyond the outfield fence the Santa Ynez Mountains provide a hazy, distant backdrop. For all its diamonds in every corner of the country, this may be summer ball's paradise.

Bret Boswell and teammates Trevor Abrams and Travis Moniot rake the infield after warm-ups. At 4:45 position players meet Pintard in the outfield grass for the familiar pregame base-running routine that many teams utilize. Pintard plays the role of the pitcher. The dozen or so players line up near an imaginary first base, taking their leads all at once. The idea is to hone in on the moment when a pitcher is either going to home or firing a pickoff throw to the bag. Pintard catches a few runners leaning the wrong way as he mimes a pickoff toss. "Got him!" he yells.

After he goes home with a few pitches in a row, he twirls for another pickoff. "Holy smokes!" he says. "With that old-man move. Got him twice."

He's enjoying this. "Got him three times! Where's my focus?"

It's last call for finding it. The infield dirt is groomed and watered. Umpires are at home plate. Starting pitcher Reagan Todd takes his final tosses in the bullpen. Pintard pulls together one more huddle on the spot, just for his hitters. He spells out the goals, trading the abstract for the concrete—100 percent execution with a man on third, pushing the envelope on the bases, staying energized in the dugout, and starting fast. "We don't win because of the *Foresters* on our chest," he tells them. "Baseball's not that kind of game."

They end the chat with hands into the huddle and a "'Sters!" rallying cry. They're about to have the chance to make it their kind of game.

◆ ◆ ◆

Kyle Isbel cracks a ground ball toward first base. The Crawdads pitcher sprints over to cover the bag, but the first baseman bobbles the ball, and Isbel beats the toss. Two pitches later he gets a good jump and steals second base. The Foresters are off and running.

Isbel has been here since day one after a good season at the University of Nevada–Las Vegas (UNLV). He batted leadoff and stole two bases on opening night. He's been on base a lot, just what you need out of a leadoff hitter. The formula this time yields a perfect result. Batting in the second hole, Lex Kaplan stings a three-ball, no-strike pitch to deep right field for a double. Isbel trots home to give the Foresters the 1–0 lead.

From the first spot on the dugout rail, Bill Pintard turns to the team in the dugout and points to Kaplan. "That's how you execute on 3-0," he says.

In the third base coach's box, Steve Schuck is multitasking—giving signs and watching everything, while doing some quick math in his head. When he returns to the dugout he'll pull out his red marker and make tally marks on a laminated sheet of paper labeled "Offensive Pressure." If winning baseball and the Foresters' hands-off approach is an art, the paper is a piece of the science behind it.

The page is headed by four offensive goals. Seven runs is the first objective, a number that means more than just a good offensive output. Paired with the meeting of a defensive goal, a seven-run output yields a win 93 percent of the time, according to the sheet.

Creating a big inning along with a defensive goal puts the percentage at 90. Earning nine freebies—defined as stolen bases, walks or hit-by-pitches, errors, and wild pitches—also puts it at 90 percent. Getting quality at bats 50 percent of the time makes it 91 percent. Base hits, hard-hit balls, well-placed bunts, and eight-pitch at bats are among the criteria for a quality trip to the plate.

There are also benchmarks that are tallied up as the game goes on, and Schuck already has a few to add. The leadoff man reached base, something they aim to make happen in six of nine innings. The Foresters picked up a stolen base and a freebie on the error, and they've already delivered two hard-hit balls. As the inning continues and the Foresters go deep into the count several times, the goal of pushing the opposing team's pitch count over 150 gets off to a good start.

The coaching staff runs through the numbers after every game. Players are aware of it during the game. It fosters an aggressive mind-set without being rigid. The tally connects an individual's performance—even a less positive one than a hit like reaching on an error or pushing an at bat to eight pitches—to the team's success. At its core baseball pits pitcher against hitter in an individual battle, but it's of course a team game. What the Foresters track underscores that combination.

There isn't much else for Schuck to add after the good start to the first inning. Keston Hiura, the Team USA invite, pops out. Pintard tells him not to chase pitches out of the strike zone. The Walnut Creek pitcher isn't throwing particularly hard, and the Foresters need to be patient. Hunter Williams follows the advice and works a walk. Kaplan gets caught stealing, though. It's bound to happen when aggression is the goal, and nobody in the dugout bats an eye. A hit-by-pitch puts two runners on, but the Crawdads escape on a groundout and keep it a 1–0 game.

At least there were no lapses. After last night, it's a start.

◆ ◆ ◆

Reagan Todd knows summer ball. The Colorado native redshirted in his first season at Arizona State in 2015. He was champing at the bit to get back on the mound that summer and was rewarded with a great experience. He pitched for the Bellingham Bells in Washington State, a team in the West Coast League. They rank in the top fifty in summer collegiate baseball attendance figures, and the town—halfway between Seattle and Vancouver—likes its baseball. Ken Griffey Jr. started his pro career there, with a Minor League club that used to play at the same home field as today's summer-ball team.

Todd made nine starts for the Bells, shaking off early rust for a strong stretch in the dog days of summer. He gave up two runs or fewer in five straight starts before a tough outing late in the season that sent his earned run average climbing to 4.88. He struck out twenty-eight, walked twenty-three, and returned to Arizona with plenty of material for off-season work.

He made his debut for the Sun Devils in the spring, starting six games and making nine appearances out of the bullpen. Like his summer, it was an up-and-down ride—he finished with a 6.44 earned run average. He struck out thirty-seven in forty-two innings but walked twenty and gave up fifty-three hits.

This is Todd's third outing with the Foresters. He pitched two scoreless innings in a relief stint and then allowed a run on seven hits a week ago in his first start.

He's logged a scoreless outing so far today when the first two Crawdads knock singles in the second inning, putting runners on first and third. It's not the situation you want to be in right after your team gives you the lead.

Todd buckles down, striking out the next batter on a fastball. Then he's out of the inning in a flash when he induces a 5–4–3 double play. The Foresters remain in front.

Walking slowly back to the dugout, Todd feels good. He's got three pitches working and is throwing them all for strikes. For now he'll work off his fastball, save heavy use of the breaking ball for later. If he hits his spots and limits mistake pitches, he'll be in good shape.

It's good news for the Foresters, and a good pitching perfor-mance starts to look more necessary after the bottom of the second inning. Though the Walnut Creek pitcher doesn't have much veloc-ity, he's got the Foresters off balance. The coaches all hit on famil-iar refrains—"Don't get greedy" and "Let him come to you"—but the hitters are reaching anyway, trying to do too much, jumping at pitches that seem too good to pass up. Lex Kaplan grounds out weakly to first base with runners on second and third to end the inning. The Foresters may have a pitchers' duel on their hands.

◆ ◆ ◆

John Martony spends his summers in the top row of Caesar Uye-saka Stadium. He's a radio guy in Santa Barbara, calling Santa Bar-bara City College and high school football in the fall and baseball in the spring. His summers belong to the Foresters. Perched at a table just outside the press box, his calls are loud enough for fans in the home-plate bleachers to hear.

Today's crowd is a little small, a reminder that baseball in paradise can be tricky. But there are Foresters diehards among the scattered groups in the stands. Under the bleachers, which are elevated, fans line a ring of stadium seats. The stands above provide shade, and the field-level view couldn't be better.

Signs posted all around the park tout the games against Team USA. Supporters can sign up for a fan bus to Dodger Stadium. The package includes lunch with the team.

The franchise makes a concerted effort to connect with fans and the community, beyond the natural host-family relationships of sum-mer ball. The hallmark of the effort is the Hugs for Cubs program. Bill Pintard's son, Eric, a former pitcher and assistant coach with the Foresters, died in 2004 when he was just thirty-two. He had battled a rare form of cancer for seven years—after he was initially given only months to live—and started Hugs for Cubs before he died. His family and team leaders have kept it going.

The program pairs Forester players with local children who have cancer. They get together for events like bowling nights and trips to Dodgers or Angels games. There are hospital visits and an off-season golf tournament to raise funds. On Father's Day this year the Foresters hosted Hugs for Cubs day at the ballpark, welcoming many of the kids in the program to a game.

It makes an impact on the kids involved, and on the players. In a chase for baseball glory and a busy summer, perspective helps.

On the field today it's still a grind. Martony calls a quick top of the third inning but an equally fast bottom half as the Foresters go quietly. The aggressive attack is hurting more than it helps, like it does sometimes. Williams gets thrown out trying to advance on a wild pitch. It's still a 1–0 game.

◆ ◆ ◆

If there's one guy in the park who doesn't mind a low-scoring affair, it's Reagan Todd. He's pitching his best game of the spring and summer combined, a shutout through four frames. The breaking ball he stayed away from early on is getting mixed in now, and it's working. He strikes out the first two batters in the fifth inning, one looking and one swinging.

The Foresters get a two-out hit in the bottom half of the fifth inning, but a line drive straight to the left fielder ends the threat. Todd trots back out for the sixth, still protecting the 1–0 lead.

The middle of the order is due up, but Todd catches the leadoff man looking for his seventh strikeout of the game. The next batter singles—the first hit for the Crawdads in their last nine at bats—but it does not start a trend. Todd strikes out the next hitter, his fourth punch-out in the last two innings.

Todd issues a two-out walk to keep the inning alive. In the dugout Pintard checks on the pitch count. It's around eighty. In Todd's first start he reached eighty-nine, so this isn't new territory. But the walk was his first of the game. The bullpen may need to get going.

Todd isn't having any of that. He fires two quick strikes for an 0-2 count on Mickey Nunes and then strikes him out swinging. Around the single and the walk, he struck out the side.

Pintard and pitching coach Tony Cougoule meet Todd outside the dugout and shake his hand. His day is done. He did his job— six innings, no runs, nine strikeouts.

With plenty of open spots on Steve Schuck's "Offensive Pressure" page, it's time for the Forester hitters to do theirs.

◆ ◆ ◆

Hunter Williams has been on base twice today. As a burly power hitter, he's a prototypical run producer, but as he digs into the batter's box to open the bottom of the sixth inning, an ability to get on base makes him a good candidate to start a rally, too. He's been on base in all but one of his games with the Foresters and is riding a streak of four consecutive multihit games.

He gets into a bad spot this time, falling behind in the count one ball and two strikes. To make it worse, he chips the end of his wood bat when he fouls off a pitch. He examines the chip and decides to step right back into the box. He'll say later that he didn't switch to a new bat because he figured it would be fine—and he's right. On the 1-2 pitch he cranks a home run out of the ballpark in left field, to the same spot where he was launching balls in batting practice. He rounds the bases quickly and meets a parade of high fives and fist bumps in the dugout, plus a few laughs about his dinged-up bat.

The Foresters have finally come back to life, and they've done it in a momentum-shifting kind of way. The fact that the home run came with two strikes makes it an even better foundation to build on. Dylan Paul, a left fielder from Texas State who's hitting over .400 so far this summer, follows the home run by smacking a single. He steals second base and scampers to third on a wild pitch. The rally—and the pressure—is on.

Colby Barrick, a junior-college star who's committed to play here next spring for UC Santa Barbara, draws a walk. Shortstop Travis Moniot gets hit by a pitch, and the bases are loaded with nobody out. That does it for the Walnut Creek starting pitcher.

Catcher Steven Coe greets the reliever with a searing line drive on the first pitch but watches it fly foul. He battles to a 2-2 count but strikes out.

It's up to ninth-place hitter Hank LoForte, a young standout from West Coast power Cal State–Fullerton. First, he gets some help. A wild pitch allows Paul to race home for the 3–0 lead. LoForte then lines a single to plate Barrick. Moniot tries to score, too, but gets thrown out at the plate.

The top of the order is up, and Bill Pintard wants the rally to continue. There might be a tendency to relax when the lead suddenly grows, but Pintard wants to keep the pressure on—for today and for the future. "Two-out hits win championships," he says from the dugout.

Kyle Isbel, the leadoff man, does his best but lines out to left field. There's no two-out magic today, but it was a good inning. The Foresters hope it's enough to snap their losing streak.

◆ ◆ ◆

Sean Chandler runs in from the bullpen with long strides from his slim six-foot-four frame. He's from Bellevue, Nebraska, a town just outside the college baseball mecca of Omaha. A late-round draft pick out of high school, he headed to the University of Nebraska to continue his career. It was a quiet freshman year this spring—just nine appearances out of the bullpen—but it's easy to see the potential, especially from the eye of a scout like Bill Pintard. He expects Chandler to bump his fastball into the midnineties in a few years.

Taking the baton from Reagan Todd, Chandler hands out a leadoff walk in the seventh inning but strikes out the next batter. The runner is erased on an interference call at the plate, and the next hitter lines out to end a quick inning.

Lex Kaplan walks to lead off the bottom of the seventh inning and stays aggressive on the bases in pursuit of an insurance run. He steals second but gets thrown out at third. Pintard isn't much for red lights, but his team has been cut down at third a few times tonight, running itself right out of rallies in the process. It's a fine line in his preferred approach, and, at this point in the season, he'll let them run. In August maybe not, but by then the goal is for all the practice on the base paths to add up. Perhaps Kaplan won't get thrown out when he tries the same thing in Wichita.

There's trouble in the top of the eighth inning when an error in center field and a misplay of a deep fly ball in right field allow Walnut Creek to plate two runs. Chandler escapes further trouble with a flyout to center.

It's a 4–2 game, and the Foresters again fail to add to the lead in a one-two-three eighth inning. Another relief pitcher, Blake Smith, takes over for Chandler in the ninth, an inning that he figures to make his own this summer. The six-foot 190-pounder is in the mold of hard-throwing closers with small frames like Billy Wagner and Huston Street. After two years at a junior college, he saved five games for Southeastern Conference (SEC) power Mississippi State in the spring.

Smith struck out two in his first outing with the Foresters two days ago, after the Bulldogs closed out their season with a Super Regional loss to Arizona. This is his first save chance, and after a momentary hiccup where he hits the leadoff man, he runs with it.

Smith strikes out the next batter swinging. The leadoff man who reached steals second and takes third on a wild pitch, but Smith is unfazed. He strikes out Marcos Valencia on three pitches.

Brady Weiss, Walnut Creek's leadoff hitter, is the last chance. He came into the game batting .267 and has a hit today. Smith gets ahead in the count 0-1 and then 1-2. He just misses the corner on a pitch that gets the count to 2-2, but finishes strong. He spins in a breaking ball that freezes Weiss for strike three and the final out.

Steven Coe, the catcher, trots to the mound and shares a hug with Smith as teammates hop over the dugout rail and join them. Pintard stations himself at the end of the handshake line. The individual messages he has for every player slow the line down a bit, but nobody minds. The Foresters are back on track.

◆ ◆ ◆

Christina Songer is very popular after games. Today the president of the team's board of directors lugs a giant delivery bag stuffed with Chick-fil-A sandwiches onto the edge of the field for the postgame meal. Bill Pintard tells the team to give her a round of applause. Seeing what's waiting for them, they respond enthusiastically.

In the corner of the dugout Steve Schuck takes a peek at his "Offensive Pressure" sheet. It wasn't a perfect day, but it was pretty good—red tally marks cover the page. The win was well earned.

While players tidy up the field, Reagan Todd climbs the bleachers for a radio interview. Just outside the dugout Pintard chats with team interns who will write a game recap for the Foresters' website. He credits Todd with an outstanding performance and cites Williams's home run as the game's turning point. The offensive struggles, he says, were partly because the Foresters just aren't used to seeing a soft-tossing pitcher. They'd rather see someone throwing eighty-eight to ninety-two miles per hour, like they do all spring and for much of the summer.

The sun remains high in the sky. It was just a two-and-a-half-hour game. The Foresters tend to play quick ones. These aren't the four-hour grinds of Major League Baseball. An aggressive style requires a team on its toes.

With postgame duties complete and sandwiches waiting, Pintard pulls the team together in the dugout. It was an outstanding effort, he says—fourteen strikeouts from the pitching staff and enough offense to get by. He wants to see fewer swings at pitches outside the zone if they run into a similar type of arm. He salutes Williams—dubbed Big Country—for providing the spark with his two-strike home run. "Better effort, better focus," he says. "Back on the winning track."

After brief comments by Schuck and Tony Cougoule, Pintard runs through the schedule for tomorrow, another game with Walnut Creek. He asks the team how things are going with their host families. Heads nod all around.

The final task is the "'Ster it up" cheer. Kaplan and Williams get sent to the center of the huddle. "'Ster it up on Tulane," Pintard says, and the cheer goes up.

The sky is still bright, another vintage Santa Barbara day drifting into a perfect evening. Just like Pintard said, it was a beautiful day at the ballpark.

5 / CAPE COD

The school bus rumbles into the parking lot at Whitehouse Field around a quarter past four, a little over two hours before first pitch. The Cotuit Kettleers, already wearing their pin-striped baseball pants paired for now with maroon warm-up jerseys, pile out of the bus, half through the front door, the other half hopping off the emergency exit in the back. They unload their bags and the team gear—coolers, helmets, buckets of baseballs.

The drive to Harwich took a while, and their ride wasn't exactly luxurious. Cape League teams catch the familiar yellow school buses for away games, taking advantage of what's available in the summer without spending big money. It's one of many quaint—and not too unwelcome—reminders to players on the precipice of big-time baseball that they haven't arrived there quite yet.

It's twenty-four miles from the Kettleers' stomping ground at Lowell Park to the home field of the Harwich Mariners, but it was a stop-and-go adventure today, as it often is once summer really arrives. It's here with a bang today—eighty-seven degrees, sunny, humid, just a slight breeze by the water—and the beach traffic has followed.

Six weeks ago, at the Kettleers' chilly first day of practice, afternoons like this seemed very far away. Mike Roberts warned his players then about how fast it all goes. The Fourth of July, what

Roberts dubbed the true beginning of summer for families and tourists on the Cape, has come and gone. For the baseball teams the holiday is more of a midseason benchmark than a beginning. As the fireworks pop, the possibilities of a summer are hardening into realities.

For a while there, reality wasn't looking too good for the Cotuit Kettleers. The temporary contract players who dominated the roster early on had to shoulder a big load, as the NCAA postseason delayed the talent influx. Infielders were in roles they weren't used to, and the defense suffered. Projected big hitters scuffled at the plate. Pitchers slogged their way through difficult outings. Nothing went right. The Kettleers started the season 1-12.

It was about as rough a beginning as anyone around Lowell Park could remember. Even Jeren Kendall, the Vanderbilt star who made a cameo before joining Team USA, couldn't spark the Kettleers. He scuffled at the plate, too.

All the while Roberts liked his team's work ethic. Despite the lack of returns, they were sticking with it, listening, working, trying to get better. He had no complaints in that department, and eventually the work started to pay off. As the third week of the season arrived, a few pitching reinforcements and some key additions to solidify the defense helped steady the ship.

By that Fourth of July benchmark, things were looking up. The Kettleers had won five of their last seven games heading into the holiday. While they lost to Falmouth on July 4, they've continued to play well since then, going 5-1-1 in their last seven games. They beat Harwich—the hottest team in the league through the first half of the season—earlier this week, and they'll get a chance for another big win on the Mariners' home field tonight.

The brutal start is a big hole to dig out of, but with eight of the league's ten teams making the playoffs—and Cotuit not alone in fighting through early struggles—possibilities remain. "Things have kind of fallen into place," Roberts says. "If each guy is getting better, then collectively, we've got a chance."

◆ ◆ ◆

Colton Hock stands in the grass down the right-field line, next to the bullpen mound, and stretches out his six-foot-four-inch frame. He is set to make his fourth start of the summer tonight, continuing the process of lengthening his innings load after a spring spent in the Stanford bullpen.

The right hander's results have been mixed but generally pretty good. He made his debut in the team's third game of the season, opening up with a relief appearance and allowing one run in two-thirds of an inning against the Bourne Braves. He stayed in the bullpen for two more outings as he settled in, going an inning and two-thirds the next time and two and two-thirds after that. He moved into the starting rotation on June 26 and pitched well, striking out five and surrendering two runs in five innings against defending champion Yarmouth-Dennis. His most recent start showcased his best stuff, as he struck out six in four-plus innings versus the Wareham Gatemen a week ago.

Whatever the numbers, Hock remains one of the more intriguing pitchers in the Cape League this summer, a prospect with tantalizing upside. Two hours before first pitch, a dozen scouts dot the bleachers, making notes and filming video as they watch hitters take batting practice. Once the game starts the radar guns will be at full attention whenever Hock toes the rubber. He's one of the main attractions tonight.

Top talent like Hock formed one piece of the puzzle as the Kettleers worked their way out of their early-season slide, with the hard-charging tone set by the temp-contract players playing a part, too.

Clay Fisher, a key player in UC Santa Barbara's College World Series run, made his debut July 3 and has started at shortstop every game since. After the Kettleers struggled defensively in that spot through the season's first few weeks, Fisher has yet to make an error. He also went 3-for-4 with a home run in his first game.

Hock's Stanford teammates Quinn Brodey and Jackson Klein have solidified the top of the batting order, getting on base at a good clip and delivering production. Brodey, in particular, has been a spark. The outfielder started his career with the Cardinal as a two-way player, hitting and pitching. Now a full-time hitter, he's starting to look the part this summer. He's tallied eleven hits in the last eight games.

Greyson Jenista, one of the few full-contract players who was here on day one, got off to a tough start. He was hitless in eight of his first nine games. A highly sought-after recruit at Wichita State, Jenista was getting the typical rude welcome to the Cape League for a freshman hitter. He could take solace in the footsteps he followed. Kris Bryant batted .223 for Chatham after his freshman year at San Diego. Two years later he was the No. 2 overall pick in the Major League Draft, and the rest was history.

Comfort also came from getting better. Jenista broke out of his slump with a three-game hitting streak. He smacked his first home run a few weeks ago and had two RBI in the win over Harwich earlier this week. The budding star is back on track.

Cal Stevenson, a junior-college outfielder who's headed to Arizona in the fall, has been a steady presence in the lineup, one of the few players who got off to a good start at the plate. Oregon's A. J. Balta and Tim Susnara have been solid contributors. Alonzo Jones Jr., the big recruit for Vanderbilt, is scuffling at the plate like Jenista was early on, another freshman finding a rude welcome.

Jason Delay, a veteran catcher from Vanderbilt who played in the Cape League for Bourne last summer, signed on with Cotuit in late June and has been a big addition, with his defense behind the plate and his ability to handle the pitching staff setting him apart. Delay's arrival came a few weeks after he was drafted in the eleventh round of the Major League Baseball Draft by the San Francisco Giants. He has to decide whether to sign or return to Vanderbilt for his senior season. In the meantime he's calling Cotuit home.

Alec Byrd, a left-handed pitcher from Florida State, made his first appearance on June 26 and has delivered scoreless outings in four of his five trips to the mound. Jason Bilous, a highly touted freshman who just won a national title with Coastal Carolina last month, made his summer debut yesterday.

The trappings of a Cape League summer have helped the cause, too. On an off day in early July, every team took a longer bus ride than usual to a different field than usual. Boston's Fenway Park hosts an annual workout for Cape League players, with scouts watching every move. Pitchers don't throw much—nobody wants to waste the innings—but the hitters get to step into the cage and take aim at the Green Monster. For all the players the time at Fenway always ranks as one of the more memorable parts of a summer in the Cape League. For once they're the ones in awe of the grass they walk, like the kids stepping onto the field at Lowell Park for postgame autographs. And they all hope they'll be back someday.

◆ ◆ ◆

Quinn Brodey is first up in the cage for batting practice. Mike Roberts throws all the pitches himself, one after another in quick succession, sweat darkening his maroon shirt. Behind him on the mound, Ross Achter is on bucket duty, collecting balls for the next round of pitches. It's an off day for him, and pitchers on off days always get stuck with jobs.

Achter is not complaining. He's here, after all.

Twelve days ago rosters were finalized. Teams still retain the ability to make changes after that date, but by the July 3 deadline they're required to dispense with the temporary contracts that filled rosters in the early part of the season.

It's a difficult day, for everybody. The numbers crunch is a harsh reality. The temp players know the deal, but an early departure still stings. For coaches and general managers, saying goodbye to a temp player often means losing someone who has been in town from the beginning, someone who has put in a month's worth of work.

The crunch wasn't too tough in Cotuit this year. A few of the Kettleers who played Wiffle ball that first day departed soon after when full-contract players who were just a day or two late began to arrive. Tanner Nishioka, the DII player from Hawaii, got three at bats in two games. Cameron Sepede from Salt Lake Community College pitched two and a third innings. Ricky Surum started at shortstop on opening night and played three more games before departing.

Many of the Wiffle-ball players stuck around, like Achter. He pitched three scoreless innings of relief in the first game of the season, striking out two and allowing one hit. It was a strong first impression, and it hasn't faded. The lefty tossed four and a third innings his next time out and picked up Cotuit's only win in the first two weeks of the season. He's been solid—a 3.05 earned run average while mixing starts and relief outings.

The pitching staff was further solidified with full contracts for temp players Eddie Muhl, Connor Simmons, and Cal Becker. Becker had become a favorite for Roberts, a kid who washed out of big-time college baseball—and ended up working in construction—looking for one last shot on a mound. He made an impression with Cotuit and signed a professional contract with the Arizona Diamondbacks just a few days ago.

Patrick Dorrian got good news, too, on deadline day. He filled in at shortstop before Fisher arrived and then slid to third base. He's had his struggles at the plate—his average just recently inched over .200—but he's a gamer. He plays backyard baseball, the brand Mike Roberts prefers. "He plays third base," Roberts says, "like a hockey goalie."

The full-contract signings trickled out throughout deadline day, popping up on the Cape League's website, which tracks transactions. David Gerics kept a close eye alongside Joe Cavanaugh, a Kettleers board member and his host dad.

His name wasn't showing up. Maybe it had always been a long shot—he was a five-foot-eleven righty from a Division III school. His earned run average was sitting at 6.55 after a bad outing in his last relief appearance, on June 28. Five days later, he hadn't been on the mound again.

Gerics went to pack his bags for home when his phone rang. It was Roberts. He was sticking around.

In the sun-splashed Harwich outfield today, Gerics shags fly balls. He returned to the mound the same day he got the call and struck out two in an inning of work against Falmouth. Last time out he went two scoreless innings against Brewster, his best outing of the summer so far.

He might pitch tonight. He might not. He fills in where the Kettleers need him. He's here.

◆ ◆ ◆

The same steamy weather that's hitting Cape Cod has descended on nearby Rhode Island, too. The Newport Gulls and Ocean State Waves are back at Cardines Field again tonight, set to meet for the sixth and final time this New England Collegiate Baseball League season.

Keeping up their hot start to the summer, the Waves won the first four matchups with their rivals to clinch the season series. They nearly made it five in a row on the Fourth of July, but the Gulls rallied from a 5–2 hole in dramatic fashion, scoring four runs in the bottom of the ninth inning to win 6–5.

The victory marked the beginning of a four-game winning streak for the Gulls, who have won eight of ten coming into tonight's game. It's the streak they've been waiting for, the kind they often deliver as they make their near-annual climb to the top of the standings.

Troy Dixon, the St. John's catcher who did end up coming to Newport, has been a welcome addition in that quest. After taking an 0-for-3 in his debut—just three days after Paiva called him and he headed north—Dixon started a six-game hitting streak. A day after it ended he went 4-for-5 with two runs scored in a victory over the Sanford Mainers, and he hasn't cooled down much since. Three days ago he had his best performance of the season, going

5-for-6 in a 14–1 demolition of the North Adams Steeple Cats. After starting the summer at home, Dixon is all over NECBL leaderboards as one of the league's top catchers.

Charlie Carpenter, whose injury first prompted Paiva to bring in Dixon, missed two weeks but came back with a bang. A recent seven-game hitting streak put his batting average at .377. He and Dixon will bat second and third in the order tonight.

Stephen Scott of Vanderbilt, one of the freshmen from power-house programs who are Newport regulars, is riding a five-game hitting streak and flashing serious power.

Mark Powell, the native of nearby Middletown, has held on to a regular gig, getting a chance to play most nights. He had three hits and two runs scored during the four-game win streak. He's one for his last fifteen, though, and he will get a day off tonight.

With the summer weather finally taking hold, the City by the Sea is buzzing with tourists. Big events like the Newport Folk Festival and Jazz Festival are on tap for later in the month. Holding their own in the busy landscape as they always do, the Gulls drew twenty-four hundred fans in their most recent home game. With a Friday-night game against an in-state rival on the docket, tonight might be even better.

◆ ◆ ◆

Two days ago you could still bask in the midnight sun in Fairbanks, Alaska, but just barely. Yesterday marked the first premidnight sunset since the solstice, at 11:59 p.m. The sun will dip at 11:56 tonight. Three minutes may not seem like a lot, but in most places the difference in sunsets from day to day during the summer is one minute. Three minutes day after day adds up. Today, less than a month later, will be forty-six minutes shorter than the day of the summer solstice.

The Goldpanners have made the most of the daylight with their best stretch of the season. Their victory in the Midnight Sun Game sparked a four-game winning streak and a stretch of eight victories in nine games.

Isaiah Aluko's hot streak has played a big part. The powerfully built outfielder with the raw tools went hitless in the Midnight Sun Game but has had at least one hit—and often two—in ten of the twelve games since. He's batting .384 on the year with ten doubles and two home runs, cementing himself as the team's best hitter.

Justin Harrer was also pretty quiet on the solstice, going 1-for-1 with a walk and a sacrifice fly. The Washington State freshman has bumped his average to .375 since and is riding a six-game hitting streak into tonight's game.

Alex Mascarenas, the former UCLA football player, has held on to the top spot in the batting order and is hitting .287. Kevin Connolly from Creighton is batting an even .300.

The Goldpanners are in the midst of their third and final long home stand against other barnstorming West Coast teams. After the Kenai Peninsula Oilers were in town for five games, it was the Barona Stars, a Western Baseball Association team based in San Diego. The San Francisco Seals swung into town next for a seven-game series. The Everett Merchants, a Pacific International League team with collegiate players and some recent graduates, are in Fairbanks starting tonight.

The opponents fit in with the Goldpanners' identity—a little more independent than franchises with long league schedules. And the NBC World Series is the end-of-summer destination all of them hope to reach.

In two weeks the Goldpanners will begin a long road trip, with the World Series in Wichita as the final stop. They'll hit Kenai for a rematch with the Oilers on their way out of Alaska and then stop for a three-game set in Washington against the Wenatchee Apple Sox. Then it's a quick stop in Hays, Kansas, for a game against a summer-ball powerhouse before NBC play begins. The nights will be shorter, but the baseball will be good.

♦ ♦ ♦

Getting a seat at Caesar Uyesaka Stadium was a little more diffi-cult than usual when Team USA made its stop in Santa Barbara. Radar gun–toting scouts filled the lower concourse underneath the grandstand, jammed in shoulder to shoulder. The Foresters' official scout count was 147. Outside of showcase events and perhaps the Cape League All-Star Game, it might have been the most heavily scouted amateur baseball game of the year.

The Team USA players were the main attraction, like the former Kettleer Jeren Kendall and Louisville's Brendan McKay, a hitting and pitching star who played for the Cape League's Bourne Braves last summer. Tanner Houck, a six-foot-five righty who struck out 106 batters for Missouri this spring, was slated to be on the mound.

But the Foresters garnered some attention, too. At the Dodger Stadium game—the first of two against Team USA—they gave up seven runs in the third inning but battled back for a 10–6 final.

On their home field the Foresters were on even footing with the visitors. In front of those 147 scouts, Texas pitcher Kyle Johnston outdueled Houck, striking out six and allowing one run on four hits in six innings of work. Hunter Williams, the Tulane slugger, mashed a home run. Texas star Bret Boswell kept up his red-hot start and smacked two hits.

The game was tied 1–1 in the tenth inning when an injury to the Team USA pitcher—and the fact that no one was available to replace him—led to an agreement to call the game. The Foresters had a runner in scoring position at the time, but tie or not, they had made their impression.

With one of the highlights of the season in the books, the Forest-ers fell into a bit of a Team USA hangover and lost their next three games. They've won six of eight since, and their top players delivered a good showing at the California Collegiate League All-Star Game earlier this week. Seven players were on the North Division ros-ter, and the team was coached by Foresters head man Bill Pintard.

Boswell had two hits in the All-Star Game and continues to be one of the best players in the league. He's hitting .356 with six home runs. Williams is batting .367 and sitting right behind Boswell for the team lead with five home runs. Lex Kaplan, his Tulane teammate, still hasn't seen his average dip below .400 all summer. Johnston had a tough time in the All-Star Game but owns a 2.54 ERA on the year. Cody Crouse has a 2.39 ERA.

Their former teammate Keston Hiura from UC Irvine successfully earned a spot with Team USA and left Santa Barbara with his new club. He had a hit last week in a game in Taiwan and is looking like one of the squad's best prospects.

Tonight the Foresters will host a nonleague game against the Valley Bears. They won 13–1 last night and would like to keep the offense rolling. The California Collegiate League playoffs loom two weeks out. Then it's off to Wichita for a championship quest.

◆ ◆ ◆

After the last swings of batting practice for the Kettleers, the Harwich grounds crew springs into action and gets the field ready. Players do most of the heavy lifting. Major Leaguers with Cape League summers on their résumés have all hosed down mounds and raked infield dirt. It's a product of the Cape League's early years, when players worked summer jobs. At one time it was a requirement for the league's NCAA certification that players be offered the chance to work. Buck Showalter served lunch in Hyannis. Mo Vaughn painted houses in Wareham. Jeff Bagwell washed dishes at Friendly's in Chatham. Most players don't take on those kinds of jobs now, but team clinics and field maintenance keep them busy.

Whether they're helping with field duty or staying cool in the dugout, Harwich's standouts hope they'll look back from a similar position someday. It's been a big summer for the Mariners. They started the season with an 8–3 win over Cotuit and won four more in a row before taking their first loss. They've been atop the league's East Division ever since.

Ernie Clement from the University of Virginia is hitting .383, threatening to become the Cape League's second hitter in as many years to bat .400—a feat that hadn't been achieved in more than twenty years before Andrew Calica of UC Santa Barbara did it last season.

Clement's Cavaliers teammate Pavin Smith is one of the most projectable hitters on the Cape, with a smooth left-handed swing. North Carolina State's Joe Dunand is an athletic infielder and has the right baseball bloodlines—he's a nephew of former Major League MVP Alex Rodriguez. Nick Feight from the University of North Carolina–Wilmington tied for second in the nation with twenty-one home runs in the spring.

As good as their top hitters are, the Mariners have really made their mark on the mound. With the deepest starting rotation in the league and a host of power arms manning the bullpen, Harwich's pitching dominated the league in the first few weeks of the season. Twelve games in—with the team's record sitting at 10-2—the Mariners had allowed a total of just sixteen earned runs, adding up to a 1.29 earned run average, a shockingly low number even in a pitching-heavy league. Two nights ago the Mariners delivered their seventh shutout of the season in a 4–0 win over Chatham. Plenty of Cape teams have gone a full summer without logging seven shutouts.

The Kettleers will obviously have their hands full tonight, but there's no doubt they'll have a shot. Even dominant teams rarely run roughshod at any level of baseball. That's especially true in the Cape League, where the season is two months long and every team boasts a dugout full of talent.

There's also a chase pack hot on Harwich's heels. The Mariners have slowed their pace—7-7-2 over their last sixteen games. Yarmouth-Dennis, the perennial powerhouse, is making another run. After an 0-5 start to the season—which included a lopsided loss to Harwich—the Red Sox have gone 17-5. Vanderbilt's Will Toffey, a Cape Cod native, is leading the charge with a .309 batting average.

In the West Division—where Cotuit is trying to make headway—the Falmouth Commodores have broken away from the pack with seven wins in their last eight games. Lipscomb's Michael Gigliotti has been one of the best players in the league and has teamed with two of his college teammates to introduce their program to the nation's top summer league. Gigliotti went 4-for-5 in the team's most recent game and is hitting .337 with five stolen bases, Jeffrey Passantino leads the league with a 0.56 ERA, and teammate Brady Puckett has a 1.33 ERA. It seems every summer a program outside the power conferences makes a mark in the Cape League and sets the course for a big spring. Lipscomb, located in Nashville and part of the Atlantic Sun Conference, may be the latest.

Falmouth has a few other stars from more typical powerhouses. J. J. Matijevic, who helped Arizona to a runner-up finish at the College World Series, returned to Falmouth on July 4 and picked up where he left off last year with hits in five of his first seven games. Star Florida freshman Brady Singer, already talked about as a future first-round pick, made his Cape League debut on July 3 and hasn't allowed a run in his first two starts.

Thanks to their recent hot streak, the Kettleers have kept themselves in the conversation. Another win over the Mariners tonight would help.

◆ ◆ ◆

In Kenosha, Wisconsin, it's a bobblehead night at Simmons Field, one of many this summer. The chosen figurine tonight is Tailgating Elvis, featuring the Kingfish mascot in a chef's hat and an apron standing behind a grill. Tomorrow night, when the Madison Mallards come to town, fans will participate in the Herbert's Jewelers Replica Championship Ring Scavenger Hunt. Vouchers hidden throughout the stadium are good for a replica championship ring that looks just like the one the Kingfish captured when they won the Northwoods League title last season.

At the height of the summer, with the turnstiles humming, promotions don't stop just because the main event is coming up. Buzz for the home run derby at the harbor has been growing louder. The field of competitors was announced two days ago. It includes league home run leader Daulton Varsho, a catcher from the University of Wisconsin–Milwaukee with big-league bloodlines. Michigan State's Marty Bechina of the hometown Kingfish will be the crowd favorite, though he enters the competition with only three home runs on the summer.

Preparations for the big night are in the final stages. Staffers and volunteers are booked. The kayaks are ready. The park by the harbor is quiet for now, just the usual dog walkers and sightseers. That will change soon. Home runs will start hitting the water in three days.

In the nation's capital the DC Grays will be trying to snap a six-game losing streak tonight. It hasn't been the smoothest summer for the club. Five of the six losses in the skid were by two runs or less, continuing a season-long trend. They haven't been able to get over the hump.

Off the field it's a different story. The new RBI program has been a success—good numbers, plenty of interest, and a lot of baseball lessons. Clinics have drawn big crowds. In addition to the weekly camps, Washington Nationals manager Dusty Baker and four of his big leaguers joined the Grays a few weeks back for a clinic at Andrews Air Force Base, where 132 children from military families got a taste of big-time baseball.

The Grays are visiting the Herndon Braves tonight in Cal Ripken Collegiate League action. They'll be on the road to Baltimore tomorrow. When they return home Sunday they'll host the members of their RBI teams for an on-field salute. The RBI regional tournament is quickly approaching, and the Grays-sponsored teams will be making their debuts.

A few hours south, the Peninsula Pilots had their second-largest crowd of the season at War Memorial Stadium a few nights ago, with the tally of 2,769 checking in just behind the opening-night crowd of 3,354.

The fans saw a good game, too. On the heels of a three-game losing streak, the Pilots broke out with a 5–4 win over the Wilson Tobs. It was another big night for Will Shepherd, a Coastal Plain League veteran who went 3-for-3 with two RBI.

The Pilots are a contender nearly every year, and this summer is no different. Two more victories followed the win in front of the packed house, running the team's record to 24-11. The team is back home tonight against the Morehead City Marlins, with a chance to make it four in a row in front of another big crowd.

◆ ◆ ◆

The large sets of bleachers on the first and third base sides fill quickly as the lineup announcement echoes across Whitehouse Field. The park is nestled in the woods behind Harwich's Monomoy Regional High School, a short path from the school's parking lot the only way in. A press box that could pass for a Bank Street Beach cottage hugs the fence behind home plate. Beach chairs are lined up two deep around the backstop.

In the springtime the Monomoy High School baseball team calls the field home. Just before the Cape League's Mariners arrive in June, the field often hosts an NCAA Division III regional, fans from New England schools like UMass Boston and Suffolk packing the metal stands.

The red, white, and blue bunting that now adorns the fences is a sure sign that summer baseball has arrived. So are the extra lawn chairs positioned down the lines. For big games, fans even set up shop at the edge of the trees that border the outfield fence. When Harwich ended a twenty-one-year drought with the 2008 Cape League championship, a crowd pegged at six thousand watched it. They must have been scaling those trees.

Pitching is the likeliest attraction for Cape League fans tonight, with North Carolina's Hunter Williams set to share the mound with Colton Hock. Williams owns a 1.82 earned run average in four starts, part of Harwich's dominant starting rotation. He beat Cotuit on opening night, the first blow in the difficult start to the season for the Kettleers.

The top of the first inning goes quickly in the rematch—a diving catch of a line drive off the bat of Jackson Klein, a chopper on the infield, a ground ball to third base. One out, two outs, three outs. Williams throws all of five pitches.

Hock trots to the mound and makes his warm-up tosses. After the throw down from the catcher to second base and the around-the-horn routine, infielders gather by the mound, and Hock bumps gloves with each one.

The leadoff man is Ernie Clement, the Virginia standout who's tearing up the league. He wastes no time, swinging at the first pitch he sees and slapping a hard ground ball toward shortstop. Clay Fisher won't make his first error here. He gathers a hop and fires to first, where Greyson Jenista completes the good play with a scoop. Two flyouts later and Hock has himself a one-two-three inning to match Williams.

Cotuit's Alonzo Jones Jr. leads off the top of the second with a broken-bat ground ball that Harwich handles for the first out. With these pitchers it might not be the first splintered lumber of the game. The presence of the wood bats in general makes the Cape a happy place for pitchers, but there's also the satisfaction that comes from cracking one of those bats. Inside fastballs that jam a hitter might get muscled into the outfield in the metal-bat world of college baseball. It's a more just result—at least for the pitchers—on Cape Cod.

Pitching has almost always dominated in the Cape League, though the growing tendency for highly touted arms to take a summer off or limit their innings has taken some of the juice out of radar-gun readings. Plenty of stars still show up, though. Walker Buehler and Phil Bickford—first-round picks the next year—pitched the Yarmouth-Dennis Red Sox to the 2014 league championship. Last year Mitchell Jordan of Stetson University—the former Ocean State Wave—matched a Cape League record with a 0.21 earned run average, a mark he shares with former big leaguer Eric Milton. Even in the one juiced-ball summer when home run records were shattered, current Oakland Athletic Sean Manaea delivered one of the best pitching seasons the Cape has ever seen, striking out a whopping eighty-five batters in 51.2 innings for the Hyannis Harbor Hawks. The total was a modern-era record, besting the number logged by flamethrower Daniel Bard of Wareham in 2005.

Harwich's pitching success this season has made Whitehouse Field a familiar stop for the scouts who pack the bleachers tonight. Along with Williams in the starting rotation, Virginia Tech's Packy Naughton has a 2.20 earned run average, Seton Hall's Shane McCarthy is at 1.50, and West Virginia's B. J. Myers checks in at 1.31. In the bullpen Notre Dame's Peter Solomon and Seton Hall's Zach Schellenger are two of the hardest-throwing arms in the league.

Cotuit's Patrick Dorrian breaks through against Williams in the second inning with a high fly ball that finds grass in deep left-center field. Flashing the hustle that played a role in Roberts's keeping him around, Dorrian races for second base and makes an aggressive dash for third. The Mariners promptly throw him out. Roberts, coaching third, chats with Dorrian before he shuffles back to the dugout.

Williams allows nothing else in the second inning, and Hock quickly returns to the mound. With one out Anthony Critelli lines a double for Harwich's first hit. A walk puts two runners on. Florida State catcher Cal Raleigh follows with a smash on the ground down the first base line, but Greyson Jenista snags it, hops up, and wins a race to the bag for the out, keeping it a 0–0 game.

Whether they're in Cotuit maroon or Harwich navy and red, fans applaud. As is the case at all Cape League ballparks, the biggest ovations in Harwich are always reserved for what happens between the lines. The Minor League–style promotions that are trademarks in other leagues are few and far between on Cape League fields. There are mascots and merchandise, raffles and autographs, but when the game is on, it gets top billing, even on a night like this. Pitchers' duel? Defense sparking the loudest cheers? They don't mind in the Cape League.

♦ ♦ ♦

Tomorrow the Cotuit franchise will celebrate one of the men responsible for the brand of baseball that the fans are enjoying tonight. The death of pioneering general manager Arnold Mycock in April left a void around Lowell Park. Kettleers leadership wanted to stage an event once baseball season rolled around to commemorate Mycock's legacy. He was the general manager for forty-four years, sprinkling in stints as treasurer, secretary, and host parent. Most of all he was a friend to everyone involved with the team.

The appreciation for what Mycock accomplished for Cotuit and for baseball on Cape Cod reflects the league's roots. It's always been about baseball and community, with little room for anything else. "I've always said that if you are doing it to get something out of it personally, you're doing it for the wrong reason," says Cape League president Chuck Sturtevant. "You have to want to do it because you're helping these young ballplayers—future Major Leaguers, hopefully—have an opportunity."

Sturtevant has seen his share of players run with that opportunity. A native of Boston's North Shore, he played baseball growing up and in high school. He and his buddies used to buy bleacher tickets for day-night doubleheaders at Fenway Park and then find their way to better seats.

When he moved to Falmouth in 1981, Sturtevant began to fill his summer nights with Commodores games. As he became a regular, he got to know the people who made the franchise go, and they steadily worked him into the fold. First, he donated baseballs. Then he started going to meetings. Soon, he was on the executive board, and in 1987 he became the general manager. One of his players that first year was future New York Yankee Tino Martinez, a pretty good starting point.

At the time the operation was small—just a half-dozen people on the board, a budget of about $18,000. Sturtevant loaned the team money a few times to cover deposits on housing for coaches.

But the baseball was good and getting better. The switch to wood bats had happened a few years before. Big-time players and big-time scouts were flocking to Cape League parks, each drawing the other. The league and its franchises were responding. Small operations began to grow. Relationships with local sponsors expanded. More and more volunteers hooked on every year.

Many of the same people who had sparked the league's modern-era growth kept pushing, like Mycock in Cotuit and Fred Ebbett in Harwich. "Arnold and Fred Ebbett were my two mentors," Sturtevant said. "I relied on them 99.9 percent of the time for assistance when I first got started. I didn't want to make a mistake. I only wanted to do what was best for the team. I would call Arnold up. I'd go over to his house, and we'd sit and talk. He'd help me out as to how he approached things, how he handled things. Fred would help me out as well, dealing with players, parents, coaches. They had had that experience."

Leaders like Mycock and Ebbett seemed to make all the right moves. In the early 1960s there were actually two leagues, the Upper Cape and Lower Cape Leagues. Robert McNeece of Chatham spearheaded the push to join forces under the umbrella of one commissioner, former pro ballplayer Daniel Silva. The move ushered in the Cape's modern era. College players and wood bats followed, and the Cape League was molded into what it is today.

The league's annual awards are a nod to its history, the league championship trophy named for Mycock, the sportsmanship award for Silva, the top-prospect award for McNeece, and many more. This summer Hyannis is naming its field after longtime league president Judy Walden-Scarafile.

Hundreds have contributed to the Cape League's growth and success over the years, most doing it as volunteers. The hard work was a labor of love, and it has yielded more than anyone could have imagined. The league now has a budget of $700,000. When the budgets of each of the ten teams are included, it's more than $2 million.

But for all its evolution, the foundation has never changed. Mycock and his contemporaries fostered the sense of community and the support for young ballplayers that still define the league.

And there was always the baseball. Even as a busy general manager, Mycock used to sit in the dugout at Lowell Park and keep score. He held on to all the old score books, even though he didn't really need to. He remembered most of it anyway.

◆ ◆ ◆

Save for a Cotuit foul ball that might have been a home run with a friendly gust of wind and two stranded runners in the third inning, offense remains elusive tonight. Harwich gets a little something going in the fourth inning, but defense and pitching win the day again. Jackson Klein holds Joe Dunand to a single on what shaped up as a double to the gap. After a bad-hop single, Colton Hock strikes out the next batter looking. A walk loads the bases, and Mike Roberts visits the mound. Hock comes back emphatically, jumping ahead in the count no balls and two strikes, going to 1-2 and then catching another hitter looking for the third out.

With four shutout innings in the books, Hock is in the midst of his best outing of the summer. Going deeper into games—making it five or six innings—is next on his to-do list. Roberts and his coaching staff noticed earlier in the season that Hock's motion changed when he started to get tired, and his velocity dipped as a result. He was standing too tall as he wound up. Bullpen sessions that followed had Hock focusing on his legs and working to stay low.

There's some activity in the bullpen as the bottom of the fifth inning gets started, but nobody's getting warm quite yet. They're just on standby. Hock keeps the relief corps at bay by striking out another hitter on a called strike three—his third straight—and getting two ground balls around a single. He's through five shut-out innings now.

Cotuit goes quietly in the top of the sixth inning as Hunter Williams continues to cruise, too. Taylor Lehman, a towering lefty from Penn State, has been throwing full bore in the Cotuit bullpen, at the ready. Roberts and his staff have a decision to make. As teammates trot to their positions, Hock hangs back in the grass outside the dugout, waiting for his marching orders. Then he gets the green light. He's feeling good—and so are his coaches.

The first batter of the bottom of the sixth inning produces hard contact on a ground ball to third, but Patrick Dorrian knocks it down and whips a throw to first for an out. Clay Fisher handles another ground ball at shortstop. Cotuit is still error free.

Harwich's Johnny Adams, a third baseman from Boston College, steps in with two outs and nobody on. Hock knows it'll be his last batter of the night, and he doesn't hold anything back. He strikes him out swinging on just four pitches, a perfect exclamation point.

After he heads to the dugout Hock walks out to the bullpen down the right-field line for hugs and handshakes with his fellow pitchers. It was his best start of the summer. The scouts were watching. And he gave his team a chance to win.

♦ ♦ ♦

Taylor Lehman and Eddie Muhl share more than a spot in the bullpen and imposing frames. They've also been the unsung MVPs for the Kettleers. Lacking a deep starting rotation, the Kettleers have leaned on the bullpen regularly. Lehman has had outings as short as an inning and a third and as long as five innings. After a rough appearance against Yarmouth-Dennis in early June, he's allowed just two runs since. Muhl is one of the league leaders in appearances with twelve. He's given up one run or fewer in every single one of them.

Lehman gets the call tonight to carry on Colton Hock's gem. In the seventh inning he's greeted by a line drive back up the middle that smacks off his leg and caroms not far from the mound. He gathers himself quickly, scooping up the ball and getting the out at first base. After a quick check by teammates and the home-plate umpire, he stays in the game and puts another scoreless inning on the board.

The day is done for Hunter Williams after seven innings, meaning neither starting pitcher will factor in the decision, despite their matching shutout efforts. Austin Bain of Louisiana State takes over for Williams. Cotuit gets base hits from Patrick Dorrian and Clay Fisher for its first threat in quite a while, but Bain strands them.

After a perfect inning from Lehman in the bottom of the eighth, Cotuit goes quietly in the top of the ninth, with William and Mary reliever Nick Brown striking out two.

Lehman stays on the mound for the bottom half of the ninth and gets two quick outs. Johnny Adams singles to put the go-ahead run on base, and Roberts makes a move, bringing on Ryan Rigby, a hard-throwing reliever from Mississippi State.

In the most recent meeting with Harwich, Rigby worked two scoreless frames for a save, and he's up to the same tricks tonight. A ground ball up the middle is flipped to second for an inning-ending force out.

It's still a 0–0 game. The pitchers' duel will need more than nine innings.

♦ ♦ ♦

Given the arrival of Zach Schellenger to the mound, the top of the eleventh inning seems an unlikely spot for the game's first true rally. Schellenger struck out an eye-popping seventy batters in 45.2 innings for Seton Hall in the spring and has picked up where he left off for Harwich, allowing one earned run this summer. He has already saved five games.

The top of the order is due up for Cotuit, and Quinn Brodey gives Schellenger a rude welcome with a base hit on a 1-0 pitch. Jackson

Klein bunts him to second, and all of a sudden the Kettleers have the go-ahead run in scoring position.

Tim Susnara, a two-year Kettleer from the University of Oregon, strides to the plate next. He came on as a pinch hitter in the ninth inning and struck out swinging. This time he smacks a 1-1 pitch back up the middle and into center field. Brodey gets a good jump, races around third—with Mike Roberts waving him home all the way—and scores easily. Finally, a run is on the scoreboard.

The Kettleers don't stop there. Jason Delay doubles, and Patrick Dorrian continues perhaps the best night of his summer with a line-drive hit to left field. Susnara scores, and Dorrian hustles to second on the throw.

In the dugout Jordan Pearce—an infielder from the University of Nevada—dons a catcher's chest protector, shin guards, and helmet and then puts a mitt on each hand. He's the rally crab, a seaside village's answer to the Angels' old rally monkey. In a good streak like the Kettleers are on, it's whatever works.

Dorrian's run-scoring hit chases Schellenger. The Kettleers get nothing else, but on this night a 2–0 lead looks pretty good.

◆ ◆ ◆

Ryan Rigby stays on the hill for the bottom of the eleventh inning. He gave up one hit in the tenth, but Delay threw the runner out as he tried for a stolen base. Armed with the lead, Rigby will have to get through Harwich's second, third, and fourth hitters to finish off a win.

More than an inning into his appearance, the side-arming righty hasn't yet recorded a strikeout. But pitching to contact is working just fine, and he continues making it work. Antoine Duplantis from Louisiana State rips a line drive to third base, but Patrick Dorrian makes a nice snag for the first out.

Joe Dunand grounds a 1-0 pitch to second base, and Ryan Hagan handles it easily with a throw to Greyson Jenista at first. As Harwich's last chance, Pavin Smith—the big-time hitter from

Virginia—works ahead two balls and one strike, but then hits a grounder back to the mound. Rigby gloves it and flips to first, and the Kettleers win the game 2–0.

Players pop out of the dugout and greet Rigby on the mound. It's about as good a win as the Cotuit Kettleers have had all year.

◆ ◆ ◆

They may have lost the season series, but the Newport Gulls get the best of the rival Ocean State Waves again tonight. Scoreless for three innings, the Gulls break through with three runs in the fourth and three more in the fifth. Stephen Scott, the freshman from Vanderbilt, provides most of the offense with a two-run home run in the fourth and a three-run shot in the fifth. Pitcher Blake Battenfield from Oklahoma State handles the rest. Making just his second start of the summer, he goes six strong innings, allowing one run on four hits.

In Fairbanks it's a rare rough night for the Goldpanners, who struggle on the mound in a 12–2 loss to the Everett Merchants. Isaiah Aluko and Kevin Connolly are the bright spots. Aluko goes 2-for-4, bumping his average even higher, up to .390. Connolly goes 3-for-3 with a double. The Panners will be back at it again tomorrow, as their long series against the Merchants continues.

Santa Barbara rolls on, the Team USA hangover fully in the rearview mirror. The Foresters get their fifth consecutive win in a 10–4 triumph over the Valley Bears. Lex Kaplan and Kyle Isbel both blast home runs. Austin Blessing, a local guy from Santa Barbara City College, tosses five scoreless innings of relief. The Foresters improve to 21-11-1, with Wichita quickly approaching.

The Kenosha Kingfish celebrate Tailgating Elvis Bobblehead Night with a walk-off win. Blake Reese, an infielder from the University of Florida, plates the tying run in the bottom of the ninth inning with an RBI triple. J. D. Hearn from UC San Diego follows with the game-winning hit. The Kingfish fail to hit a home run, but the long balls will be flying soon enough.

The DC Grays drop another close one, falling 7–5 to the Herndon Braves, as a late rally comes up empty. Leadoff man Lamar Briggs gets three hits and Tyler Thomas bests him with four, but it goes for naught, as the Grays leave nine men on base. They fall short despite outhitting the Braves 14–7. Playoff hopes aren't dead yet, but time is running short.

The Peninsula Pilots make it four wins in a row with a 4–3 victory over Morehead City. Sam Sinnen from nearby Old Dominion University tosses six strong innings for the win. Two more home games are up next. The playoffs are still three weeks away, but the Pilots—as usual—have put themselves in a good spot.

◆ ◆ ◆

As they pack up their bags for the school bus ride back to Cotuit, Roberts chats with most every player individually, sharing praise or encouragement. It was a good night, and the way things have turned around, it's worth celebrating. "Honestly, I'm as pleased as a coach could be—and my assistants, too—with any team we've ever dealt with up here," Roberts says as he reflects on the strides the Kettleers have made in the past few weeks. A lot of work was needed, and they've put it in.

Roberts reiterates to Colton Hock that this was his best start and that the improvements made from his last time out were obvious. When Hock got tired, Roberts thought he almost threw the ball better. It's a step forward, one they'll try to build on for his next start six days from now.

Patrick Dorrian finished the game 3-for-5, the first three-hit game of his summer here. He continues to earn his keep. "I'm amazed," Roberts says. "He has just blossomed."

Ross Achter and David Gerics join their fellow pitchers on the walk to the bus. They didn't see any action tonight, but they'll be available whenever the Kettleers need them.

Roberts is happy they both got the chance to stick around. Their opportunity is what a summer in the Cape League is all about. "You just love working with the kids, and you hope and pray they buy into what you're trying to teach them and you see them improve," Roberts said. "I think that's what all ten coaches in the league are here for."

6 / KENOSHA

A kayaker is towing a plastic baby pool through the waters of Kenosha Harbor. It would be a strange sight any other day. Today? Perfectly normal. You have to keep the home run balls somewhere.

There's also a Jet Ski with a large fishing net on board. Two sailboats double as foul poles, foam-covered rope tied between them and buoys every twenty feet to represent a fence. Beyond the fence line, not far from a sign on shore that tells fans not to save spots, there's no such rule in the water. A small speedboat is already anchored for the perfect view of the spectacle to come.

In the park that frames the harbor, food trucks and beer tents, merchandise booths and ice cream stands dot the grass. Tables line the shore in the VIP area, providing front-row seats for sponsors and league officials. A concert stage is set up for a local country music cover band.

This day that started as a wild idea—difficult to execute, certainly, but too tantalizing not to try—is actually happening tonight. Eighteen Northwoods League sluggers will be hitting baseballs into Lake Michigan in about two hours. The balls will splash down. The kayak and Jet Ski will give chase. Thousands of people will cheer.

In bright-red Kenosha Kingfish polo shirts, Conor Caloia, Rich Marks, and Vern Stenman haven't stopped moving all day. Linked by headsets to each other and other Kingfish personnel, they're directing an army of a hundred or so yellow-clad staffers to turn the Kenosha waterfront into a home run–themed carnival. Every detail has been meticulously planned out. Events are what they do, though they've never done anything quite like this. They're not sure anyone has.

Caloia came up with the idea. He's the chief operating officer and a managing partner for Big Top Baseball, which owns and operates four Northwoods League franchises in Wisconsin. When Kenosha was chosen to host the league's All-Star Game, Caloia started brainstorming. A few years ago the professional Class A South Atlantic League held the early rounds of its all-star home run derby on the deck of an aircraft carrier docked in Charleston, South Carolina. They wouldn't be able to do that here—no aircraft carriers on Lake Michigan—but Kenosha's waterfront park, Caloia mused, would make a pretty good home plate.

Stenman, the Big Top president, usually goes back and forth with Caloia when they're spitballing ideas. This won't work. That will. Concepts develop. The brainstorming never stops. But this time the answer was simple and resounding. They had to find a way to do this. Rich Marks, the Kingfish general manager, was on board, too.

Tonight the vision becomes reality, right down to the perfect weather. The lake sparkles in the sun. Passersby on the Sixth Avenue sidewalk slow their pace as they catch sight of the yellow shirts, the tents, and the—is that a home plate on the pier? It is tonight.

♦ ♦ ♦

Before there were home runs splashing into the harbor, before the Kingfish came to Kenosha, before Big Top Baseball even had a name, there were the Madison Mallards. They were the flagship and the template, a marvel in summer baseball. It's a wonder they didn't stage a home run derby on one of Madison's small lakes long before the Kingfish ran with the idea.

The Mallards made their mark with dozens of other promotions. Some worked great. Some did not work great. All of them drew people to the park. Blind as a Bat Night, where one fan wins LASIK eye surgery. Singles Night, with every other seat sold to men and women. The world's largest first pitch, five thousand strong, all around the diamond, everyone a pitcher. Short People Appreciation Night, with ticket prices on a sliding scale of height. Pay What You Want Night, whatever you think the tickets are worth. Beetle Eating Night—free tickets if you down a bug. A game against the Swedish national team. The Diamond Dig, with one real gem nestled somewhere in the grass. Bacon Appreciation Night.

The list goes on, and it's always growing. "We do goofy things and keep trying to do something new every game, every home stand," says Mallards owner Steve Schmitt. "Sometimes they flop, but we never sit back and say, 'Oh, let's not try anything this week.'"

Schmitt founded the Mallards in 2001. He owns the Shoe Box on the outskirts of Madison, touted as the Midwest's Largest Shoe Store. The brand that made Big Top Baseball has easy-to-spot roots there, both in the giant cow statue sitting out front and in the service you'll find inside. The customer really is always right. Schmitt recalls a man coming in recently with a pair of boots and saying they weren't holding up. He had purchased them in 1994. The store gave him full credit.

At the park the same philosophy means fans come first. That was the idea when Schmitt started the team. A lifelong St. Louis Cardinals fan, he had gotten into the sports business on the side when he joined an ownership group for a Minor League hockey team. The team didn't last, but he learned a lot. Before that some close friends were on the front-office staff of the Madison Hatters, a Minor League Class A franchise. When the Hatters left in 1994, it was the end of affiliated baseball in Madison, a history that included a long stint for the Madison Muskies. An independent-league team dubbed the Madison Black Wolf called Warner Park home for four years but departed in 2000.

Schmitt didn't want the city to lose baseball. It seemed plenty big enough to support a team, unlike some smaller communities in the area that had met the same fate. At the same time, Northwoods

League founder Dick Radatz Jr. was aiming to put a team in Madison. The state capital with a metro area population of a half million, it would be the largest market in the fledgling league, then six years old, with a growing footprint in the upper Midwest. Radatz sold the franchise to Schmitt and watched the takeoff begin.

Schmitt directed a makeover of Warner Park, which had taken on the dark colors of the Black Wolf independent-league club. Bright green and yellow soon replaced navy and gray. The Mallards had a fireworks show on opening night.

It was a bumpy ride at the start, as any sports franchise launch typically is. That first year there were more than a few crowds numbering in the hundreds, fans scattered among empty seats in a big, old, and quiet Minor League ballpark. "What the hell am I doing?" Schmitt remembers asking himself.

On the last day of the first season—Fan Appreciation Night— Schmitt got his answer. Nearly three thousand fans streamed through the turnstiles. As crowds grew to an average of a thousand a night the next year and two thousand the year after that, the rest was history.

The Mallards now pull in about six thousand fans per night, tops among summer collegiate teams by a significant margin. In *Ballpark Digest*'s combined rankings of Minor League, independent, and summer-league teams, the Mallards crack the top thirty. Matched up with the colleges their players call home, they would rank in the top ten. Madison has become a summer-ball mecca.

◆ ◆ ◆

The guests of honor arrive in uniform about an hour before the start of the baseball festivities, home run hitters piling off a coach bus. As they grab their gear from the baggage compartment and descend the steps from the park's Sixth Avenue entryway, many of the players pull out their cell phones and snap pictures of the panorama before them. They share can-you-believe-this looks with each other, all while taking in every inch of their unusual baseball home for the evening. The green mat with two batter's boxes flanking home plate fits snugly onto the concrete pier, a mesh screen behind it for a backstop. Twenty feet away is a pitcher's screen and a bucket of baseballs.

The gates opened at 5:30 p.m. It's a Tuesday night, not exactly prime time, but getting outside is an easy sell on a night like this, with hardly a cloud in the sky and none of the humidity that can sneak in this time of year. The grass and the sidewalks next to the water are starting to fill up quickly.

The park borders the water in an almost perfect setup for baseball. Its long promenade along the channel from the shore of the harbor to Lake Michigan doubles as a right-field line. Fans grab spots at the edge, legs dangling over the water. The home-plate pier juts out from a smaller section of the park—the backstop for today's purposes—that sits at a ninety-degree angle to the promenade. In what's essentially deep center field, well beyond the buoy fence, the deck of the Kenosha Yacht Club provides distant bleacher seats.

Of course, Steve Schmitt and company didn't consider Kenosha Harbor's baseball dimensions when Big Top Baseball made its move to the town. It's a welcome accident, but the lake and the family fun perfectly fit into the brand.

Expansion for Big Top Baseball started with the Wisconsin Rapids Rafters in 2010. Then came the Green Bay Bullfrogs in 2013. They play their games at Joannes Park, a few miles from famed Lambeau Field, home of the National Football League's (NFL) Green Bay Packers.

Building franchises is a streamlined process now, headed by Big Top leadership. Where Schmitt is a businessman with a baseball passion, Conor Caloia and Vern Stenman are sports-management veterans. The Northwoods League's for-profit model means they can do their jobs on a full-time basis, as if they were in the front office of a Minor League team.

Stenman grew up in Minnesota and interned with the Northwoods League team in St. Cloud. It was a small operation, and by the time he left he had become the assistant general manager. He found it to be crucial experience for a career in sports. He had done everything—press releases, player contracts, sales, marketing.

When the National Hockey League made its return to his hockey-mad home state, Stenman took a job with the Minnesota Wild. It was a position hockey people in Minnesota would have killed for—something like five hundred people applied, Stenman heard—but Stenman didn't love the big, corporate machine, and he missed the hands-on work of summer ball. He quit and found his way back to the Northwoods League, signing on to work for Dick Radatz Jr. in Madison. When the club was transferred to Schmitt, Stenman was in limbo, having just quit a supposed dream job for a sudden unknown. Radatz told him not to worry—he sold Stenman with the team.

As the years went by in Madison and the baseball boom began, Stenman approached Schmitt about an opportunity to build a team in Wisconsin Rapids. He wanted to do it together, and Schmitt was on board. That was the first step in Big Top Baseball becoming Big Top Baseball.

Caloia, who had been an intern in Madison, came back and ran the Mallards, while Schmitt and Stenman focused on the expansion club. It went so well, they did it again in Green Bay, as Caloia became a partner.

The same do-it-all jobs that drew Stenman back to summer ball brought in others with similar goals. Not every intern can become a Northwoods League owner just a few years later—especially as the league has been molded into a bigger operation—but the path to having an impact on a franchise, rather than being a cog in a professional machine, is still there.

Kenosha joined the fold in 2014. The team's home turf at Simmons Field, a few miles from the harbor, is nearly one hundred years old with a history to match its time served. It was once home to the Kenosha Comets of the All-American Girls Professional League, which was made famous in the film *A League of Their Own*. Thirty years later, the Class A affiliate of the Minnesota Twins moved in and stayed through 1992, bringing the likes of Chuck Knoblauch and Denny Neagle through town. Once the Twins departed, the Northwoods League made an initial foray to Kenosha with the Kroakers from 1994 to 1999.

Over the next fifteen years—while Simmons Field hosted semi-pro and high school teams—the Northwoods League and summer collegiate baseball really picked up steam. When Big Top Baseball came to Kenosha, it had a blueprint. Simmons Field was renovated in a partnership with the city. Its cozy confines remained—you can easily see green grass from the street—but new seats obtained from Baltimore's Camden Yards, a grass berm down the right-field line, and two suites enhanced the experience. The port side of a dry-docked boat provides a small portion of the left-field fence and the all-important party deck.

The team was a hit immediately. A sellout crowd of 3,218 watched the inaugural home opener in 2014, and the Kingfish averaged 2,200 fans that first summer, good for fourth in the league.

Connecting with the community likely had a big impact. Big Top leadership knew it couldn't just show up with a baseball team and hope for the best. Prior experience had taught them that. So before the franchise even had a name, focus groups were gathered in Kenosha. It would be the community's team through and through.

One of the conclusions was that the brand had to be heavy on the city's ties to Lake Michigan. The fish-themed name, the mascot, and the boat would do the trick. The colors are predominantly red, with Lake Michigan blue alongside. The fish mascot is Elvis themed, fitting with the usual part of a Big Top brand—fun.

Three seasons in, the Kingfish are still going strong. They own a Northwoods League championship and steady attendance numbers. And the connection to Lake Michigan? It's about to get stronger tonight.

◆ ◆ ◆

Nobody knows exactly what it will be like to watch home runs splash down in the harbor, but a crowd estimated at three thousand is here to find out. Viewed from the home-plate pier, the right-field promenade looks jammed. It's four or five deep along the water's edge. In the park area lines are long for food and merchandise. On the water a few more boats have made their way into the harbor, dropping anchor beyond the fence line. A two-masted tall ship that offers public and charter sails out of Kenosha has a full crowd aboard, with the fans seated on the edge ready to keep home run tallies with numbered panels.

Judging by the ovations as home run–derby participants are announced, much of the crowd has a hometown flavor. The fans save their loudest cheers for Marty Bechina, the Kenosha Kingfish representative in the competition. The Chicago native just finished his freshman season at Michigan State University, where he batted .260 with two home runs. He has hit three long balls this summer, tied for the Kenosha team lead.

Bechina wears Kenosha's cream-colored home uniform. When his name echoes on the speakers situated throughout the park, he walks out on the pier to join his derby teammates from the league's South Division. Eighteen players are in the competition, nine from the South and nine from the North. They're competing individually for home run supremacy, but also in a team battle between North and South. Players from the two divisions will alternate turns at the plate, with one round amounting to an inning. Anything that isn't a home run is an out. Hitters get six of them to work with.

The players mill around behind the pier, waiting to be introduced. The shared challenge and experience that awaits makes them fast friends. Their baseball paths have hit similar mileposts, with vastly different starting points. They are here from Boston, Massachusetts, and La Jolla, California. Their schools contend in the Atlantic Coast Conference (acc) and the Summit League, with recent College World Series trips alongside quests for Division II glory.

Daulton Varsho is one of the stars of this Northwoods League summer, and his baseball bloodlines could have predicted it.

His father, Gary, played eight seasons in the bigs with the Cubs, Pirates, Reds, and Phillies. His uncle, Dale, manages the league's Eau Claire Express, for whom Daulton is suiting up this summer. It's been a fruitful season, just as the spring was. The slugging catcher—who stayed in his home state to play for the University of Wisconsin–Milwaukee—won Horizon League Player of the Year honors after hitting .381 with eight home runs. He was only the second sophomore in league history to win the top award. So far this summer Varsho is batting .304 and has slugged nine home runs, which has him tied for the league lead. He'll be one of the favorites tonight.

Griffin Conine has Major League roots, too. His father, Jeff, was a seventeen-year veteran who played until 2007, when he was forty-one years old. He won two World Series titles with the Marlins. Griffin was drafted in the thirty-first round by his dad's old team out of high school but opted for the college ranks at Duke University. He saw part-time duty as a freshman but is heating up in a full-time role with the La Crosse Loggers. He's batting .279 and is one home run behind Varsho for the league lead.

Zach Jarrett grew up in the national sports spotlight, but on racetracks, not baseball diamonds. His father, Dale, and paternal grandfather, Ned, are NASCAR Hall of Famers, though there's a baseball branch of the family tree, too. His maternal grandfather played in the Brooklyn Dodgers organization. Zach just completed his sophomore season at the University of North Carolina at Charlotte, where he batted .248. He's playing in front of the big crowds in Madison this summer and has blasted six home runs.

Jake Shepski is giving Varsho a run for his money atop the home run leaderboard this season. The Notre Dame standout has nine of them and has been on base a lot in between the long balls. He's batting .369 and has emerged as one of the top players in the league at the season's halfway point.

Steve Passatempo, from the University of Massachusetts–Lowell, is red-hot, too. He's batting .330 for the Wisconsin Woodchucks after leading his college team with eleven home runs in the spring. Logan Mattix has eight home runs this summer. He plays at DII Georgia College but has more than held his own against mostly DI competition.

They trot out to the pier, one by one, taking it all in as they go. Wood bats in hand, they pose for official pictures with their North and South teammates, shimmering blue water behind them.

◆ ◆ ◆

Dick Radatz Jr. envisioned nights like this. Well, maybe not exactly like this—what with a player taking warm-up swings on a pier— but the feel is right. A perfect summer night. Thousands of fans. Baseball.

Twenty-two years ago he just didn't know exactly how to get there. Baseball had always been in his blood. His father, Dick, was a flamethrowing reliever for the Boston Red Sox in the 1960s, whose nickname—the Monster—and six-foot-six frame earned him cult-hero status. Dick Jr. played baseball at Albion College in Michigan. He hung up his spikes after graduation but didn't stray far from baseball diamonds. He worked with the Los Angeles Dodgers organization and then ran the Red Sox's spring-training operation and their Class A Florida State League team. He was the league's executive of the year in 1986, and his teams set multiple attendance records.

After seven years with the club, though, he found himself out of a job. A friend and colleague, George MacDonald Jr.—the long-time president of the Florida State League—was in the same boat. Through his baseball travels MacDonald knew that the affiliated Minor League teams in Kenosha and Wausau, Wisconsin, were about to depart, joining many others that had retreated from the northern part of the country. It made sense, even if it robbed good baseball towns of their baseball teams. Drawing good crowds on cold spring nights was always a difficult proposition, and the communities struggled to provide the economic infrastructure necessary to support a new brand of Minor League clubs, with their multimillion-dollar budgets and corporate-sponsorship needs.

Radatz and MacDonald saw an opening. "We knew how to promote baseball," Radatz says. "And we knew those towns were losing their teams."

On a leap of faith and $150,000 from investors, Radatz and Mac-Donald started the Northwoods League with five teams in Kenosha, Wausau, and Manitowoc, Wisconsin; Dubuque, Iowa; and Rochester, Minnesota. John Wendel, who was the general counsel for the Florida State League, and Bill McKee, who had bought and sold a number of Minor League franchises in the 1980s, were the primary investors, but there wasn't a lot of cash to go around. "We started five teams from scratch—no office space, no uniforms, no website, no nothing," Radatz says. "I'm not sure how we kept the pencil that sharp, to tell you the truth."

From the beginning the league followed a different blueprint than every other summer collegiate circuit. It was a for-profit venture, with the franchises and even the league itself—unlike typical sport-governing bodies—pulling in revenue.

There were sleepless nights while the revenue streams trickled. Eight years in, the investors hadn't gotten a dime back. But Radatz believed the league had tapped into something and that brighter days were ahead. "At that point, I told my three partners, we're going to start making money," Radatz says, "and I honestly don't think they believed me."

He made what he calls generous offers to buy out the investors, and they accepted. The league was officially his baby, and he was right about its prospects. It grew fast. In 2002—the year Radatz bought the investors out—there were eight teams. It expanded to ten soon after and began establishing a presence in the summer baseball world around the same time. A league all-star team beat Team USA in an exhibition game. Average attendance across the league soared to more than a thousand. Alumni like Max Scherzer started popping up on Major League rosters.

Soon enough, Radatz was pinching himself. "It's gone beyond our wildest dreams," he says. "We've got a tiger by the tail, and we're just trying to hold on, make good decisions, and go forward."

The growth has been spurred further by a unique twist on the league's leadership structure. Most leagues have a board of directors composed of the owners of each team. In contrast, the teams in the Northwoods League share one seat on the five-person board, a product of an initial instinct that the founders' baseball experience would steer things in the right direction. The league also takes a 5 percent royalty on teams' gross revenues.

It takes trust from the owners, Radatz says, but it works because those royalties and league dues are invested back into the franchises. It's why every team has its website, mobile app, high-definition video production, and ticket system taken care of by the league. "I think people that invest in sports teams, they want some say," Radatz says. "For people to emulate our concept, it takes a great deal of trust and some years to develop that trust that, 'Hey, the league and the board of directors is going to act in our best interest. And we don't need to have a seat at the table.' We've apparently gotten by that. People who invest a lot trust our judgment in how we operate and run the league."

In turn Radatz trusts the franchises. When the Big Top Baseball crew broached the idea of hitting home runs into the harbor, Radatz—a self-professed baseball purist—felt a little trepidation but ultimately gave the green light. "These guys know what they're doing," he says. Looking out at the water now, he just may be a believer.

◆ ◆ ◆

It's time for the home runs. Fans who have been here a while saw some swings earlier—VIP tickets for event sponsors included a chance to take a few hacks—but no long balls. That will change quickly. Or at least that's the hope. Is it hard to hit home runs when the back of the batter's box is six inches from the edge of the pier?

Is the air different down by the water? Is it difficult to see the pitches? Nobody really knows.

Daulton Varsho is the first to give it a try. With his league-best nine home runs, he's about as good a bet as anybody to start the proceedings with a bang. He's listed at five-foot-ten, 190 pounds, a powerfully built catcher through and through. In his black Eau Claire jersey with orange numbers, he settles into his left-handed stance. His uncle, Dale, the Eau Claire manager, will throw to him.

As the public address announcer introduces him and the buzz of the crowd ticks up, Varsho watches the first pitch go by. He takes the second and the third and lets the fourth go, too. On the fifth pitch he whips his bat through the zone and smacks a ball to the opposite field. The contact sounds solid, but it's a line drive that splashes into the water well short of the fence line.

Varsho swings again on the next toss and bounces it off the concrete pier, sending it ricocheting into the water. He goes to center field on the next pitch and gets enough lift, but the ball ends up about ten feet short of the rope.

He catches his breath while he takes the next two pitches. Then it happens. On the tenth pitch, with three outs to work with, Varsho smashes a deep drive to center field that plunges into the water fifteen feet beyond the floating fence. It's the first home run in the first home run derby at the harbor. A guy standing on the bow of his black fishing boat nearly caught it with a net.

Varsho goes to the opposite field for his next one and watches it sail past the kayaks and into the water for his second home run. A foul ball draws the fourth out, but the long balls keep coming. Varsho belts one to left-center field, his longest of the day, and then peppers the same spot with another one. From a boat nearby a fan dives into the water, swims to the ball, and grabs it for a souvenir, to the delight of the crowd.

With four home runs on the board, Varsho narrowly misses a fifth with a deep fly to center that lands just in front of the line. A foul ball ends the round.

Varsho and his uncle stop for a picture as they make their way off the pier. Fellow players greet him on the grass, wanting to know what it was like. He admits he was a little nervous. He noticed the breeze was moving right to left, so he tried to avoid pulling the ball and getting high fly balls caught up in the wind. He would have liked that fifth home run, but he had a blast.

Last summer, which he also spent playing for Eau Claire, he competed in the Northwoods League home run derby at Witter Field in Wisconsin Rapids. It was fun, but nothing like this. "The atmosphere was unbelievable tonight," Varsho says.

He'll watch the rest of the proceedings from a front-row seat, family and friends by his side. He's not sure four home runs will be enough.

♦ ♦ ♦

Steve Passatempo walks onto the pier. He'll be the first hitter from the South Division, where the hometown Kingfish reside. After a good freshman year at UMass Lowell he's been one of the break-out stars of the summer in the Northwoods League. In June he hit for the cycle. Tonight he brings five regular-season home runs into the derby.

Things are moving fast, with Passatempo stepping into the box just moments after Daulton Varsho's final out. With fans scattered across the park and not right on top of the action, organizers want to avoid dead time and keep the splashdowns coming.

Passatempo obliges. He takes two pitches, makes two quick outs, and then blasts a rocket over a boat in left-center field, the longest home run of the day so far. After two more outs he pulls the ball down the left-field line. The kayaker near the sailboat foul pole holds up a yellow Kenosha Kingfish flag to signal that it's a fair ball. Two home runs.

With another line drive into the lake leaving him only one out left to work with, Passatempo gets hot. He belts two straight deep ones to the same spot in left-center field to pull even with Varsho. Then a towering drive sends him ahead with five home runs.

He lines out to end his stay on the pier on the next pitch and then breaks his wood bat over his leg, à la Bo Jackson. He shares a few laughs with his fellow home run hitters as he makes his way back to dry land.

Adam McGinnis steps in next. Another powerfully built catcher like Varsho, he plays for Western Illinois and has spent two summers with the Waterloo Bucks, Iowa's lone representative in the league.

McGinnis is second in the league in home runs this season with eight, but he's struggling to get into a groove today. He makes one out on a foul ball and then two on a swinging strike, taking a few pitches here and there. A line drive falls short of the line. A high fly comes up shy, too, before McGinnis knocks a home run to left-center field.

There's no comeback, though. McGinnis ends his round with one home run. Passatempo is still the leader with five. Varsho has four. The hometown favorite is next.

◆ ◆ ◆

Last summer, in their second season, the Kingfish won the North-woods League championship. It was a dominant season—their record was a gaudy 48-24—and the offensive lineup featured plenty of pop. The team hit forty-seven home runs, one of the best totals in the league.

If there had been a home run derby at the harbor last year, the Kingfish might have sent UCLA star Eric Filia, who hit six home runs and drove in fifty-five runs. Ohio State's Nick Sergakis and his six homers would have been a good choice, too. Jason Scholl, a catcher from Eastern Illinois, might have been the best option. He blasted ten home runs.

Halfway through the 2016 campaign, the Kingfish aren't having as much luck in their title defense—and they aren't hitting as many home runs, either. Marty Bechina and Pete Schuler lead the team with three each. Neither looks like a hulking power hitter. Schuler is a six-foot-three, 180-pound catcher, Bechina a six-foot, 190-pound infielder who can also play the outfield. It was Bechina who got the call for the derby. He enters it tied for the lowest home run total among derby participants. He's telling everybody he chats with that he just wants to hit one today.

Bechina is close to home this summer. Kenosha is about an hour and a half north of Chicago, where Bechina grew up and starred for St. Rita in the city's Catholic league. His freshman season at Michigan State offered a big opportunity. He started all but one game, though he wasn't thrilled with how he finished.

He's seizing his chance with the Kingfish, leading the team in a host of offensive categories. He's currently on a twelve-game hitting streak that started on the Fourth of July. He'll be in the All-Star Game tomorrow.

Today it's not about grinding out a hit streak in the dog days of summer. As Bechina steps onto the pier, he hears the ovation again. A Kingfish employee, Zac Pallissard, who's in charge of the logistics on the pier, gives him a fist bump as he gets the screen behind the plate set.

Bechina takes two pitches and then mashes one to straightaway center, the deepest part of the harbor field. It splashes down a few feet short of the fence line. On the next pitch Bechina gets on the board with a deep drive to left-center field that nails a boat, but his next two swings are near misses, too. The second one is so close that the splash clears the fence line, but close doesn't count for much.

Maybe he isn't quite cut out for this. Maybe the Kingfish crowd won't have much to cheer for. Bechina has three outs left with one home run to his credit.

The next pitch is letter high, up just a bit from the pitches that yielded the close calls, and Bechina crushes it out to left-center. He does the same on the next one—another letter-high toss—and belts it ten feet past the fence, just in front of a green kayak. The crowd favorite is heating up.

Bechina doesn't take any pitches or step out for any warm-up swings. He's in a groove, and the pitches are coming in where he wants them. His next swing lifts a line drive down the line in left field that gets out for his fourth home run. A high drive to left-center ties him for the lead.

The crowd is into it, the buzz as loud as it's been all night. With the chance to take the lead, Bechina gets another pitch in his wheelhouse and hits his longest home run yet, past the kayaks in left-center. Five swings, five consecutive home runs, and the Kingfish have a slugger after all.

Bechina's hot streak finally ends with a line-drive out. He takes a pitch and then tries another line drive and comes up just short. Down to his final out, a liner to left ends it.

If the near misses had gone just a little bit farther, Bechina would be in the lead by a mile. But six is enough for the top spot, one ahead of Steve Passatempo.

Bechina is all smiles as he walks off the pier. "My goal was one," he says. "And six is better than one."

◆ ◆ ◆

After three more hitters Marty Bechina is still at the top of the leaderboard. Greg Lambert from the Willmar Stingers hit two, and Daniel Jipping from the Battle Creek Bombers—who has eight homers on the season—also hit two. Andrew Fregia from the Thunder Bay Border Cats blasted three. The South Division has a 13–10 edge as Zach Jarrett makes his way to the pier.

At six-foot-four, 226 pounds, he looks the part. His Mallard green socks are pulled high. Jarrett took an 0-for-4 night just a few days ago in Kenosha, when Madison visited, but the Mallards are outdoing their Big Top brethren with a 30-18 record.

Jarrett takes one pitch and then flies out short of the fence line in right-center field. He pulls the ball on his next swing, and his first home run splashes down just in front of one of the boats in left field.

In June Jarrett hit four of his six home runs over a two-week stretch, but he can't get on a hot streak today. He flies out before lining one over the fence for his second home run. After another out his third and fourth homers come consecutively, but that's as far as he gets, bowing out with four blasts.

With four hitters down and five to go on each side, Bechina is announced as the leader, drawing cheers from the Kingfish fans. But there's a long way to go, with a lot of big hitters left, one of whom Bechina knows well. Jake Shepski was a high school teammate in Chicago at St. Rita. They were pretty good, with a dozen other teammates playing college ball, too. Shepski and Bechina both won their high school league's Outstanding Player Award.

No hitter in the Northwoods League is having a better summer than Shepski. If he keeps it up, he'll be an MVP favorite, especially if his Mankato Moondogs stay hot. They're eleven games over .500 at the all-star break. Shepski is on a roll, too, with eight hits in his last four games. He knocked out his ninth home run of the season two days ago.

A switch hitter, Shepski opts to bat from the left side for the home run derby. His first swing produces a hard line drive, something that's been pretty common off his bat this summer but not exactly what he's looking for today. It skips into the water well short of the fence.

Two fly balls come close, while another liner dives in shy. Another flyout puts Shepski on the brink of a shutout before he pulls one down the line that clears the fence by fifteen feet. It splashes into the water just in front of the fans lining the edge of the harbor.

On his next swing, Shepski lines out to finish his round. Hitting home runs at the harbor is proving not so easy.

◆ ◆ ◆

Like the lazy middle innings of a pitchers' duel, it's getting a little quiet on the waterfront. Laren Eustace from the Green Bay Bullfrogs follows Shepski to the pier and matches him with one home run. Ricky Ramirez from the St. Cloud Rox does the same.

The Northwoods League doesn't really do quiet. As the outs pile up, public address announcer Aaron Sims shifts into hype-man duties. Sims is a play-by-play announcer in the American Hockey League and handled PA work for the Madison Mallards for many years before coming over to Kenosha. Tonight he's giving shout-outs to the fans on the right-field side and wants to hear how loud they can get. He gets waves from the fans on the tall ship sailing beyond center field. He gets a call-and-answer chant going for local grocer Festival Foods, with their slogan "Great stuff for not a lot of money." Right field handles "great stuff." The home-plate fans answer with "not a lot of money." Dancing to "YMCA" is next on the list.

There's some power looming, too. Logan Mattix has six home runs for another Big Top team, the Wisconsin Rapids Rafters. He hit two in one game a few weeks back, and his team is in the midst of a big season. They're 32-16 and entering the all-star break with four straight wins.

Mattix blasts three home runs in his turn on the pier. The South still leads it 21–12, but one of the top challengers left is due up next. Beyond his baseball bloodlines, Griffin Conine fits the mold of a Northwoods League star. Much of the league's talent has midwestern roots, but some of its top alumni in pro ball have played here the summer after their freshman year at power conference schools. A long season with a lot of swings—or pitches—accelerates the growth process. Star turns often follow.

Major League All-Star Chris Sale played for Conine's La Crosse Loggers after his freshman year at Florida Gulf Coast. The next year he emerged as the best pitcher in the Cape Cod League and was selected in the first round of the Major League Baseball Draft the next summer. The top college pitcher chosen in last month's draft—A. J. Puk—pitched for the Waterloo Bucks after his freshman year at the University of Florida and then played for Team USA the next summer.

Conine's path is yet to be determined, but he's been red-hot lately, with home runs in two of his last three games before the all-star break.

In the left-handed batter's box, he takes a cut on the first pitch he sees and fouls it directly into the screen behind the plate. His next swing produces a better result, as a high drive toward the tall ship just clears the fence line.

Every ball he hits looks good, but two of the deep flies land just short. With four outs he sneaks one over the buoys in center field for his second home run. He takes the next pitch out to right-center for his third home run, but his hot streak stops there. A line drive and a foul ball down the left field line end his round.

With five hitters left, Marty Bechina still leads the field.

◆ ◆ ◆

Interviews on the mic with Aaron Sims and the all-star-team managers prompt a break in the action. Home runs are still tough to come by. Jonah Davis from the Green Bay Bullfrogs gets shut out in his turn. Alex Fitchett—spending his summer in Rochester, Minnesota, after spending his spring in Hawaii—hits two homers. Matt Johnson from the Lakeshore Chinooks hits a few towering shots but finishes with three.

Before the ninth and final round of hitters, the Kingfish staff decides to have a little fun. Zac Pallissard, who has spent his night sliding the home-plate screen back and forth when hitters come and go on the pier, grabs a bat. As Sims explains to the crowd, Pallissard mentioned in the office a few days ago that he thought he could hit a home run if he was given a shot. A few players called him on it, and a friendly wager was placed. One swing. If he didn't hit it out, he'd have to dive in and swim to the foul pole.

With his board shots perhaps a sign of preparation, Pallissard lives up to his word when he smacks a home run to left field. Amid the loudest cheers of the night, he dives into the water anyway. A Jet Ski scoops him up.

"If this were the 1980 Olympics," Sims says on the mic, "Al Michaels would have asked us if we believed in miracles."

With the Big Top promotional playbook nearing its final pages, all that's left is the business at hand. Two hitters remain—and one Kingfish player waiting with a smile to see what they do.

Anthony Brocato from the Thunder Bay Border Cats is first up. He strides onto the pier with a headband in place of his uniform hat. The flair goes along with some home run credentials. He's played in only twenty-three games but ranks in the top ten in the league with six home runs. Five of the blasts came in an eight-game span.

His first swing yields a high fly ball, but it falls short of the fence line. He bounces one into the water for the second out. A short pop-up makes him 0-for-3.

Brocato is the North Division's last chance to rally in the team race. They're down 24–17. He breaks through with two home runs, but it's not enough to get the North back to even or to beat Bechina.

The last man up is Connor Heady from the Wisconsin Woodchucks and the University of Kentucky. He has five home runs this summer and hit two in one game a few weeks ago, but tonight is not his night. His fifth out lands just shy of the fence line. Down to his last chance, he skies a fly ball to right. The final splashdown of the night is twenty feet shy of the fence.

Standing with family near home plate, Marty Bechina smiles and shares a high five. His goal was one. He got six. And he won.

Sims announces Bechina to the crowd and chats with him over the speakers. When the interview concludes, Kingfish teammates shower Bechina with bottles of water.

His uniform still wet, he quickly pulls himself away from photos and congratulatory high fives. Kids are lined up for his autograph.

◆ ◆ ◆

As twilight fades the country music cover band hits the stage, and it looks like plenty of fans will be sticking around to hear them. When it gets dark fireworks will light up the sky. The home run hitters mill around with teammates and family, eating from the VIP buffet. They'll stick around for fireworks, too.

Kingfish staff estimates the crowd at around three thousand, right in the neighborhood of what they hoped for. The event went off without a hitch. "Better than expected, in all honesty," Conor Caloia says.

Vern Stenman picks out a good spot for the fireworks, which he'll watch with his young daughter. Caloia receives congratulations from friends and coworkers. Dick Radatz Jr. sits in his seat by the pier, spinning a baseball in his hand as he chats with friends. Rich Marks finally takes a deep breath.

It was a good night. "I don't think Kenosha has ever seen anything like this," Marks says.

7 / WASHINGTON DC

From the U.S. Capitol building, it's a seven-minute drive through city streets to the home of America's pastime in Washington DC. Nationals Park will be packed this evening for the first game of a three-game weekend series with the San Diego Padres. The Washington Nationals are humming along eighteen games over the .500 mark and fully capturing the imagination of the city they've called home for just over a decade now.

From the right-field corner of Nationals Park, across the Anacostia River, up Minnesota Avenue, and past a different block of Pennsylvania Avenue than the one most people know, it's about thirteen more minutes to another home for baseball in the nation's capital.

The Nationals Youth Baseball Academy sits nestled on the edge of Fort Dupont Park in the area of the District called Southeast. The neighborhood, Ward 7, is one of the city's poorest areas. Public housing complexes sit alongside small homes, some perfectly kept, others with peeling paint and overgrown yards. The river serves as a kind of dividing line for the Washington of postcards and politics and the Washington of the people who call it home.

In the steamy midmorning, views of the skyline already shrouded by haze, the small turf fields by the entrance to the baseball academy buzz with the ping of metal bats, the smack of balls hitting gloves, and the din of children playing the game. Local kids fill the fields and the neighboring indoor facilities year-round, even when it's not baseball season. There are clinics, lessons, community events, after-school care, tutoring—all orbiting around baseball but making an impact outside of the baselines, too. There is no cost for children to attend any of the programs. The aim is to provide them with opportunity in baseball and beyond. The $17 million facility was the big-league team's end of the bargain when the city chipped in public money for Nationals Park.

On the pristine main field, where the green artificial turf glistens and bakes in the sun, the DC Grays have their own camp going for local kids. This is their home, too. They share the facility—and a mission—with the youth baseball academy.

The Grays' final game of the regular season is tonight at 7:00 on this field, the last stop on a forty-game Cal Ripken Collegiate League slate that flew by even faster than usual. The Grays were on the wrong end of a string of close games and found themselves out of playoff contention by the final week. Tonight's game is it. Players will pack up and leave town tomorrow.

First pitch is nine hours away, but six players are already on the field to lend a hand with the clinic. They wear gray baseball pants and navy-blue warm-ups, big-mirror images of the half-dozen kids who are here for the clinic, all wearing their own Grays gear. The kids are regulars, usually part of a bigger crowd at the free camps, but perfectly fine with getting some one-on-one attention today.

The kids are lined in up in left field, throwing back and forth to one another from one knee. Ken Robbett, a Grays board member, sets up orange plastic bases around the infield. A few employees from Katten Muchin Rosenman, a law firm with offices nation-wide, make their way to the field. They're the latest in a steady stream of volunteers who work the camps all summer—and they brought their gloves.

Grays president Mike Barbera stands at the top of the bleachers, on the concourse that overlooks the sunken diamond. He gazes out at his crew. Robbett is an attorney in DC. The Grays players hail from as far away as Idaho. The Katten employees look ready for a Tuesday-night rec softball game. All six kids are black, from the neighborhood.

"People like to be a part of things," Barbera says. Turns out, you can build something that way.

◆ ◆ ◆

The ball whips around the horn, first base to second to third to home. The campers and two Grays players time how quickly the kids can get it back to the plate. Then they're all jogging to right field to hit off tees. Then they're hustling home for live hitting. "On the hop," Robbett says on every switch, and he moves faster than his charges.

When he's not working, Robbett can often be found on a baseball field. It's been that way for a long time. When his son was climbing the baseball ranks, he founded a developmental youth program in northern Virginia. His son then went on to play in college and joined the Grays in the summer. Robbett found himself pulled into the orbit and happily latched on to a new baseball team. He's now a board member and runs all the clinics with a deft touch.

The volunteers from the law firm grab spots on the infield for the live hitting drill. Drake Hollingsworth, a catcher from the University of Alabama–Huntsville, gets on a knee halfway between home and the pitcher's mound and sends soft tosses toward the plate. He gives quick pieces of advice to the hitters between his soft tosses.

Soon, swings and misses turn into line drives. The smallest kid in the group crushes a ball onto the outfield grass. He gets a high five from Grays catcher Evan Pace as he dances to first base.

It's common practice for summer-league teams to host daytime clinics. They represent a chance to give back while building the brand and setting the summer-ball players up with a part-time gig. For the DC Grays, clinics go much deeper—they're a core part of the franchise's foundation. Antonio Scott and Brad Burris, former baseball players at Washington's Howard University, started the franchise in 2007 in tandem with the DCBaseball.org initiative.

The goal was to rebuild the sport in the city, with a summer team of college players serving as the ambassador. The Grays played four seasons in the Clark Griffith League.

When the league folded, the team did, too. A year later, out of the blue, Scott got a call from Mike Barbera. A Washington lobbyist and a former baseball player at Williams College in Massachusetts, Barbera had an itch for summer ball. He wanted to team up with Scott and Burris to get the Grays back up and running, community mission and all. They joined the Cal Ripken Collegiate Baseball League in 2012, with their purpose in the city unchanged by the new start. The manifestations of it have only expanded—from the clinics to sponsoring a middle school team to the biggest leap yet. This year the Grays are running the DC chapter of Major League Baseball's RBI program.

It's a big undertaking for a nonprofit franchise manned by baseball moonlighters. Barbera and Scott—who now serves as the general manager—are enmeshed in every part of the operation, from player recruitment to clinics to fundraising. Burris, now a board member, is helping to spearhead the RBI program.

The good news is they have plenty of help. Like Robbett, new supporters and volunteers sign on every year and find themselves doing more and more with every passing summer. Many make it official and join the board, with baseball tying together their diverse backgrounds. Paris Inman started a Little League program in Washington a few years ago and is a fixture in the local youth baseball scene. Bob Duff founded the Diamond Dream Foundation, which offers baseball clinics and nutritional outreach in DC. Thom Loverro is a columnist for the *Washington Times* and hosts a sports-talk radio show. Gary Wilcox played baseball at Texas Tech. Thurgood Marshall Jr.—the son of the former Supreme Court justice—grew up a Washington Senators fan and has served on the U.S. Olympic Committee. Barry Direnfeld, a retired attorney who leads fundraising efforts for the Grays, played baseball at Kenyon College. Scott Burr, the housing coordinator for the collegiate team, played Division III college ball.

Whether they stop in for game nights or swing by a clinic during their lunch breaks, they're hooked. Direnfeld has stopped in at the field today. He and Barbera are heading outside the Beltway this afternoon to catch up with two of the RBI teams. The summer-ball squad may be down to its final game, but the RBI teams are playing in their first regional tournament, making today a big day.

As the Grays' clinic moves to another drill, the youth academy's camp breaks for lunch. A few minutes later a Nationals staffer walks one of the kids down to the field where the Grays' camp is happening and pulls Robbett aside. Soon the kid is playing catch near the first base line with Zach McCrum, a pitcher and designated hitter from Eastern Kentucky University. The clinic has grown by one.

Turns out the kid didn't want to eat lunch. He just wanted to keep playing.

◆ ◆ ◆

When Antonio Scott and Brad Burris were originally getting the franchise off the ground and picking a name, they settled on the Grays for a meaningful reason. The choice was a nod to the Homestead Grays, the Negro League team that split its time between Washington and Pittsburgh. Legendary players Josh Gibson and Cool Papa Bell once wore the Grays uniform.

For a team aiming to make a big impact in the African American community, it was the perfect name. And Scott and Burris knew the need for that impact was only growing. With the integration of Major League Baseball in the late 1940s, the percentage of African Americans in the big leagues grew steadily. In 1959, 17 percent of big leaguers were African American. It was 27 percent in 1975. The number has fallen significantly since then, to 8 percent in 2016.

Whether symptom, cause, or both, there's a feeling that participation in general has waned, all the way down to youth levels. Major League Baseball's RBI program started as a concerted effort to bring the game back to inner cities, and by extension to African American youth.

The nation's capital needed a boost more than most. In 2008 Washington native Emmanuel Burriss—once a star in the Cape Cod League during his summers at Kent State University—made his Major League debut with the San Francisco Giants. In a *Washington Post* article telling his story, baseball people in the city came to the consensus that he was the first DC baseball player to make the bigs in thirty-eight years. Over the same span the city has sent dozens of players to the National Football League and the National Basketball Association.

Scott had a front-row seat as baseball faded. He finished his baseball career at Howard—a historically black college—in 2001. The next year the school cut its baseball program.

A native of Chesapeake, Virginia, on the state's southern border, Scott stayed in Washington after school. Even as his alma mater moved on from baseball and he hung up his spikes, he stayed in the game, getting involved with the DCBaseball.org nonprofit and taking over operations.

The initial mission wasn't much different from what the Grays eventually embraced—camps, clinics, donated equipment, enthusiastic baseball volunteers matched with enthusiastic baseball players. It all revolved around creating opportunity. The advent of the summer-ball team provided a spark for the young players to run with the opportunity and start creating goals, expectations, and paths forward. College baseball players were natural role models, someone to look up to outside of the coaches and organization leaders whom kids saw every day. "It goes back to the basic concept—use our college ballplayers to give those kids aspirations," Scott said. "Even if they don't want to become a baseball player, it's aspirations of going to college or doing something that's not just in DC."

The summer games weren't glamorous in the team's early days. The Clark Griffith League had its share of history, with alumni from as far back as the 1950s making the Majors. By its final season it was down to five teams in the DC area.

Scott and Burris did it all, a two-man show dedicated to making it work. They hired a manager their first year, but it didn't work out, so Scott stepped into the dugout, adding the on-field coaching to his general manager duties.

When the league folded, the franchise and the Grays' brand was in limbo until Barbera called. He had been on the hunt for a summer-ball opportunity ever since a trip back to his baseball roots. In 2009 Williams College and Amherst College celebrated the 150th anniversary of their 1859 meeting, which holds a place in the record books as the first-ever collegiate baseball game.

While he was in town Barbera struck up a conversation with fellow Williams grad Jim Duquette, a former Major League general manager. His cousin Dan—now the Baltimore Orioles general manager—owned a New England Collegiate Baseball League franchise in Pittsfield, Massachusetts. He started the team after departing as Boston Red Sox general manager and would stay involved until his return to the big leagues with the Orioles. Barbera and Dan Duquette shared several long chats about summer ball. "He said summer is a really fun way to stay in baseball," Barbera recalls.

Barbera reached out to Cal Ripken League officials. They were looking to expand, and DC was a prominent hole on their league map, with teams circled around the capital but nothing in the middle. League officials were on board. As soon as Barbera started doing research in earnest, he learned about the Scott and Burris–led Grays, and the snowball was off and rolling.

It was a perfect fit. Scott and Burris had been hoping to keep the brand and mission alive. Barbera thought that, with a beefed-up fundraising effort and more volunteers, the model could work. Together, they recruited a board of directors, and the new Grays played their first Cal Ripken Collegiate League game in 2012.

There were some adventures that first year, just like the ones Scott and Burris had dealt with the first time around. When a pizza place pulled out of a concessions deal, Barbera found himself cooking hot dogs on a hibachi grill.

For their first two seasons the team played at Gallaudet University in DC. It was a good home except for the lack of lights, which limited game-time options. When the Nationals Youth Academy opened, it was another perfect fit, and the Grays made the move in 2014.

Results in the win-loss columns have been mixed. The team had a winning record in its second year but needed until 2015 to make its first playoff appearance. A fair amount of talent has come through. One of the best players last year was slugging Brigham Young University catcher Colton Shaver, who's playing in the Cape League this summer.

Success off the field isn't as easy to measure as wins and losses, but from the front office to the board to the players leading the clinics, the impact feels real. There's a need for baseball, for opportunity, for bats and gloves, for role models.

One story still resonates among the franchise's leaders. Chris Spera, the public address announcer, a board member, and the father of a former Gray, was at the academy for a meeting before the Grays' first season there. It was springtime, and the baseball team from neighboring John Sousa Middle School was practicing on the field. Spera was chatting with coach Brie Whitmire when she told a player to sub in for the shortstop. The departing shortstop left his glove on the dirt on his way to the dugout. When the sub got there he picked it up and put it on. "I said, 'Wait, what just happened?'" Spera says. "She said, 'Well, we don't have enough gloves.'"

Spera and the Grays board reached out to some connections. Soon the team had all the gloves it needed. Then bats and helmets the next year. This summer the Grays went all in and sponsored the team.

It all happened organically, fitting with the mission but not part of a coordinated effort. When a team is in the community and open to helping, good things happen.

The story is also a reminder of what the Grays are doing. "Out there in the suburbs," Spera says, "you forget."

◆ ◆ ◆

It's not hard to tell that this will be their first tournament. Their uniforms, with the DC Grays logo emblazoned on the breast, are a gleaming white with barely a speck of dirt to be found. The dust from slides into second and the grass stains from dives in the outfield have yet to make their mark, but that will change quickly. The first pitch of their first tournament is in a few minutes.

For now the DC Grays Junior RBI team is trying to stay out of the midday sun, finding relief in a shaded stand of bleachers. The field at Cosca Park in Clinton, Maryland, just outside DC in Prince George's County, awaits. Barbera navigated the usual traffic snarls on his way out of the city and is here for the team's tournament debut. As the players lounge on the bleachers, he tells them to pull together for a photo. Parents in attendance crowd beside him to get their own cell phone shots.

The event is an RBI regional tournament, featuring the Grays and other teams from the mid-Atlantic area—Baltimore, Philadelphia, Harrisburg, and a local team from Prince George's County. The winner of each region will punch a ticket to the RBI World Series, set for later this summer in Cincinnati, Ohio.

RBI teams have a home in two hundred cities worldwide. The program began in 1989, and a number of alumni have gone on to play big-league baseball, including CC Sabathia, Jimmy Rollins, and Justin Upton. Local chapters in the United States are often affiliated with the Major League teams that share a city. Others are smaller outfits, like the program in Harrisburg and an early incarnation of a DC program that was run for many years by the Batter Up Foundation.

The Nationals Youth Academy changed the landscape of youth baseball in DC's neighborhoods, bringing its own programs that didn't necessarily have the same focus as RBI teams. Clinics and community events took priority over games and tournaments. With that as the backdrop, Barbera and Grays board members decided to explore the possibility of taking on a new DC RBI program.

It was a natural step for the franchise, a way to take clinics and donations to a higher level. And as with everything else, there was a need. There are successful Little Leagues operating in Wards 7 and 8, but kids aren't eligible to play Little League once they're older than twelve. "You lose the kids when they turn thirteen," Barbera says.

RBI fills that void, with its junior program for players ages thirteen to fifteen and its senior level for sixteen- to eighteen-year-olds. There is also a girls softball program.

The Grays jumped in headfirst, taking on all of it at once. On a spring day this year they announced the partnership and went to work. There is no cost for kids to play. Teams practice and play a league schedule. Seven teams played under the Grays umbrella—five baseball and two softball squads. Local leagues were brought into the fold as partners, like Ward 7 Baseball, a group founded by a DC police officer who himself was a product of an RBI program in Harlem. The regional tournaments amount to a postseason.

Brad Burris, the original Grays cofounder, coaches the thirteen-to-fifteen-year-old team along with Corey Jordan, who founded a Little League in the city, and Jabari Graham, a former college baseball player. Shane Davis, a former player at George Mason University, is a volunteer.

With first pitch approaching, the players hop off the bleachers, cleats clanging on the metal. Burris pulls them into a huddle near the dugout. "Confidence," he says. "Grays on three."

◆ ◆ ◆

The summer collegiate team's finale is about five hours away. Barry Direnfeld will be there, but he cares more about the game he's watching right now on the sun-splashed field at Cosca Park. A retired lawyer and the franchise's chief fundraiser, Direnfeld jumped on board initially because he's a baseball guy. It was the mission outside the summer nights that kept him around. "To me, it's a vehicle for a different end," he says of the college team.

A big piece of that end is on the field now, the reality of all the mission's possibilities. The Grays Junior RBI squad is the home team against Harrisburg in the tournament opener. After a score-less top of the first inning, they're in a jam in the bottom half on a leadoff walk and a stolen base. But the Grays pitcher buckles down, spinning for a pickoff throw that gets the runner at second and calms the rally.

After another hitter reaches and moves into scoring position on a rundown gone wrong, the Grays head to the dugout trailing 1–0. Brad Burris, the head coach, watches from just outside the dugout, his back leaning against the aluminum fence post at the edge. He's not entirely sure what to expect from his team today. The oppo-nents are veterans of RBI baseball and beyond, while some of his players are just getting their feet wet in baseball and competitive situations. There's some baseball talent, though. The shortstop's got a great glove. The middle of the order has some pop. How it translates today remains to be seen.

The situation is the same a few hundred yards away, on one of the complex's smaller fields. The Grays RBI softball squad is also in action, wearing light-blue uniforms with the Grays logo. Direnfeld and Barbera make their way over and watch a few innings. The soft-ball team is playing from behind, too. It has more beginners even than the baseball program. If baseball opportunities dry up when young players hit a certain age, girls softball chances can be even harder to come by. Not only is this tournament the first for the Grays program, it's the first of anything like this for the softball players.

Back on the baseball diamond, the Grays have fallen behind 3–0, but they're threatening in the bottom of the second inning. Runners lead off of first base and third base, with just one out on the board. As a pitch gets away from the catcher, the runner at first hesitates, stops, and shuffles back to the bag. Burris leans away from his spot on the fence and shakes his head. He tells the runner that he should be on second, feeling the familiar nagging tug of a looming missed opportunity, the kind any baseball vet knows too well. Sure enough, a few pitches later, the Grays ground into an inning-ending double play. It could have been avoided if the runner on first base had moved up to second.

As the players head back to the dugout and grab their gloves, Burris implores them. "Play smart baseball," he says.

He wants a win today, competitive instincts taking over. But he also wants a win in the bigger picture. As much as the opportunity itself is important, Burris wants his players to seize it—play the right way, work hard, and see what happens. It's up to them to do it. The Grays' RBI program aims to give them all the tools.

As Direnfeld and Barbera watch through the chain-link fence, a parent finds them and offers a thank-you, both for the opportunity and for the tools. It's not the first word of thanks they've heard this summer. They can see the signs of progress—big clinic crowds, kids starting to identify themselves as ballplayers, parents taking a ride to Maryland on a Friday afternoon to watch. "I'd say we've lit a fuse," Direnfeld says.

◆ ◆ ◆

Brad Burris gathers his players on the right-field grass after the final out. They take a knee, still looking unhappy after what turned into a tough debut. Harrisburg pulled away and won by the ten-run rule in five innings. There was a bright spot near the end as the Grays—with one of their least experienced pitchers on the mound—wriggled out of a bases-loaded jam to keep the deficit from growing.

Burris reminds the players that they've still got two games left in the tournament. More opportunity awaits. "Got to bounce back," he says. "We want to compete here."

Assistant coach Shane Davis highlights the late pitching change and the escape from the bases-loaded jam as a success. He thinks it can be a potential rallying point for the team going forward. "We asked our catcher to go out on the mound," Davis says. "He ran out there and got outs. That's being a ballplayer. No matter where I put him, he's going to go out, bust his butt, and execute."

Paris Inman, the board member and one of the driving forces of the RBI program, stopped in for the late innings. He talks to the players with a big-picture perspective. They're part of something special, he tells them. He's talked a few times with John Young, the founder of the Major League Baseball RBI program. "He's in his seventies," Inman says, "and he's still excited."

The team huddles and sends up a cheer. Barbera chats with the coaches and says thanks and good luck as he heads out. The other Grays are up next.

◆ ◆ ◆

As the late-afternoon sun starts to dip, the city is still hot and the academy is still busy. There's youth baseball on one of the small fields and batting practice for the Grays collegiate squad on the big one. Prep is underway in the concession stand. Interns are setting up the main gate and planning out giveaways. Hats, shirts, seat cushions—with the season ending tonight, it's all got to go.

On the field the grind of the summer—forty games in forty-five days—has given way to a last-day-of-school kind of feeling for the players. With batting-practice swings taken, a few of the Grays toss a football back and forth.

It hasn't been the team's best summer in terms of victories on the field. The Grays' playoff fate was sealed with an eight-game losing streak earlier this month, a slide that was full of brutal missed opportunities. Two of the games were decided by a single run, five by two runs.

The numbers are frustrating for the Grays coaching staff and front office, a representation of a season that could have been better. Jason Woodward, the commissioner of the Cal Ripken Collegiate League, knows the numbers for a different reason. They're a good reflection of the parity the league likes to see. The Grays will miss the playoffs but could have easily been in. The team visiting the

Nationals Youth Academy tonight—the Baltimore Dodgers—are still in contention for the final playoff spot in the North Division. Ten teams are in the league, with the top three from each five-team division qualifying for the postseason.

Woodward has stopped in for a quick hello as he makes the rounds in the league tonight, and he chats with Mike Barbera in the press box as the Grays go through their pregame routine. It's the final day of the regular season for most teams, with a handful of games left tomorrow.

Between the parity and the talent, Woodward believes it's been a good year for the league. A number of players are lined up to go to the Cape Cod League when their Cal Ripken seasons end. One Grays pitcher, Jacob Erickson, is already there, having gotten an early call from the Cotuit Kettleers. "You know you're getting the right players when the Cape wants them," Woodward says.

A nonprofit like the Cape League and the New England Collegiate Baseball League, the eleven-year-old Cal Ripken circuit—named in honor of Cal Ripken Sr.—has found a niche with a blend of young players from big-time programs and veterans from smaller schools. The list of alumni in pro baseball isn't as long as those of some other leagues, but it has standouts like Major League vets Brett Cecil and Brian Dozier. And the list is likely to grow. In 2011, 2012, and 2013 the league had a former player selected in the first round of the Major League Baseball Draft.

Powerhouse teams have helped the league's profile. Like the Grays, the Bethesda Big Train used to play in the Clark Griffith League and then moved to the Cal Ripken circuit when it debuted in 2005. In the eleven years since, they have won four championships. The best run came in 2011, when they went 33-9 and earned the No. 1 spot in well-known national rankings put out by a summer-ball website. This year they lead the South Division with a 27-12 record.

In Baltimore—home to three Cal Ripken teams—the Redbirds carry the torch. They've won four consecutive championships and own the best record in the league this year at 28-11.

Off the field the Grays aren't the only community-minded organization in the league. The Big Train was founded in part as a fundraising vehicle for improving youth sports fields all around the DC
metro area. Since the franchise's founding in 1999, hundreds of
thousands of dollars have been doled out. In Baltimore the Redbirds run a youth baseball program. "Those are two franchises that
everyone is trying to emulate," Woodward says. "And I think you're
seeing everyone step their game up as a result."

♦ ♦ ♦

The football tossing has morphed into a punting contest. A few of
the players talk politics in the dugout. They've spent a summer in
Washington, after all.

In the batting cage Marques Inman hones a right-handed swing
that has produced three home runs and fourteen doubles for a
team-high seventeen extra-base hits this season. The more significant number for his career trajectory, though, may be thirty-nine.
That's the number of games he's played—every single one—a welcome sign for a player who's been patiently waiting for his chance.

Inman starred in high school in Elyria, Ohio. He was on the
radar of Major League scouts but went undrafted after his senior
year. As a freshman at West Virginia University, Inman started only
seventeen games and played in thirty. He hit fairly well, but addi-
tional opportunities were tough to come by. With the Grays the
regular playing time has helped him become one of those young
Cal Ripken League players whose star is rising. He'll bat cleanup
tonight in game number forty. "It's been fun for my first summer
college program," Inman says. "It's been a good experience and a
good learning curve. Just polishing my skills and getting better
from an overall standpoint."

Draft talk will pick up again for Inman in two years. It's easy to
imagine the doubles becoming home runs and the athleticism shining through. He's primed to carve out a bigger role with the Moun-
taineers next year, and when he leaves DC this week his summer

will continue. Inman is headed to Cape Cod as a late reinforcement for the Cotuit Kettleers.

While the team hasn't had as much success as it hoped, Inman isn't alone as a bright spot. In his third summer in the Cal Ripken League, Tyler Thomas has found a home with the Grays. He played twelve games with the Bethesda Big Train in 2012 and then saw limited time as a pitcher there the next year. Last summer he was sidelined after surgery.

Thomas hails from Woodbridge, Virginia, south of DC, and plays his college ball at Division II Shepherd University in West Virginia. Injuries have limited him in his collegiate career, but he's making the most of a healthy summer this year. Heading into the finale, he leads the team with a .340 batting average.

Lamar Briggs is getting healthy, too. He was a preseason first-team all-conference pick heading into his sophomore year at Jackson State but missed about half the season with an injury. He's played in thirty-six of thirty-nine games with the Grays and has flashed the talents that earned him that all-conference nod. Briggs is hitting .274 with five extra-base hits.

On the pitching side, two of the league's top strikeout artists this summer have called the Nationals Academy home. Bo Burrup, a towering lefty from Brigham Young, has fanned forty-two batters in 36.1 innings, good for third in the league. Simon Rosenblum-Larson, the starting pitcher for tonight's season finale, has struck out thirty-nine with a 3.24 earned run average.

Since ending the costly eight-game losing streak, the Grays have won three of their last five games. Playoffs or not, they'd like a good finish tonight.

◆ ◆ ◆

Forty-five days ago Simon Rosenblum-Larson started the season opener for the Grays. It was his first action since April 2 with his college team, Harvard, and it didn't go particularly well. He allowed five runs—three earned—in 4.2 innings. When he departed it only got worse for the Grays, who lost 13–1 to the Bethesda Big Train, an inauspicious start to the season for the team and its pitcher.

But things have gotten better. Like Inman, Rosenblum-Larson has benefited from opportunity this summer. By his third start with the Grays he'd already surpassed his innings total from the entirety of his freshman year in Cambridge, shaking off the rust and becoming one of the team's top arms. His best outing came his last time out against the powerhouse Baltimore Redbirds. He struck out nine and surrendered two runs in six innings. His 0-4 record belies the way he's pitched.

Tonight, the lanky, six-foot-three right-hander is closing the season where he started it. He winds up for the first pitch of the game and gets a swinging strike. In an odd twist the home-plate umpire rules that the bat hit the catcher's glove on the swing. After one pitch the leadoff man is awarded first base on an interference call.

The next batter—the Dodgers' best hitter—fouls off the first two pitches he sees. Rosenblum-Larson then gets him swinging for a quick three-pitch strikeout. Two pitches later the No. 3 hitter flies out to Lamar Briggs in right field. A passed ball with the cleanup hitter at the plate puts a runner in scoring position, but Rosenblum-Larson gets a groundout to end the inning.

The Dodgers look poised to match the scoreless first frame in the home half of the inning. Lamar Briggs and Jawan McAllister, a center fielder from Pittsburgh, fly out to start the inning, and Marques Inman falls behind in the count 1-2. He's been a tough out all summer, though, and he plays the part again. He fouls off a pitch, takes a ball, and then fouls off two more. On the eighth pitch of the at bat, he singles.

Tyler Thomas makes the battle count. On the first pitch he sees he smashes a deep fly ball to right-center field that clears the fence for a two-run home run.

That big finish is lining up well.

◆ ◆ ◆

From his spot at the edge of the dugout, Reggie Terry greets Marques Inman and Tyler Thomas with high fives. He isn't surprised to see his team making one last push, even with nothing to play for. They've played hard for him throughout the summer. "Out of all the games, there was only one game where we quit," the Grays manager says. "I talked to the guys, and they responded. When things get tough, you've got to keep trying to punch through the bag."

Terry is in his second summer as the head man in the Grays' dugout. Before that, he spent three seasons as an assistant coach with the Cal Ripken powerhouse Big Train. A former player, his own career on the field was cut short by an injury after a brief stay in the Texas Rangers organization. Before that Terry starred at Norfolk State University, where his career totals in a number of offensive categories still rank in the school's all-time top ten.

Terry has also coached high school ball in Woodbridge, Virginia, and a connection there led him to his first stop in the Cal Ripken League. When the Grays came calling, he jumped at the chance to manage. The opportunity to join in the team's mission made it an even better fit. "Getting kids to play baseball—a game that I grew to love—is important," he says.

In the dugout beside him Jimmy Williams watches the action with a baseball lifer's eye. He was born and raised in the District and grew up watching the old Washington Senators at Griffith Stadium. Baseball took him to dozens of stops in the Minors for the Orioles, Dodgers, and Giants. He even spent two seasons in Japan.

Back home he coached at Howard University until the program was cut. He still spends his springs on diamonds, as an assistant with the Prince George's Community College baseball team.

The Grays offer a chance to work with high-level players, something Williams relishes. He also wants local kids to come out and watch those high-level players, often inviting youth coaches and players to games. "We're having a hard time with baseball," he says.

"Kids are always telling me they want to play pro ball or play DI. Well, they need to come out and see what it is. You've got to be exposed to it to see what it really takes."

The role models themselves are here to play baseball, but the community impact they can make isn't lost on them.

Bo Burrup is used to lending a helping hand. He did his Mormon mission in inner-city Baltimore. Mixing baseball with the same kind of effort for the Grays has made for a memorable summer. "That's honestly one of my favorite parts is being able to help kids," Burrup says. "We worked with some kids today who are on a team, and they were pretty good. We've also had some that didn't even know how to put on a glove. It's pretty cool to help those kids learn about baseball."

Lamar Briggs is part of a tradition with the Grays as a player from a historically black college. The franchise tries to recruit a few such players every year. He knows that he can perhaps make an even more significant impact. "A lot of places, they don't reach out to the community," Briggs says. "Here, they're trying to keep these kids on the right path. I enjoy that, too, being out here with the kids."

The way Terry sees it, it's not a one-way relationship. "I think when you bring a lot of people together, everybody is built up," he says, "even the people who you think might be on top from the first glance."

◆ ◆ ◆

The crowd is small tonight, board members and host families accounting for most of it. Fan support is still a work in progress, but as community efforts go, it's not the top priority anyway. Thanks to the last-game giveaways, the fans who are here will go home with a lot of gear. Seat cushions, hats, and shirts are handed out between every inning.

The fans are seeing a pretty good game for the home team, too. The top of the order is up again in the second inning and picks up where it left off. With a runner on and two outs, Lamar Briggs smacks a single, and Jawan McAllister reaches on an error to load the bases. Marques Inman empties them in a flash, crushing a 2-0 pitch over the right fielder's head for a three-run double.

Tyler Thomas gets on with a hit-by-pitch, and Zach McCrum—the designated hitter from Eastern Kentucky—takes out the frustrations of a summer-long slump on a 1-2 pitch, belting it out to left for a three-run home run.

It's 8–0, and Simon Rosenblum-Larson doesn't even need all the run support. He gives up an unearned run in the third inning on a sacrifice fly but is spotless from there. He ends up going seven innings and striking out seven.

Inman stays hot with a single in the fourth and scores on a base hit by McCrum, finishing the night 3-for-3 with three runs scored and three RBI. Tyler Thomas provides the exclamation point on his big summer—and a big finish for his team—with a two-run home run in the sixth, giving him two homers and four RBI in his last game.

Relievers Kasey Gast from Iona and Marlon Pruitt from Grambling close it out, and the Grays coast to an 11–2 win, one of their best performances of the summer.

♦ ♦ ♦

After one final handshake line, the Grays huddle up on the left-field grass. Jawan McAllister sneaks up on Terry and douses him with a water bottle. It's not quite a Gatorade shower, but it'll do.

Terry's final speech of the season starts with a thank-you—for not quitting. He knows this win means next to nothing, but it doesn't matter. "We muscled through it," he says.

Terry salutes Simon Rosenblum-Larson, whom he calls "Harvard," for a great outing. "You're 1-4!" he says.

Chris Spera, Antonio Scott, and Mike Barbera take turns addressing the team, too. Spera tells the players to go back home better citizens and with a little swagger for coming to a good league and working hard all summer. Scott talks about guys he played with ten years ago whom he still calls friends and encourages the players to stay in touch.

Summer isn't over for everybody. Rosenblum-Larson and teammates Lucas Martinez and Vinnie Catanza are headed to Cuba for a barnstorming tour with a team of Cal Ripken League all-stars. Marques Inman will pack his bags for Cotuit.

Closer to home, the Grays RBI teams will be back in action at the regional tournament tomorrow. Plans for fall ball and off-season clinics are already in the works.

On the field Terry calls for a group hug and one last Grays cheer. Slow goodbyes follow. Barbera shakes the hand of every player. "Proud of you guys," he says.

8 / HAMPTON

In orange warm-up shirts and navy-blue mesh shorts, the Peninsula Pilots are trying and mostly failing to stay cool. Between swings in the batting cage, they crowd into the only hiding place from the late-afternoon sun, a thin sliver of shade by the third base dugout. On the mound head coach Hank Morgan throws batting-practice tosses, a damp T-shirt wrapped and draped over his head, a cross somewhere between a turban and a hat. Infielders fight the sun to get their ground-ball work done. Pitchers mill around; they can do their running after the game, when the sun is down. The steady beat of the ceiling fans hanging from the grandstand mixes with the crack of the bat echoing out of the batting cage, country music blaring from the speakers as a backing track. The song is the summer anthem "Sunny and 75." It is indeed very sunny, but the thermometer soared past seventy-five before the sun even came up.

This is summer—this has always been summer—at War Memorial Stadium in Hampton, Virginia. Hot. Humid. Kids on their way up the baseball ladder calling the field home.

The tradition of pro baseball in southeastern Virginia began more than a century ago, but it found its true home when War Memorial Stadium was built in 1947. Long before summer collegiate baseball settled in, Hampton and the city of Newport News, neighbors on the Virginia peninsula, teamed up to fund construction of the stadium. The story goes that legendary Brooklyn Dodgers general manager Branch Rickey had a hand in designing the charming park, around the same time he was ushering Jackie Robinson into Major League Baseball. The Dodgers' Class A Piedmont League team moved in when construction was completed. For the next forty-five years, with only a few gaps, professional baseball filled the peninsula's hot summer nights.

The end came in 1992 when the Seattle Mariners' Carolina League franchise departed for Wilmington, Delaware. The stadium and the town weren't big enough in the eyes of the owners, a sign of the same trend that took Minor League clubs out of Kenosha and Madison in Northwoods League land.

The team went out with a championship in its final season, but that didn't ease the sting much for local baseball fans. The field was quiet for the next eight years, with local teams and a pro softball club as the only tenants. There were even rumblings that the stadium's days might be numbered.

Then the new Pilots came along in 2000. Sixteen years later they're the old yard's longest-tenured home team.

◆ ◆ ◆

Early birds amble in when the War Memorial Stadium gates open around a quarter past five, the same time the bus with the team from Holly Springs on board pulls into the parking lot. Prime spots in the section behind home plate have been claimed with seat cushions. A few of the early arrivals climb to the top row, where a slight breeze sneaks through the fence. Regulars pore over the stat sheet they grabbed at the gate and chat about last night's game. The Pilots split a doubleheader on the road against the Edenton Steamers, their closest neighbor in the Coastal Plain League and their chief rival. Peninsula scored two runs in the top of the ninth to power a win in the opener. The Steamers walked off in the bottom of the ninth to win the second game.

Pilots staffers are hoping for a big crowd tonight—it's Saturday night, school is still out, the home team is playing well—but they're a little worried the heat might keep people away. Even if it's an off night, though, it's been a typical summer here. The Pilots pull in 1,961 fans a night, third in the Coastal Plain League behind the Savannah Bananas and the Gastonia Grizzlies. They rank in the top fifteen nationally, a fixture among the most successful summer collegiate teams in the country.

"If you build it, they will come" didn't quite apply when the newest Pilots moved back in. It was just the baseball that had been missing. War Memorial Stadium and its long history were already stitched into the fabric of the community. When the games returned, so did the fans, and the ballpark has served as the perfect home for a summer-ball team.

The standard hallmarks of a 1940s ballpark have drifted—and have also been molded—into a rustic charm over the years. It's easy to picture games from decades gone by, when Satchel Paige, Johnny Bench, Gary Carter, César Cedeño, and Darren Daulton played here. Snap a photo at a game, and the right Instagram filter might make it hard to tell the year.

The brick backstop is straight out of Wrigley Field. Behind it small boxed sections include permanent stadium seats and patio chairs, a nod to the laid-back feel at Pilots games. A low-slung concourse runs between the box seats and the gently rising wooden bleachers. It's sixteen rows to the top, where a black slat fence connects to the grandstand roof. The underside of the roof is exposed wood and metal rafters, with ceiling fans spinning and warm-toned lights shining up from the metal posts. After the sun sets the stadium almost glows.

New styles and features blend the old with the new. For a while in the 1990s the bleachers were blue and red, Minor League chic all the way. The new Pilots stripped them back to the bare wood. There's a tiki bar down the left field line, with merchandise and concession stands under the bleachers. A kids play area outside the first base line features a small artificial-turf Wiffle-ball field and an inflatable slide.

A renovated press box is perched on the grandstand roof. On the field new dugouts feature a brick facade. Two stands of lights that were originally rooted inside the fence—Branch Rickey, upon seeing them, is believed to have quipped, "Well, boys, I guess we made a couple of mistakes"—were moved outside the field of play in 2005.

The outfield wall is emblazoned with logos of local companies, leaving just enough room for orange banners commemorating the team's 2013 and 2014 league championships. The scoreboard, complete with a video screen that towers over the left-field fence, went in a few years ago.

The stadium does show its age. Drainage on the playing field is a constant battle. Restrooms are cramped. Parking is limited. The field is sandwiched by a neighborhood on one side and an industrial area on the other, a far cry from the preferred downtown location of a modern stadium. An engineering study released earlier this year recommended millions in renovations, and the city—which owns the park and leases it to the Pilots—is mulling options.

No matter what happens, the Pilots plan to call Hampton home, and nostalgia is a major factor in any discussions. There's an old photo from the local newspaper archives that shows the ticket booth outside the gate, which still greets fans today. Prices were painted on the facade back then—box seats five dollars, reserved seats four dollars, general admission three dollars, senior and military two dollars, children under five free.

At Pilots games nowadays, five bucks still gets you in.

◆ ◆ ◆

There's a good chance you'll meet Henry Morgan if you come to a Peninsula Pilots game. He'll walk past your seat and ask if you're enjoying the night. He'll introduce himself if he hasn't seen you before, shake hands, make sure the kids know about the Wiffle-ball field, make sure you know about the tiki bar. Or maybe he'll be lending a hand in the ticket booth. If you happened to drive by in June, you would have seen him laying sod on the field.

Morgan owns the Pilots, but he refers to himself as the franchise's caretaker, and he views the differing labels as an important distinction. All those Minor League franchises that came and went—they had owners, most of whom were out-of-towners. Morgan was born and raised in Hampton. He was on the city's stadium authority in 2000 and helped the push to attract the Coastal Plain League. The Pilots moved in under owner Dave Dittmann, who would buy the Newport Gulls a year later. Morgan purchased the Pilots from him in 2001 and has been at the helm ever since. Head coach Hank Morgan is his son.

Henry's caretaker identity is rooted in the time when his hometown didn't have baseball, when War Memorial Stadium sat empty and quiet on summer nights. "When softball left here in 1999, I was on the stadium authority," Morgan says. "I had to get a team here because I was afraid they were going to turn it into an industrial park."

As Morgan was well aware, the wrecking ball would have knocked down a lot of history. The Class A team that Branch Rickey and the Dodgers moved into the new stadium were called the Newport News Dodgers and were affectionately known in the area as the Baby Dodgers. They won two Piedmont League championships, with lineups featuring future big leaguers Gil Hodges, Johnny Podres, and Clyde Mashore. The team stayed until 1955.

The Washington Senators brought baseball back to the peninsula in 1963 with the Peninsula Grays. A team with the same name played under the Cincinnati Reds' umbrella and stayed for three years, with big talent on display, including Major League Hall of Famer Johnny Bench and longtime manager Lou Piniella.

That era also spawned one of the park's legendary stories. Satchel Paige had been released by a team in Greensboro in 1955. He was forty-nine years old and slated to be the first black player in franchise history, but an opponent's front office protested his presence. Eleven years later—at age sixty—Paige pitched for a Peninsula team against the same Greensboro squad and threw his last professional pitch at War Memorial Stadium. Three thousand fans turned out to watch him. He pitched two innings.

One more Major League club—the Kansas City Athletics—used the Grays moniker, their farm team playing at War Memorial from 1967 to 1969. Then it was the Houston Astros for a few years before the Philadelphia Phillies began the first of their two stints in town. The Montreal Expos also made a stop.

The Phillies returned in 1976 and brought the peninsula its golden era. They were the first team to use the Pilots name, and they stayed for ten years, winning two Carolina League championships. They won one hundred games in 1980 with a power-hitting shortstop named Julio Franco blasting eleven home runs.

When the Phillies left in 1985, the Chicago White Sox stepped in with a team that would earn a few mentions in the baseball flick *Bull Durham*. The Seattle Mariners brought the Pilots name back before their departure in 1992 ushered in the end of pro baseball on the peninsula. A women's professional softball team called the Virginia Roadsters was the primary tenant from there.

Summer collegiate baseball represented a chance to bring the game back. Morgan knew Hampton would embrace it. The closest big-time baseball before the Pilots moved in was across the water in Norfolk, where the Triple A Tides play. The Pilots brought baseball—and a different brand of baseball—home. "Triple A across the water, those guys might pull up on their way to first because they've got that contract," Morgan says. "These guys want that contract."

◆ ◆ ◆

With first pitch in about an hour, the picnic tables and bar stools in the tiki bar are full, pregame drinks and dinner from the barbecue tent on the menu.

Similar scenes are playing out across the Coastal Plain League tonight. Its slogan is the "Nation's Hottest Summer League." The weather certainly fits, and attendance numbers do, too. A new team, the Savannah Bananas, is drawing the biggest crowds in the league. Ten of the league's fifteen teams average more than a thousand fans per game.

The league made its debut in 1997 and filled a hole in the summer-ball map. Florida now has a league, but at the time the southeastern United States—home for a huge amount of college players—had few summer-ball destinations.

The footprint stretches from Savannah in the South to the peninsula and Martinsville, Virginia, in the North. Two teams play in South Carolina, and the bulk of the clubs call North Carolina home.

The league itself draws its name from a former Class D circuit that played in North Carolina from 1937 to 1952. Like the Pilots, many of the franchises brought baseball back to old Minor League outposts.

The Wilson Tobs played in the Eastern Carolina League as far back as 1908, with a rich history. Ted Williams and Rod Carew once played at Fleming Stadium, which the Tobs still use for their home turf. Teams in Edenton and Fayetteville, North Carolina, have roots in the original Coastal Plain League.

The High Point–Thomasville HiToms played in the Carolina League. The Lexington County Blowfish followed a long string of Minor League squads in South Carolina's capital city. Wilmington, North Carolina, had teams play short stints in the Piedmont, Southern, and South Atlantic Leagues before the Coastal Plain's Sharks arrived and stuck. Savannah's new franchise picked up the slack after the legendary Sand Gnats left town in 2015.

With farm-team roots for its hometowns, games have a Minor League flair. The league follows the same model as the Northwoods League—for-profit franchises with full-time front-office staff—and promotional schedules reflect the similar approach. The Gastonia Grizzlies held a Midnight Madness game in 2011, with first pitch right when the clock struck midnight, though there was no Alaska sun to help. Tickets for Savannah Bananas games go for fifteen dollars and include all-you-can-eat status at the concession stands.

The baseball's been good, too. Twelve players from the league's inaugural season were selected in the 1998 Major League Baseball Draft. In this year's draft the number was eighty-nine, including No. 8 overall pick Cal Quantrill of Stanford University, who played for Morehead City in 2014. The alumni list is highlighted by Major League All-Stars Ryan Zimmerman and Justin Verlander and even one NFL star. Seahawks quarterback Russell Wilson played a summer with the Gastonia Grizzlies, when he was a two-sport athlete at North Carolina State.

Pete Bock and Jerry Petitt cofounded the league in 1997. Like Dick Radatz Jr. of the Northwoods League, Bock was an experienced sports executive, having worked as the general manager for the Durham Bulls and other Minor League clubs. In the movie *Bull Durham*, he played the minister who married Jimmy and Millie at the ballpark. Petitt is a veteran of the hotel industry and remains heavily involved with the league every summer.

The spark for the creation of the Coastal Plain League came from Bock's experience with another league. His son, Jeff, who pitched at Boston College in the early 1990s, spent a season in the Valley League, based in the Shenandoah Valley of Virginia. Bock wondered about starting a league closer to his North Carolina home, and the idea soon became reality.

The league's proximity to dozens of powerhouse college programs was a strong selling point. As the talent on the field rose and the infrastructure off of it expanded, those programs jumped on board. The University of North Carolina sends seven or eight players every year, sometimes a larger crew than it sends to the Cape Cod League. Clemson, Georgia Tech, and North Carolina State are regulars, too. And there's room for good players from smaller programs—stars from the past few summers hailed from Miami of Ohio and Division II Lander University.

As the league grew, communities with deep baseball pasts embraced their new baseball presents. Hot summer nights in the South had the crack of the bat again.

◆ ◆ ◆

The clubhouse down the right-field line provides a bit of respite from the heat. Pilots players trickle out slowly, a few at a time, bound for center field and an official team picture before game time. Their uniforms are a tip of the cap to the Phillies, the parent club of the original Pilots. The pinstripes and bubble-script *P* on the breast that Mike Schmidt and Steve Carlton wore in the early 1980s have been tweaked, with the Pilots' signature orange replacing maroon. Over the years the Pilots have channeled other former War Memorial Stadium tenants in designing new uniforms, with the famous one-stripe Chicago White Sox look of the 1980s and the old Houston Astros rainbow both making an appearance.

The players and coaches line up in three rows for their photo, on a knee in front, on their feet in the middle, standing on benches in the back. The scoreboard, with the Pilots logo on the big screen, is in the background.

For posterity's sake, it might be an important team photo. The 2016 Pilots are 28-15 with twelve games left in the regular season. With the best record in the Coastal Plain League's East Division, they're primed to contend for the franchise's third league championship.

Hank Morgan, the last one out of the clubhouse, jogs to the outfield and hurries to find a spot where he can squeeze in. They were waiting—the photo wouldn't be complete without him. Morgan took the reins on an emergency basis midway through the summer of 2007, when the Pilots' head coach got a Division I college job and had to start the new gig immediately. At the time Morgan was the general manager. He stepped in, and the team won his first game in the dugout. They've won about 300 more with him at the helm. Last summer he broke the Coastal Plain League record for career wins as a head coach with his 289th.

Baseball has long been in his family's blood. Henry coached Hank in Little League and American Legion ball. Hank went on to play shortstop for Hampton High School and then earned a walk-on spot at Virginia Military Institute, a Division I program. He transferred for his last two years to Christopher Newport University, a Division III club in Newport News, not far from home.

When his playing career ended, coaching was a possibility, but he already had a wife and baby, and so he joined the working world. Around the same time, his father took over ownership of the Pilots. After their first season Henry asked Hank about becoming a part of the front office, and Hank ran with the opportunity.

Six years later came the emergency call to the dugout—and it was a true emergency. The Pilots had a bus to catch but no head coach. Their pitching coach, the second in command, was out of town. Hank hopped on the bus. The rest was history.

♦ ♦ ♦

The Pilots put out a full set of baseball cards every summer, keepsakes to hold onto as players' careers continue into pro ball. A young fan perched on the first base line fence holds a sandwich bag full of them in one hand and a permanent marker in the other. As they stretch on the field and wait for the pregame festivities to get underway, players stop by and sign their cards.

This year's stack of cards includes some players who are in the midst of big summers. Seven Pilots were picked for the Coastal Plain League All-Star Game a few weeks ago, which was held in Fayetteville, North Carolina. Kurt Sinnen blasted a two-run homer and won the game's top hitter award.

Sinnen is here from nearby Virginia Beach and Old Dominion University, just across the water in Norfolk. It's been a fun summer, and not just because of the .300 batting average. Kurt's brother, Sam, also plays for Old Dominion and is also with the Pilots this summer as a pitcher. He owns some of the best strikeout numbers on the team. Kurt, who catches and plays designated hitter, has been behind the plate for several of his brother's starts.

Will Shepherd is likely at the top of autograph wish lists. In his third summer with the Pilots, the Liberty University slugger has maintained a batting average north of .400 for most of the season. He saw an eleven-game hitting streak snapped in the doubleheader last night. While he's getting the night off this evening, he will surely be back in the lineup for the all-important stretch run.

First baseman Darian Carpenter of Virginia Commonwealth University, infielder Cole Austin from West Virginia, designated hitter Kyle McPherson from James Madison, catcher Franco Guardascione from Jacksonville, and pitcher Devin Hemmerich from Norfolk State were also all-stars.

Plenty of others could have gotten a nod, too. Joe Poduslenko, an infielder from Seton Hall, has been one of the team's hottest hitters lately, and he'll bat leadoff in tonight's game. Chris Gau, a righty from Jacksonville University, has an earned run average under 3.00 and is striking out around a batter per inning. He's spent time in the bullpen and the rotation and will get the start tonight.

A win would be nice after last night's finish. And in the big picture the team has been treading water—after losing consecutive games just once in the first month of the season, the Pilots suddenly dropped three in a row, and they're just 7-7 since hitting a high-water mark of thirteen games above .500.

The stands are filling in, and the public address announcer welcomes the fans with a nod to the historic park they've walked into. The pregame read includes the familiar names of Peninsula alumni, and the game tonight, he says, will bring back memories and stir new passions here at 1889 West Pembroke Avenue.

As the players gather outside the dugout for a pregame ceremony, Henry Morgan pulls them together. The franchise caretaker sometimes doubles as a motivator, when the time is right. Tonight—on the heels of a loss and with the final weeks of a long summer looming—he paraphrases a quote from Winston Churchill: "Success is moving from failure to failure without losing your enthusiasm." His Pilots will give it a shot.

◆ ◆ ◆

The Pilots are set to honor the memory of a beloved part of the team's family tonight. Henry Morgan's Churchill quote could apply to the ups and downs of a baseball season or to the indelible mark former bat boy Kevin Eadie made on the franchise. Enthusiasm amid trying circumstances was a defining characteristic.

Before grabbing the microphone to set the pregame ceremony in motion, Morgan takes a second to fill in the players on the story. He tells them about Kevin and his time with the Pilots, about how he never missed a game that first year, how he wouldn't let anybody help him up when he fell, how he charmed Morgan into giving him the bat-boy gig in the first place, and how he courageously fought the rare disease—Niemann Pick Type C—that took his life in 2008, when he was just fourteen years old. "He had the same dreams as you," Morgan says to the current Pilots, many of whom would have been right around Kevin's age in 2008. "He didn't get a chance—you do."

The neurodegenerative disease has no cure. Kevin, who grew up in nearby Williamsburg, Virginia, was diagnosed at the age of three. He played youth baseball but had to give it up once severe symptoms took hold. When his mother approached the Pilots about staging a fundraiser at a game, Kevin found a way back to the field, convincing Morgan to let him be the team's bat boy. He was just eight years old, five years younger than the usual age limit the team employed, but he and Morgan hit it off immediately—kindred spirits in their love of the game—so the rule was suspended. "He embodied everything that's right about baseball," Morgan says. "He was energetic. He loved the game."

Morgan gave his new charge a few conditions—his mom had to approve of the job, he always had to do his best in school, and he would take home exactly one dollar a game, with potential raises based on his dedication. Kevin wholeheartedly agreed to everything, telling Morgan he would happily do it for free. Morgan replied that he would have happily given him two dollars.

Over the next seven seasons Kevin was a constant presence at War Memorial Stadium even as the disease progressed, stumbles by the dugout giving way to seasons with a walker. In 2008 he was confined to a wheelchair and spent more time in the hospital than the dugout, but he was there on an emotional Kevin Eadie Night, with the team pushing him around the bases after the game.

Kevin's time as the bat boy impacted everyone in the organization and every player who came through town, Morgan says. In the time since, the Pilots have done all they can to return the favor. The Morgans have worked hand in hand with Kevin's family in forming the Kevin Eadie Foundation, which has raised more than $1 million for efforts to find a cure for the disease.

Beginning when he was still in the dugout and every year since his death, the Pilots have dedicated a game to him, with proceeds going to the foundation. They also present a Kevin Eadie Spirit Award, which carries more cachet around War Memorial Stadium than any most valuable player or top pitcher honor. Fans donate one dollar for one vote and can vote as many times as they want. The ballot boxes are always stuffed.

Kevin's mother, Brenda, is on the field for the ceremony tonight, along with the foundation's board members. She echoes Morgan's sentiments about her son's connection to the Pilots, saying to the newest crop of players, "He loved this game, and he loved this team."

Three years before Kevin's first summer here, the Pilots didn't exist. If they ever needed a reminder of what their presence could mean, they got it every time Kevin scooped up a bat.

The memory lives again tonight as Morgan grabs a microphone and welcomes the fans to Kevin Eadie Night. The video board shows a short piece detailing his story and his time with the Pilots, but a lot of the fans don't need the introduction. War Memorial Stadium is its own little community, and this is that community's cause. "His spirit lives on in this ball field," Brenda says.

◆ ◆ ◆

The five minutes between the ceremonial first pitch by a student and headmaster from a local school and the actual first pitch by the Pilots' Chris Gau are a bit of a circus.

Home Run Hershey, a small dog who's been trained to run the bases, breezes around the horn, collecting a treat on every bag and leaping into his owner's arms at home plate. Hershey is a new addition to the Pilots family this year, following in the footsteps of the team's original base-running dog, Holly.

A birthday party hosted by the Pilots takes center stage next, kids circling the mound and joining players on the trot out to their positions in the field for the national anthem. The Pilots' mascot, a giant bird named Slyder wearing an old-fashioned pilot's hat and goggles, follows with his grand entrance. More kids, pretty much anyone who wants to, get the honor of yelling "Play ball!" into the microphone at a significant volume.

When it's finally time, Gau fires in the real first pitch, the radar gun on the scoreboard flashes 85, and the Pilots are off and running. The leadoff man for the Salamanders slaps a hard ground ball to third base, where Nick Walker makes a nice snag and whips a throw to first base for the out.

Gau's fastball bumps up to 89 by the time the second batter, Brandon Riley, digs in. He lines a single to left field to bring up Dillon Stewart, one of the top hitters in the league, a guy who made the finals of the Coastal Plain League All-Star Game home run derby. Gau battles him and gets him to fly out to left field. Riley steals second to reach scoring position, but a nice play at shortstop by Kyle Wrighte ends the inning.

Joe Poduslenko, the infielder from Seton Hall, stays hot for the Pilots to lead off the bottom of the first inning, cracking a double.

After a flyout by Kurt Sinnen, Poduslenko steals third base. When the throw from the catcher to third gets away, Poduslenko scampers home, and the Pilots nab a 1–0 lead.

Players perched on the window wells of the dugout hop off to greet Poduslenko at home. Coaches on folding chairs bump fists with Poduslenko on his way through. In the stands Henry Morgan is making the rounds, sitting down to chat with several groups in the first few rows.

The tiki bar, jam-packed before the first inning, is all quiet now. Pilots fans have a game to watch.

◆ ◆ ◆

The Salamanders start the top of the second inning with two consecutive singles, and an outfield error on the second hit pushes a runner to third base. The third single in a row plates a run and ties the game at 1–1.

Jeffrey Scott watches from one of the grandstand entranceways. Fans shuffle past, hands full of soft drinks and snacks. As the Pilots' general manager, Scott oversees the behind-the-scenes logistics that are making those fans smile tonight—and making the franchise a success—but on game nights he watches as much of the action on the field as he can. "It's about making sure we do enough to break even, but baseball is still A1," he says. "We're all about trying to win, too. That's awesome because it gets those competitive juices flowing."

Scott grew up twenty minutes from War Memorial Stadium. He remembers going to a few games when the Single A Mariners team was here. His baseball career ended after high school, but he never lost his passion for the game. His wedding band is engraved with baseball-like stitches.

In 2005, while a student at James Madison University, he hooked on as an intern with the Pilots. The next summer he came on full-time as the assistant general manager to Hank Morgan. When Hank was forced to the dugout, Scott stepped into the general manager job and has been doing it ever since.

He laughs when regulars catch him early in the season and ask if he's glad to be back at the ballpark for the summer. "I'm like, 'Man, I'm here year-round,'" Scott says.

Chasing down sponsors is a big part of the job, and the Hampton and Newport News area has been receptive. Advertisements cover almost every inch of the outfield fence, and every promotion is sponsored. Scott also handles player signings, host families, concessions, interns. It's a full-time job.

Summer nights are the reward. Scott joins in the applause when Gau escapes the jam, leaving runners on second and third, thanks to a groundout and a flyout. After an inning and a half, it's a tie ball game.

◆ ◆ ◆

The Pilots plan to mix and match pitchers today, with Devin Mahoney from St. Louis taking Gau's spot in the top of the third inning. He opens with a quick frame but finds trouble in the fourth. With two outs, four consecutive walks push the go-ahead run home for Holly Springs.

The Peninsula offense awakens soon after. Two singles and a bunt load the bases for Connor Sorge from Central Missouri, and his base hit scores a run. The Pilots regain the lead an inning later when Joe Poduslenko tallies his second hit of the night and eventually comes around on a sacrifice fly.

Holly Springs continues the back-and-forth with two runs to go up 4–3 in the top of the sixth. Reliever Colton Harlow—from Scott's alma mater, James Madison—keeps it from getting too much worse by escaping a two-on, one-out jam. A strikeout and a groundout do the job.

The Pilots hold up their end of the bargain in the sudden slugfest with three more runs in the home half of the inning. An error and two straight bunt singles bring the first run to the plate. Poduslenko comes up with runners on second and third and delivers again, getting a base hit to right-center field to score two runs.

The middle of the order goes quietly after that, but the Pilots have a 6–4 lead as the game heads into the seventh inning.

In his spot behind home plate, decked out in a Pilots T-shirt and hat, Wayne Gianettino tries to get the crowd going. It's his job, unofficial though it may be. After all, his nickname around here is Super Fan Wayne.

The Newport News resident used to come to watch one of the Phillies Minor League clubs years ago. He remembers Julio Franco, Ozzie Virgil, and Juan Samuel coming through town. About ten years ago, when the new Pilots were picking up steam, he came back to the ballpark with some friends and has essentially never left. "I fell in love," he says. "It's a family atmosphere, and Henry accepts everyone the way they are, no matter their walk of life. And where can you spend five bucks and see this? It's the best fun for the money."

When Henry Morgan took control of the team, he led a two-pronged effort to establish its place in the community and get people like Wayne out to the ballpark. Local businesses were a big piece of the budget puzzle, but building the fan base was the primary goal. "We're selling entertainment," Jeffrey Scott says. "We're competing against movie theaters, bowling alleys, Putt-Putt courses. Avid baseball fans are going to be out here regardless. It's trying to get the families. Little by little, we've built it. As we continue to make the place better, the people around here have just been tremendous. The community support we get from people is just outstanding. It's been really cool to see that growth."

Even now, sixteen years in, the work never stops. The Hampton area has deep military roots with Langley Air Force Base and Naval Station Norfolk nearby, so there are always new fans out there just waiting for a team to adopt.

Marketing efforts and branding make up the top-down part of the approach. From the bottom up, Morgan's handshakes in the ballpark seal the deal. "Our philosophy was to build it one fan at a time," Morgan says.

One super fan at a time, too. Wayne has missed two games this year, one because he was sick, the other due to work commitments. Otherwise, his booming voice is a constant on the soundtrack of the summer at War Memorial Stadium.

◆ ◆ ◆

The Pilots haven't needed Will Shepherd's big bat tonight. Before the top of the seventh inning, he's on the field with a rake instead of his usual lumber, as bench players and the coaching staff double as the War Memorial Stadium grounds crew. Even coach Hank Morgan is out there, scraping dirt around the first base bag.

Shepherd pulls the second base bag out as a teammate smooths the dirt around it, but he may need to grab a bat after all. Holly Springs greets a new Peninsula pitcher with a triple and an RBI single that make it a one-run game. With runners on first and second and one out, the Pilots nearly get out of the inning with their lead still intact, but a double-play ground ball turns into an error, and the Salamanders make the blunder sting. Four more hits and a sacrifice fly plate five more runs, and all of a sudden the Pilots trail 10–6. They hadn't played great baseball tonight—three errors, seven runners left on base—and it finally caught up to them. They might still salvage a win, but they know they've got to play better as the games start to get more and more important.

The rough inning takes a backseat for the seventh-inning stretch. The video board plays a clip of Kevin Eadie singing "Take Me Out to the Ballgame," and the crowd joins in. Four players emerge from the dugout as finalists for the Kevin Eadie Spirit Award, and Shepherd is announced as the winner. As a veteran of the team—he's practically found a second home in Hampton—he's a big part of the Pilots' family, and the award reflects that. His popularity with the baseball card–carrying crew doesn't hurt.

An inning later players pass their hats through the stands for donations to the Kevin Eadie Foundation. Shepherd leads the way.

✦ ✦ ✦

Super Fan Wayne leads the crowd in the singing of Neil Diamond's "Sweet Caroline" after the bottom of the eighth inning. It's near the end of a long, hot night at the ballpark, and there hasn't been much to cheer about lately—Holly Springs tacked on two more runs in the eighth—but the dwindling crowd is singing along nonetheless.

Two more errors—the fifth and sixth defensive miscues of the night for the Pilots—set up two more runs for Holly Springs in the top of the ninth. It's a 14–6 game heading into the bottom of the ninth.

As the Pilots get set for their last at bats, Henry Morgan eases the tension of a rough night by yelling from the stands, "We've got 'em right where we want 'em!"

But a comeback isn't meant to be. After a leadoff single, the second batter grounds into a double play. Morgan is back at it— "*Now,* we've got 'em right where we want 'em"—but a ground ball to third is the final out.

After the handshake line, players and coaches head quickly to the clubhouse. It's two straight losses now, this one the worst yet. The Pilots need a big rebound tomorrow when they host High Point–Thomasville. They're still in first place, but challengers are hot on their heels.

Showered and dressed, players stop for more autographs from a few persistent young fans. Others mingle with host families and friends or walk across the field to the tiki bar, where they'll grab a postgame meal. The clips of Kevin Eadie continue to light up the video board.

The old ballpark has seen plenty of bad nights for the home team. Even the 1980 Pilots team that won one hundred games still lost forty. For the fans filing out under the stadium's glow, maybe it wasn't such a bad night anyway. "If people come once," Jeffrey Scott says, "they're coming back."

9 / CAPE COD

In his regular pregame greeting at Cotuit Kettleer home games, public address announcer Roy Reiss welcomes fans to "Cape Cod's Field of Dreams." A former sportscaster in Boston, Reiss has been on the mic in Cotuit since 2012. His welcome is the same as always today, and Lowell Park is truly looking the part, a scene that a baseball movie director might wait weeks for.

The thermometer reads seventy-eight degrees. The sun blazes, barely a cloud in the brilliant blue sky. It's the kind of crisp, clear beach day that makes Cape Cod the tourist destination that it is, but Kettleers fans have dusted the sand off their feet early today. They've arrived at Lowell Park in droves, packing the wooden bleachers and marking every spare spot of grass outside the fences with blankets and chairs. Even the space under the wooden bleachers is claimed. The fans know it's their last chance to see the Kettleers this summer.

Cotuit's midseason surge hit a high point with the extra-innings win in Harwich in July, when Colton Hock shone and the offense broke through late. All the momentum of the good stretch, all the pieces that were coming together, faded into another slide immediately after. The Kettleers lost five games in a row following the win over the Mariners. Three of the games were close and two were not, but they counted the same in the standings. The Kettleers stopped the skid with a win over Orleans on July 22 but lost three more in a row right after, giving them eight defeats in a nine-game span.

As the final week of the regular season hit, the Kettleers were still clinging to playoff hopes, aiming to take advantage of the Cape League's large postseason field. They forced themselves into the picture with two wins over the Hyannis Harbor Hawks—the team they were chasing in the West Division standings—and a shutout of the Chatham Anglers. But a 6–1 loss to Yarmouth-Dennis yesterday, in the penultimate game of the season, sealed their fate. Cotuit will miss the playoffs.

It's not something they make a habit of around here, and fans know it. They need only look around on their way to their seats or the concession stand. On the facade of the bleachers is a giant poster of the 2013 team posing with the Cape League championship trophy. In glass cases behind the bleachers, the team's history is on full display—letterman jackets, plaques, trophies, newspaper clippings. The rich and winning tradition of Cotuit's baseball club is readily apparent.

The 2016 Cotuit Kettleers will not have a prominent spot in any record books, but for those closely involved, it's a different story in memory banks. "Are there years you wish you had executed better on the field? Of course," manager Mike Roberts says. "But every summer is a great summer."

The reasons are many. In player development—a key part of any summer team's mission—positive steps can be taken whether games are won or lost. Bonds are forged when a team plays nearly every day, competition bringing out the camaraderie. Players will stay in touch, always looking out for their former Kettleer teammates when their paths cross in the spring. And if all else fails, what could be better than a summer of baseball in a beautiful place?

The other reason is a unique part of summer ball—players become part of the Cotuit baseball family. They've slept under the roofs of Kettleer host families. They've given pointers to Little Leaguers at weekly clinics. They've spent off days at the beach, barbecued with board members, fished with fans. There's no detached frustration like Cotuit baseball fans might be feeling about their other team, the Boston Red Sox. You keep cheering for family.

First pitch for today's season finale is at 4:30 p.m., an hour earlier than usual for Cotuit home games. Late in the season the league doesn't want any games cut short by darkness, in case of playoff implications. Even without those ramifications, it's still a chance to soak in a perfect day for baseball.

Soon after Reiss's greeting, Roberts's "Hey, Hey, Cotuit" song comes over the speakers with about forty minutes to first pitch. The fans, of course, sing along.

♦ ♦ ♦

His father and his cousin can trade plenty of stories from their summers in the Cape Cod Baseball League. Ross Achter will have quite a few of his own now, and, in terms of what happened on the field, yesterday's game may be the headliner.

Achter drew the start for Cotuit's biggest game of the year, the must-win against the Yarmouth-Dennis Red Sox. He had been pitching mostly out of the bullpen lately as the staff gained some depth; he hadn't made a start since July 3. But with his team in need of a win to stay alive in the playoff race, it was Achter who got the ball.

Staked to a 1–0 lead in the top of the first inning, the left-hander tossed a one-two-three bottom half. He worked around a single for a scoreless second inning. He notched his second strikeout of the game in a perfect third. The defense turned a double play to erase a leadoff single in the fourth inning. His catcher caught a runner stealing in the fifth, and Achter ended the inning with another strikeout. Five shutout innings. "I didn't really change anything," he says of his performance. "I just went out there and attacked from the get-go—got ahead of hitters, and that allowed me to throw three pitches the whole game."

He went back to the mound for the sixth inning and allowed a leadoff single. After a sacrifice bunt and a pop-out, he was on the cusp of escaping the jam, but Will Toffey from Vanderbilt singled home the tying run.

Still, Achter had given his team a chance. It was by far his best outing of the summer. It came against one of the league's best teams, on a field that is not kind to pitchers.

The chance to win faded, though. The Kettleers didn't score again after the first inning—they stranded ten runners on base— and Yarmouth-Dennis broke through against the Cotuit bullpen once Achter departed. The Red Sox pulled away for the 6–1 win.

For Achter, perspective has been easy to find all summer, from the journey with his dad, to the Wiffle-ball game, to pitching well and earning a full contract. He finished the summer with a 3.44 earned run average in ten appearances. He earned two wins and struck out nineteen in 31.1 innings. He wasn't dominant, but he held his own, and he'll draw some confidence from that as he goes back to Toledo for one last collegiate season. He hopes he caught some eyes.

Achter will watch today's season finale from the dugout and will head home soon. Even after the loss, it hasn't been hard to tap into the perspective again. "I can honestly say I wasn't really expecting to come out here and last the whole summer," he says. "It's definitely one of the best summers of my life, and I wouldn't trade it for anything."

◆ ◆ ◆

The win last night over the Kettleers was the second in a row for Yarmouth-Dennis, and it looks as though the two-time defending champs are primed for another playoff run. This is the Red Sox's time of year, almost regardless of what comes before—they won the title as the East Division's No. 3 seed each of the last two seasons. In one of those years, they went an even 22-22 in the regular season before the playoff push.

This year the Red Sox started the season 0-5, with a 9–1 loss to the Harwich Mariners mixed in. From that point on, they've played well above the .500 pace, winning twenty-five of thirty-eight games, with one more game remaining today.

Continuing to ride its dynamic pitching, Harwich has managed to stay just ahead of Y-D for the top spot in the East Division standings. After their shutout loss to Cotuit on July 15, the Mariners outscored their next two opponents 23–4. Their top hitter, Ernie Clement from Virginia, has never cooled off. In contention for the batting title, he might be the league MVP favorite.

Y-D and Harwich have looked like the two best teams in the league for much of the season, but with the playoffs bearing down, it's actually Falmouth that owns the Cape's best record. The Lipscomb University trio continues to sparkle. Michael Gigliotti is batting .310 with two homers and eleven stolen bases. Brady Puckett leads the league in wins. Jeffrey Passantino tops the ERA leaderboard.

The Commodores will be the top seed in the West. Wareham—Cotuit's opponent today—will be the No. 2 seed. The Gatemen own a 25-15-4 record and have won seven of their last nine heading into the season finale.

It's anybody's game come playoff time, momentum and roster changes combining to make an eight-team bracket even more wide open than it already would be. In Cotuit's last championship run, a cast of reinforcements arrived at the perfect time, and the Kettleers caught fire.

The magic ingredient for every Cape League playoff ride seems to be desire. In college baseball, it's a given that teams want to win. Omaha is never far from anyone's mind, even at small schools. In summer ball winning isn't so primary. But the right group of competitors with the right mix of chemistry can flip the switch when a championship is on the line. Eight Cape League teams are aiming to do just that this summer.

Cape League president Chuck Sturtevant has stopped in at Lowell Park tonight. The playoffs will take him almost everywhere else over the next week and a half, so tonight's finale is a good chance to catch up with the Kettleers.

It's been a good year from the league's perspective. Attendance always seems to hold fairly steady. The All-Star Game in Chatham was a success, with an announced crowd of 7,243 at Veterans Field.

As always there are trends to monitor. The leashes on pitchers seem to get tighter every summer. Only nineteen pitchers logged enough innings to qualify for the ERA title this summer. Many pitchers departed early, a practice that could snowball as an increasingly high-stakes college baseball world moves to protect its assets. The Cape League and the scouts who watch it don't want that. Players whose future might be paved by summer success shouldn't want it either.

The league is looking at expanding rosters to give teams more flexibility. A shorter schedule could be in the works down the line. The league has evolved before and won't stop now. "It's something we need to always maintain," Sturtevant says.

Whatever changes happen, an eye will always be kept to the field. The Cape League has something special—and knows it. "To me, it's almost like what I would call hometown baseball—what baseball was all about way back when," Sturtevant says. "You've got the fans right next to the field. They have contact with the ballplayers before and after the games. They get their autographs. The kids look up to the players like they're the stars. It's a great family atmosphere."

♦ ♦ ♦

Patrick Dorrian is not in the starting lineup today, but he moves through his pregame routine as if he were—batting practice, ground balls, stretching. He didn't take much of anything for granted this summer, from day one on. Here, on the final day of the season, he still won't. "I tried to play the whole time like I wasn't on a full contract," Dorrian says.

That attitude, combined with opportunity, kept Dorrian in the Cotuit lineup more often than not, even though he never quite put it all together at the plate. He finished with a .194 batting average but played in thirty of the team's forty-four games. And he seemed to come up big when chances arose. Seven of his eighteen hits went for extra bases, and his twelve RBI ranked fourth on the team.

With his time in the junior-college ranks complete, Dorrian is headed to Division II powerhouse Lynn University in Florida next season. The school won the national championship in 2009 and is a perennial contender. It should be a good fit, and a summer's worth of improvement will be packed with the suitcases. "Personally, I got so much better and had so much fun," Dorrian says. "Met all these guys. It was amazing. It was an awesome summer."

As first pitch approaches, Dorrian stakes out a spot at the far end of the dugout, on the railing. He'll cheer as if he were playing.

◆ ◆ ◆

Colton Hock has been snapping his fingers a lot the past few days. It's a nod to something Mike Roberts said way back in June, in summing up how quickly a summer in the Cape League flies by. "Coach said on one of the first days, that it's going to be like a finger snap," Hock says. "Sure enough, I've been snapping my fingers."

Hock made his final regular-season start on July 29. That lined him up to pitch a potential playoff game, but, with no postseason for his club, he'll settle for going out on a high note. Facing Hyannis— the team the Kettleers were chasing for the final playoff spot—Hock went six scoreless innings, striking out six and allowing three hits. Together with the win over Harwich on July 15, Hock logged six shutout innings in two of his final three outings.

Scouts had to like the finish. Frankie Piliere, who scouts the league for the college baseball website D1Baseball.com, posted on Twitter in July that Hock looked like the number-one pitching prospect on the Cape.

For his part, Hock tried not to notice the radar guns behind home plate. He was not always successful, but he found the right balance in his final start, and big success followed. "It's a lot—sometimes there are thirty or thirty-five of them back there," Hock says. "It's hard not to take a peek and start thinking about what they're looking for. The biggest thing I learned—and it took me until my last start pretty much—is if you just pitch the game like you grew up doing and not try to impress anyone, you're going to have success." He adds, "I think that's something all of us had to learn."

Hock finished the summer with a 3.44 ERA and thirty-one strike-outs in 36.1 innings. Maintaining his velocity deep into games remains a work in progress, but the summer with Roberts and the Cotuit coaching staff was a step in the right direction. He'll remember several key points as he returns to Stanford. "It's a great stepping-stone going back to school," he says.

He'll take plenty of memories, too. Hock and his Stanford team-mate Jackson Klein lived with the Lawson family, two very big kids squeezing in with five little Lawson kids. The Cape Leaguers weren't sure what they were getting into at first, but they were all Lawson kids by the end of it. Their host brothers and sisters are wearing homemade Kettleers jerseys today, Hock's and Klein's names scrawled on the back. "It was an unreal summer with them," Hock says.

At the tail end of a whirlwind two months, Hock can understand why some players might want to take a summer off or head home early, but he was never tempted. "I could see how it just feels like too much—you go right from the spring into summer ball," Hock says. "It's a grind. But everything here is just incredible."

Hock worked the Kettleers baseball camp most days, arriving at the field by nine o'clock and not leaving on game nights until more than twelve hours later.

The days were long, but the summer was short. Like a snap.

◆ ◆ ◆

As they did last summer when Colton Hock played for them—as they do almost every summer—the Newport Gulls appear to be peaking at just the right time. The Gulls won five of their last seven games in the regular season and earned the No. 2 seed from the New England Collegiate Baseball League's Southern Division. They'll host game one of a first-round series against the Danbury Westerners tonight at Cardines Field.

The statistics say the Gulls will be a postseason contender. They finished the season ranked second in the league in runs scored behind Mystic, the Southern Division No. 1 seed. The pitching staff ranked fourth in team ERA.

The offense was led all season—or at least from the time Paiva called him on the phone from the front row at Cardines Field—by Troy Dixon. With a 1-for-4 night in the regular-season finale two days ago, Dixon clinched the NECBL batting title. The St. John's catcher hit .371, adding two homers, fifteen doubles, and eighteen RBI. He became the first Gull to win the batting crown since 2012. It was a dream summer for Dixon, especially since it started at home.

Jake Brodt, one of the team's late arrivals, hit .288 with six homers. Stephen Scott showed as much offensive potential as any freshman in the league, batting .285 with ten home runs. Hometown kid Mark Powell finished with a .193 batting average, never quite heating back up after his midseason slump. He did have two hits in a game against New Bedford earlier this week, and he'll be in the starting lineup tonight.

Newport's neighbor, the Ocean State Waves, won't be in the playoffs. The best start in franchise history gave way to an injury-plagued finish. They tumbled down the standings and lost a one-game playoff to New Bedford for the final postseason spot. Though there wasn't as much talent on the field by the end of the season, there was no denying its presence—seven players have inked temporary contracts with Cape League teams as playoff reinforcements.

The Gulls will keep playing, and they're expecting one of the best crowds of the season to pack into Cardines Field to watch it. The Gulls led the league in total attendance and finished second in per-game average. The signature moment came on July 17, when 3,116 watched the NECBL All-Star Game on a perfect Newport night.

♦ ♦ ♦

The final bit of pomp and circumstance at Lowell Park this season belongs to Heroes in Transition, a local organization that provides support to military veterans in need. The ceremonial first pitch from one such veteran is a perfect strike, and Kettleers players tip their hats to him as they take the field for one last pregame huddle.

Wareham's place in the playoffs is secure, just behind Falmouth and with a cushion on third-place Bourne. With the playoffs looming and nothing at stake, the Gatemen won't go deep into their pitching staff today, but their lineup looks as fearsome as usual. The middle of their order has hit fourteen home runs this year, led by former DC Grays catcher Colton Shaver, who has eight of them.

Sure enough, there's trouble not long after the ceremonial first pitch gives way to the real first pitch. Josh Roberson, a valuable reliever in the Cotuit bullpen from North Carolina–Wilmington, is making his first start today. He walks the first two batters he faces and watches both runners move up on a wild pitch. They score on a base hit by Georgia Tech's Joey Bart, one of the league's top prospects. Wareham leads 2–0.

Bart is on third base when Roberson induces a ground ball to shortstop. Ryan Hagan fires home to get Bart, who had run on contact, and the tag is applied by catcher Cory Voss. With something to cheer about after a shaky first few moments, the big Lowell Park crowd suddenly gets loud. After a single by Shaver, Roberson induces a double play to end the inning, and the crowd gets into it again.

Quinn Brodey leads off the bottom of the first inning for Cotuit. Unlike some Kettleers who have taken important steps but might be missing the good numbers, Brodey's summer story comes with no caveats. When he played alongside Colton Hock with the Newport Gulls last summer, he was still a two-way player, as he was in his freshman year at Stanford. He pitched in eight games and had a 2.27 ERA that season with the Cardinal. At the plate he hit .293 in fifty-eight at bats.

He focused exclusively on hitting as a sophomore this spring, with solid results—a .280 batting average and seven homers—and his summer in Cotuit has removed any doubt that a singular focus on hitting was the correct choice. Brodey has been the team's top hitter and ranks among the league leaders with a .336 batting average. He went 4-for-5 with a double in yesterday's loss to Yarmouth-Dennis.

Brodey was one of two Cotuit players named to the West Division team for the Cape League All-Star Game, along with pitcher Eddie Muhl. "Here's a young guy who came in and was kind of timid with the bat and timid in the outfield," Roberts says of Brodey. "He's really bought in and worked on some things. Did I ever think Quinn Brodey would lead off here? No." But here he is.

Brodey was the team's only all-star position player. Other Kettleers had their moments, even as the team struggled to produce. Clay Fisher, the slick-fielding shortstop from UC Santa Barbara, batted .231 with a home run in fourteen games before being forced to leave Cotuit early due to an injury. He finally made one error, but only one. Brodey and Hock's Stanford teammate Jackson Klein is tied for second on the team with two home runs, though it's been a struggle in the batting-average department. Arizona-bound Cal Stevenson is batting .254, second on the team behind Brodey. The Oregon duo of A. J. Balta and Tim Susnara ranked second and third on the team in runs batted in. Vanderbilt's Alonzo Jones Jr. never broke out of his slump, hitting .175 heading into the season finale. Catcher Jason Delay batted .191. A month after his draft call, he opted to play one more season at Vanderbilt.

Greyson Jenista, the big freshman from Wichita State, continued to make strides as the season went on and turned in some of his best performances as the Kettleers made their last-ditch playoff push. Jenista had two hits in a win over Chatham this week and two more in the key victory over Hyannis. He made it three straight two-hit games in yesterday's loss to Yarmouth-Dennis.

Jenista will finish with an average in the low .200s, but with a lot to build on as he heads back home. He also has another summer to look forward to—Jenista is set to return to the Kettleers next year.

The pitching staff has had its share of ups and downs as well. Muhl, the lone all-star, has a 1.84 earned run average. His fellow jack-of-all-trades Taylor Lehman is at 3.19. Ryan Rigby, who closed out the big win over Harwich, has a 2.16 ERA. Alec Byrd, out of Florida State, led the team in earned run average with a 1.62 mark in 16.2 innings.

The Kettleers will keep watch from a distance on another of their pitchers. Cal Becker, who signed his pro contract in July, is headed for Montana and the Missoula Osprey of the Pioneer League.

In the batter's box today Brodey can't carry over yesterday's success into his first at bat. He flies out. Jordan Pearce and A. J. Balta also make outs as the Kettleers go down in order. After one inning they trail 2–0.

◆ ◆ ◆

The Santa Barbara Foresters won the California Collegiate League championship on July 31—the twenty-first title in franchise history—but the real prize is what they'll start chasing in a matter of days.

The Foresters are bound, as always, for the National Baseball Congress World Series in Wichita, and they may well be the favorite. The run to the league championship was part of a six-game winning streak and a stretch of ten wins in eleven games. They finished league play with a 24-12 record. There were moments when the team wobbled earlier this year—a slow start, some missteps. They didn't look quite like last year's team, which lost all of seven games in the regular season. But they're starting to look like a juggernaut now.

In the double-elimination California Collegiate League playoffs, the Foresters cruised through the winners bracket and won the title with a 5–2 victory over the Conejo Oaks.

Bret Boswell from Texas won playoff MVP honors and finished the regular season with gaudy numbers—a .391 batting average, a .467 on-base percentage, eight home runs, fifteen doubles, and two triples. He'll likely win the league MVP Award when postseason honors are announced later this week.

Tulane stars Hunter Williams and Lex Kaplan rounded out the meat of the order for the playoff run. Williams homered in the championship round, his seventh blast of the summer. He finished with a .319 batting average. Kaplan closed with a .330 average.

Kyle Johnston may join his Texas teammate Boswell in winning top league honors. The hard-throwing pitcher struck out five and allowed one hit in the first game of the playoffs, finishing league play with a 1.74 ERA and forty-one strikeouts. He'll start the opener in Wichita.

Once they get to Kansas, the Foresters may run into the Alaska Goldpanners. Now on Lower 48 soil, they're matching up with the Jayhawk Collegiate League's Hays Larks in a World Series tune-up today, not far from Wichita. In their return to barnstorming this summer, the Panners own a 25-18 record. They won five straight games a few weeks back.

Isaiah Aluko never cooled down, carrying the offense all summer. He takes a .366 batting average and three home runs into tonight's game, and he's hoping to catch the attention of scouts at the World Series.

Justin Harrer from Washington State continued a late-season surge with a 3-for-4 performance and a home run in the team's most recent game, a win over the Wenatchee Apple Sox in Washington. Kevin Connolly from Creighton is batting .325.

Joe Fernandez, the Midnight Sun Game starter, will get the ball tonight against the Larks, back in action after he was sidelined for much of July. He has a 3.86 ERA on the summer.

The Goldpanners last won the NBC title in 2002. It was their sixth, which remains the most all time. But the Foresters are right behind them with five, all since 2006.

If either one of them wins this year, they'll make history.

♦ ♦ ♦

The lines are long at the Lowell Park concession stand, hot dogs and burgers at the park replacing for tonight the usual cookouts at the rental cottage. As they stand in line fans can look at the framed posters of summer scenes hanging on the bleachers. The shots are of the current Kettleers in places around town. Though the players look a bit out of their element—lined up in the town square, perched on a dock and a boat, walking through the village—the photos are a sign of how much the players are welcomed as part of the community.

Ross Achter meanders through the bleachers with an intern, a roll of raffle tickets in tow. It's a common job for pitchers on off days—their presence helps the raffle sales while enhancing the closeness that fans can feel to the players on Cape Cod. Kids trail behind Achter, waiting for an idle moment to ask for an autograph.

On the field the Kettleers are suffering from something that's been a common problem this year—they aren't hitting. Cotuit owns the worst team batting average in the league and has scored the fewest runs of the ten teams. The wood bats and power arms tend to make it a pitcher's league—the top hitting team this summer is at .265—but you have to hit at least a little bit to win.

It's not happening—even with a low bar—through four innings. The Kettleers don't have a single hit. Josh Roberson has settled in after the shaky first inning. Wareham tacked on a run in the third. Roberson pitched a quiet fourth, but the 3–0 deficit feels bigger than that.

◆ ◆ ◆

After the South Division's win in the Home Run Derby at the Harbor, the North Division got a little revenge when the action returned to an actual baseball field. The night after the show on the water, the North won the Northwoods League All-Star Game 9–5 at Simmons Field. Steve Passatempo from UMass Lowell had the best game among the home run–derby participants, cracking a two-run homer for the South team.

The Kingfish carried the festival atmosphere back to Simmons Field, with concessions and games in the parking lot. Pregame autographs were a hit. It was another perfect-weather night, and the stands were packed. So were the picnic tables and the party boat.

The Kingfish won in their return to the field after the all-star break, and home run king Marty Bechina stayed hot with a two-hit game. Three days later he homered—into the stands, not the water.

The team still hasn't hit its stride, but the fans keep coming. The Kingfish are at home tonight against Madison. It's team-poster giveaway night. And there's a petting zoo.

◆ ◆ ◆

The powerhouse Bethesda Big Train captured the Cal Ripken Collegiate League championship earlier this week. Members of the DC Grays saw the score from afar, at home or back at school or even on Cape Cod. Marques Inman is in Cotuit and starting for the Kettleers today, following up his big summer in DC with a short stint in the Cape League. Some even watched from Cuba. The Cal Ripken League all-star team that traveled to the island for a goodwill barnstorming trip is playing a Cuban Major League team today.

Back in DC it's already time to think about next year, for the baseball and beyond. The RBI teams held their own in the regional tournament, and interest continues to build. The Grays board is planning a fall-ball program that will start in a few weeks. Winter training and clinics are also in the works.

A little farther south the Peninsula Pilots are still going strong—and there's reason to think they may play for a while. After their lopsided loss to Holly Springs on the steamy night in July, they've reeled off six wins in a row. The latest was the biggest, a 19–2 demolition of Petersburg that clinched home-field advantage for the first round of the playoffs.

Five games remain in the regular season, and then the quest for another league championship begins. All of a sudden the Pilots lead the league in team batting average and team ERA. Will Shepherd is in position for the league batting title with an average hovering around .400. The Pilots may be peaking at the perfect time.

◆ ◆ ◆

With one out in the fifth inning Wareham puts a runner on base thanks to a single off Roberson. On the bullpen mound down the left-field line, David Gerics keeps an eye to the field and the corner of the dugout as he accelerates his warm-up tosses. A wild pitch sends the runner to second, and a walk puts a second runner on base. Mike Roberts climbs the dugout steps and heads to the mound. He motions for the right-hander.

Gerics gets one final warm-up toss in, slips through the gate, and jogs toward the mound. It's been a while. He last pitched on July 18, about two weeks ago, in the late innings of a 12–0 loss. He allowed three runs in three and a third innings, a bit of a step back after he went two scoreless frames in a game nine days before. His season earned run average is over 6.00, but he's shown flashes of potential.

Joe Cavanaugh, his host dad and the team photographer, hustles to get in position for a few last shots. The radar gun readout on the scoreboard flashes 90 while Gerics warms up.

He's due to face Joey Bart, the slugger from Georgia Tech. That's Division III Pomona-Pitzer against an Atlantic Coast Conference power. It's a reminder of what Gerics accomplished just by sticking around. "I always thought I didn't get my fair shake out of high school," he says. "It was nice to prove that I could hang around with these guys."

It was nerve-racking at the beginning of the summer, he says, not knowing if he'd be packing his bags at a moment's notice. He took it day by day. He'll always remember the moment when the full contract came through. "Honestly, one of the happiest moments of my life," he says.

Gerics misses the strike zone on his first pitch to Bart. The next pitch is grounded to shortstop, and the Kettleers get a force at third base for the second out on a nice play by Ryan Hagan. Pomona-Pitzer wins the first battle, but another is coming fast as Wake Forest's Gavin Sheets—another big hitter from the ACC, and Wareham's cleanup batter—steps in. After Gerics misses the strike zone on the first pitch, Sheets fouls off the next two. Gerics thinks he gets a strikeout on the fourth pitch of the at bat, an 89-mph fastball on the outside corner, but it's called a ball by the umpire. Sheets fouls another pitch off before an off-speed pitch that also just misses the corner pushes the count to three balls and two strikes.

Gerics kicks dust from the rubber. He takes a deep breath and looks in for the sign. He checks the runner at second.

The pitch is a good one, cutting inside. Sheets chops it into the ground, and it caroms toward first base. Marques Inman scoops it and steps on the bag to end the inning. Gerics strands both runners, getting two ACC sluggers—likely two future pros—along the way.

He describes the Cape League as a dream. Sometimes, even when you haven't pitched in two weeks and your ERA is over 6.00 and the game doesn't matter a lick, it's even better.

◆ ◆ ◆

The dream is never easy, though, as the Kettleers have found out all summer. Colton Shaver, the league's home run leader, greets David Gerics with a single to start the sixth inning, and Alex Destino launches a home run to make the score 5–0.

Gerics doesn't allow much else—just an unearned run charged to him after he departs in the eighth inning. His final pitch of the summer yielded a walk. He'll finish his Cape League career with a 6.19 earned run average, but he knows scouts lean more on what they see through the fence than the numbers they find on a stat sheet. "Hopefully, someone saw something this year and I get an opportunity," he says. "That's the reason we're all here."

The possibilities are never far away. Between innings the final installment of the team's alumni segment plays over the speakers. Roy Reiss, the pubic address announcer, checks in with as many former Kettleers as he can, recording their memories. Ben Rowen, a side-arming reliever who pitched for Cotuit in 2009 and made his big-league debut in 2014, is the feature today. He talks about his experience, the people he met in the town, his host family. He was a guy who started his career at Los Angeles Harbor College. Anything is possible.

♦ ♦ ♦

The Kettleers break up Wareham's no-hit bid in the sixth inning, and outfielder Jackson Klein actually pitches fairly well when given a chance on the mound. A former temporary-contract player with Cotuit, Cam Sepede, who returned to the league as a late add for Wareham, pitches well in relief for the Gatemen. But that's about as good as things will get for the home team tonight.

Jordan Pearce singles to start the bottom of the ninth, but the team's old rally crab is off duty tonight. A Wareham reliever retires the next three batters in order. Cal Stevenson, one of the guys who was here on day one, makes the final out of the season.

Mike Roberts and his assistant coaches greet the Wareham staff by home plate, congratulating them on the season and wishing them luck in the playoffs. Stevenson leads the Kettleers to the mound, where they line up for handshakes with the Gatemen.

Host families and fans have already descended on the field as the Kettleers finish up, kids racing around the bases. The Kettleers gather in shallow left field for one last huddle. It's emotional for Roberts and the players. It always is, and it's even more so for Roberts this year. It was a tough summer, the first without his wife. "Every exit day, no matter when it is—even when you win—is very difficult if you've built family with these guys," Roberts says. "And my priority has always been to build family." The family may be growing by one today—his fourth grandchild is on the way. He's waiting to hear the news.

His baseball family was particularly important this summer. "This little village," Roberts says, "is a great place."

Roberts has few criticisms for his players despite their early ending and their playoff miss, saving it all for himself. The team struggled mightily in close games, and Roberts is a firm believer responsibility for that lies with the manager. "I did not do a great job this summer," he says. "The players did a great job."

There were success stories all around—the temps who earned full contracts, Quinn Brodey and his .326 average atop the order, growth for young players, confidence to take back to school.

A few players in addition to Greyson Jenista may be back next summer; the 2017 roster will start to take shape almost immediately. Most will not play on this field or for Roberts again. This time next year, some will be in pro ball.

Roberts leaves them with familiar messages—be positive, live with passion, help others. Baseball is secondary amid the big picture. His Kettleers heard a lot of the same words almost exactly two months ago, when they sat on the dugout bench in their college hats and warm-ups, a summer of possibilities—and a game of Wiffle ball—ahead of them. Under a still bright-blue sky, as they share hugs with teammates and coaches and send up one last Kettleers cheer, it all resonates.

◆ ◆ ◆

Shade stretches over home plate, the mound, the infield dirt, and most of the outfield grass. A bit of sun still catches the right-field foul pole, back where it all began this summer, on Mike Roberts's makeshift Wiffle-ball diamond.

The goodbyes are long. A few kids still want autographs. Roberts chats with every player and intern. Board members mingle on the field. On the pitcher's mound Colton Hock and Jackson Klein try their best to corral their brood of host brothers and sisters for a Lawson family photo.

In the middle of the scene there's a familiar pop of bright yellow. One of the Lawson kids grips the handle of a Wiffle-ball bat.

10 / EXTRA INNINGS

Sinsheimer Park sat quiet in the first week of August. The San Luis Obispo Blues played their last game of the season there July 27 and did not qualify for the California Collegiate League play-offs. Their players headed back to Western Carolina, UCLA, Texas Tech, and beyond.

Some teams at the National Baseball Congress World Series may have wanted to track those players down, maybe sign them to a late contract or at least ask a question that had grown increasingly important. How exactly does one beat the Santa Barbara Foresters?

The Blues were the last team to have an answer. On July 22 at Sinsheimer Park, the Blues scored two runs in the bottom of the seventh inning to break a 2–2 tie in a regular-season tilt with the Foresters. The bullpen followed with two scoreless innings of relief. The Foresters ended up stranding fourteen runners on the bases, with missed opportunities looming large, especially in the late innings.

As they settled in for the two-hour bus ride south to Santa Barbara, the Foresters knew what they were capable of but couldn't know they were about to live up to every bit of the promise. It would be their last quiet bus ride.

The Foresters won the next two in the three-game regular-season set with the Blues. Stranded runners were a thing of the past as they racked up a combined twenty runs in the two contests. Pitching dominated, with the Foresters winning 8–0 and 12–1. The second of those wins clinched the regular-season division title and provided a fitting end to an era. Late in the season the team announced it would be moving to a new home in 2017. Caesar Uyesaka Stadium, the Foresters' home turf for twenty-five years, saw one last win.

The Foresters kept rolling in the California Collegiate League playoffs, with their sixth consecutive victory securing the league championship on July 31. With the loss to the Blues as their only blemish, they won ten of their final eleven games.

The trip to Wichita and the NBC World Series included four days off. Teams would encounter a new format, with the tournament scrapping its old double-elimination bracket in favor of pool play.

Nothing—not the break or the format or their opponents—slowed the Foresters down. In their World Series opener, they blasted the Haysville Aviators of the Jayhawk League by a 9–0 score. Fresh off a postseason most valuable player performance in the California Collegiate League playoffs, Bret Boswell started his Wichita run with a home run and five runs batted in as part of a 2-for-4 night. Joe Moroney from the University of Kansas, a late addition to the roster as the Foresters tried to fill an injury gap, fit right in with a 3-for-3 performance in his debut. On the mound Boswell's Texas teammate Kyle Johnston was dominant, just as he had been in the opener of the league playoffs. This time he struck out seven in six scoreless innings and gave up just a pair of hits.

Game two was even better for Santa Barbara. Facing Sharp End Baseball of the CenTex Collegiate League, the Foresters mashed their way to a 13–1 win, blowing the game open with eight runs in the eighth inning. Boswell was at it again with two runs batted in. The Tulane duo of Hunter Williams and Lex Kaplan combined for five hits and four RBI. Hank LoForte, a Cal State–Fullerton standout who had become a key player for the Foresters as the summer progressed, went 4-for-4. After four solid innings from starter Matt Hartman of Arizona, five Santa Barbara relievers combined to shut out Sharp End the rest of the way.

Before their final game in pool play, the Foresters received some good news from back home. Boswell was named the California Collegiate League MVP, and Johnston was voted as the Pitcher of the Year. Williams, Kaplan, pitcher Connor Mayes, and pitcher Jackson Sigman earned spots on the all-league team.

Things couldn't have been going much better. But for that last game in the pool-play round, the Foresters had to line up against the only other team at the World Series that could truly call itself summer baseball royalty.

The Alaska Goldpanners of Fairbanks were playing pretty well in their own right. They beat Sharp End 10–1 in their World Series opener, pounding out thirteen hits. Isaiah Aluko went 2-for-5. Keaton Smith of Nevada, one of their hottest hitters down the stretch, went 3-for-3. Two days later the Goldpanners won a 10–9 thriller over Haysville, winning on a walk-off single by Austin Atwell in the bottom of the eleventh inning. Atwell finished with three RBI, while Aluko racked up five.

In the matchup with the Foresters, the Goldpanners struck first with a pair of runs in the first inning and one more in the second. Joe Fernandez, the Midnight Sun Game starting pitcher, didn't need any help from the twilight this time, striking out three in two scoreless innings.

The Foresters went to work against the Goldpanners bullpen, with Williams knocking a two-run single in the third inning to make it a one-run game. Boswell singled home the tying run in the fourth inning. After two scoreless innings each, the Foresters broke the tie in the seventh on another RBI single by Williams. The Goldpanners couldn't rally against the Santa Barbara bullpen, getting just two hits over the final five innings as the Foresters closed out a 4–3 victory.

Despite the loss, the Goldpanners still earned a ticket out of pool play, but their run ended in the quarterfinals with a 13–7 loss to the Hays Larks. Aluko had three more hits and a home run, finishing the tournament with seven hits and nine RBI, but the Goldpanners couldn't keep up in the slugfest.

The Foresters had no such trouble. Facing the Northwest Honkers, a barnstorming team from the Pacific International League, Santa Barbara romped to an 11–0 victory in the quarterfinals. Williams and Boswell both went deep, with Williams driving in four runs. Kaplan added three hits. The offense was more than enough for Connor Mayes. In his final start of the summer, the Texas right-hander lit up the radar gun and tossed six shutout innings with ten strikeouts. The win earned the Foresters a trip to the World Series semifinals for the fourteenth consecutive year.

The next game was the toughest of the tournament, maybe the toughest in those fourteen consecutive semifinal trips. The first semifinal matchup between the Hays Larks and the Kansas Stars ended up as a seventeen-inning game. With the championship set for the next day, the other semifinal had to be played whenever the marathon ended. The Foresters and the San Diego Force took the field after midnight Wichita time.

An early 4–0 deficit added to the tension for the Foresters, but they rallied with three runs in the fifth inning and tied the game in the eighth inning on an RBI double by Colby Barrick. Their own extra-inning marathon ensued, with the teams playing scoreless tenth and eleventh innings to keep it a 4–4 game.

San Diego scored two runs in the top of the twelfth inning, but the Foresters had one more comeback in them. Boswell singled home two runs to tie the game in the bottom of the twelfth, and Kaplan won it with a walk-off single to right field. As the Foresters celebrated their title-game berth, the clock read 4:26 a.m.

About thirteen hours later, the Foresters played for the NBC World Series championship and made sure there was a little less drama than their win in the wee hours. Kaplan stayed hot with an RBI single in the first inning, and the Foresters raced to a 4–0 lead after two innings. They added single runs in the fourth and seventh innings and let their pitching do the rest. Making his first start, Jacob Patterson of Texas Tech—a World Series reinforcement—went seven shutout innings. Reliever Cody Crouse of Florida International gave up two runs in the ninth but eventually closed the door. With two outs Williams scooped a ground ball at first base and flipped to Crouse for the final out.

The Foresters raced onto the field and leaped into a dog pile. Their twelfth consecutive win had yielded championship number six.

"These guys from the beginning of the year, they just worked so hard and cared for each other so much," manager Bill Pintard said in postgame interviews. "They genuinely loved each other. They were consistently unselfish. I knew in my heart that this team was going to do it."

The Foresters left Wichita with a new spot in the record books: a tie with the Alaska Goldpanners for the most championships in NBC World Series history.

◆ ◆ ◆

While the Goldpanners watched the Foresters claim part of their summer-ball throne, it was a strong season for the team in Fairbanks and outside the forty-ninth state's borders. In the return to their barnstorming roots, they finished with a 25-18 record. Their NBC showing was their best in Wichita in several years. They hope to be back next summer, chasing their first World Series crown since 2002.

Many stars emerged for the Goldpanners, ready to return to school and maintain an upward trajectory. Justin Harrer from Washington State tied for the team lead in batting average with a .357 mark and also stole fifteen bases. Kevin Connolly from Creighton hit .317 with five home runs. Alex Mascarenas, the former UCLA football player, hit .286. Joe Fernandez finished with a 2.75 earned run average and twenty-seven strikeouts in 19.2 innings.

No Goldpanner made his summer count more than Isaiah Aluko. He batted .357, hit four home runs, and stole fifteen bases. His eye-popping numbers at the NBC World Series caught some important eyes. On August 18, exactly one week after his three-hit performance in his final game for the Goldpanners, Aluko signed a Minor League free-agent contract with the Minnesota Twins. Scouts had watched him in Wichita. Aluko reported to rookie ball with the Gulf Coast League Twins the next day. He played his first game on August 22 and stayed hot with a home run in a 2-for-4 performance.

For the rest of the Goldpanners, it's back to school. For the team, it's on to next summer. The plan is to stick with the barnstorming approach and remain outside of the Alaska League. The board hopes to continue making improvements to Growden Park.

Sunset is still after nine o'clock in Fairbanks these days. Summer won't last long, but it will be back soon enough. The 2017 Midnight Sun Game is set for June 21 against the San Diego Waves. Tickets go on sale soon.

♦ ♦ ♦

As the calendar flipped to August, the Peninsula Pilots didn't slow down. Fully regrouped after their bad loss to Holly Springs, they finished the month of July with five consecutive wins and opened August with five more in a row for an even ten. Only a one-run loss to the Petersburg Generals in the regular-season finale stopped them from hitting the playoffs on an eleven-game winning streak. As it stood the Pilots finished with the best record in the Coastal Plain League—38-17—by a wide margin. They led the league in team batting average and earned run average.

The Petitt Cup Playoffs—named after league cofounder Jerry Petitt—began with a one-game, win-or-go-home division semifinal round. The Pilots beat the Morehead City Marlins 8–3. They trailed 3–1 after two innings but turned the game around with a seven-run sixth inning. Will Shepherd, the Liberty University star and the team's top hitter all summer, had a hit and two runs batted in. Nick Walker and Kyle Wrighte also drove in two. Pitchers Chris Gau and Devin Mahoney, the same combo that had a rough time in the big loss to Holly Springs, got it done this time. Gau allowed one earned run in three innings, and Mahoney tossed 5.2 scoreless innings of relief.

The same white-knuckle format endured in the division championship round as Peninsula hosted the Wilson Tobs in a one-game playoff. Again, the Pilots prevailed, scoring five runs in the middle innings and holding off the Tobs for three scoreless frames down the stretch. Shepherd had a quiet night, but Charlie Cody of the University of Virginia picked up the slack with three hits. Colin Nowak from the University of Southern Indiana earned the win with five solid innings, and the bullpen dominated.

The win earned the Pilots a trip to the best-of-three championship series. Their opponent would be the Savannah Bananas. The Coastal Plain League newcomers were the top team from the West Division and beat Asheboro in the semifinals before topping Forest City in the division title round.

While the Bananas are new on the scene—and the Pilots are anything but when it comes to the championship round—history had little bearing on the matchup. In game one of the title series at Grayson Stadium in Savannah, the Bananas rallied from an early 2–1 hole with three runs in the fifth inning and four in the sixth on their way to an 8–4 win.

Back at War Memorial Stadium in Hampton the next night— with 2,292 fans packed in—the Pilots scratched and clawed to stay alive. They took a 3–0 lead in the third inning, gave it up in the eighth as the Bananas tied the game, but pushed through to score the go-ahead run in the bottom of the eighth inning. James Madison University's Kyle McPherson did the honors with a solo home run. Michael Parmentier from Norfolk State pitched a scoreless ninth for the save.

After the rough start to the series, the Pilots had momentum and home field. Game three would also be at War Memorial Stadium the next night. And though it was a Tuesday and the temperature soared to ninety-five degrees, nothing could keep Pilots fans away. An announced crowd of 3,342 settled in for the winner-take-all championship game.

Unfortunately for the Pilots, they went home unhappy. With both teams running low on pitching, the game turned into a slugfest. The Bananas took a 6–0 lead in the second inning. The Pilots came back with four in the home half, but they would be chasing all night. A two-run rally in the eighth inning made it an 8–7 game and Mahoney did yeoman's work in relief, but the Bananas added an insurance run in the top of the ninth and set the Pilots down in order in their last at bats. In its first summer in the league, Savannah celebrated a championship.

It was an unusual feeling for the Pilots and their fans. They had won their last two championship appearances, in 2014 and 2013. They hadn't tasted defeat in the final round since Forest City swept them in 2009.

The summer was a memorable one all the same. Nine players batted over .300, as the Pilots lit up opposing pitching staffs all season. Mahoney, Gau, Devin Hemmerich, and others starred on the mound.

In postseason awards Shepherd was named the Coastal Plain League's Hitter of the Year. He finished with a .407 batting average, five home runs, and forty-seven runs batted in, adding sixteen stolen bases for good measure. He'll go down as an all-timer with the Pilots. In three summers in Hampton, he had a career batting average of .344 with thirteen home runs.

While the fans went home unhappy after the finale, those 3,342 will surely be back next summer.

◆ ◆ ◆

The Newport Gulls won New England Collegiate Baseball League championships in 2012 and 2014. Hoping to continue the even-year trend, they entered the 2016 postseason with five wins in their last seven games and earned home-field advantage for the best-of-three Southern Division semifinals.

Game one of the series on August 3 started with a bang as the Gulls surged to a six-run second inning at Cardines Field.

League batting champ Troy Dixon from St. John's had two hits, and Vanderbilt slugger Stephen Scott mashed his eleventh home run of the season. Middletown native Mark Powell started at designated hitter and chipped in a run batted in. The pitching staff, which improved steadily as the year went on, got eleven strikeouts in seven strong innings from NECBL veteran Hunter Schryver of Villanova.

The bats stayed hot the next day. Dixon went 3-for-3, Jake Brodt had three hits, and Chris Chatfield drove in four runs. But the Danbury Westerners had more offense and evened the series with a 10–8 win.

Back at Cardines Field for the decisive third game of the series—with 2,105 fans watching—the Gulls were shut out for four innings before rallying with two in the fifth, one in the sixth, and three in the seventh to take a 6–2 lead. Powell, moved up to second in the order, continued a solid playoff run with a hit and an RBI. The Westerners made a comeback push with three runs in the eighth, but the Gulls held them off, winning 6–5 for a spot in the Southern Division finals.

The Mystic Schooners, the Southern Division's regular-season champion, awaited, with a berth in the league championship series on the line. On the road in Connecticut, the Gulls took a 3–1 lead in the fourth inning of game one and made it a 5–2 game in the seventh, with Scott homering again, but the Schooners scored two runs in the seventh and three in the eighth to take their first lead. The Gulls couldn't score in the final two innings, as Mystic took a one-game lead.

Another big crowd of 1,976 greeted the teams at Cardines Field the next night, but the home team again fell victim to late-inning magic by the Schooners. The Gulls had regrouped after falling behind 2–0 in the first inning and had grabbed a 3–2 lead. But Mystic tied the game in the seventh and then exploded for four runs in the top of the ninth for a 7–3 advantage. Powell led off the bottom of the ninth with a walk, but a strikeout and a fielder's choice short-circuited comeback hopes. The Gulls eventually got runners to second and third, but Mystic ended the game with a strikeout.

The Schooners went on to beat the Sanford Mainers for their first NECBL championship. Gulls players headed home, many with a lot to build on. Scott was among the league leaders in home runs and RBI. Andrew Gist, the pitcher from the University of Georgia, led the league in strikeouts. Powell finished with a .177 batting average, one home run, and a memorable summer as part of his hometown team.

Dixon ended his surprise summer in Newport with a .394 batting average, a two-month heater that could have a huge impact on the trajectory of his baseball career. When NECBL postseason awards were announced in late August, Dixon was named the league's Most Valuable Player. Chuck Paiva was glad he called.

◆ ◆ ◆

The end of the summer was quieter in Washington DC and Kenosha, Wisconsin, with the Grays and the Kingfish both missing out on the playoffs.

In DC the work of expanding the team's community mission went on, even as summer drifted into fall. With so much interest in the RBI program, the Grays board decided to do all it could to keep players on the field. They're putting a 15U boys team into the city's Metro Fall League and softball teams into the Northern Virginia Girls Softball Association's fall circuit. In the winter the players will keep at it, with indoor training sessions every Friday night for softball and every Saturday morning for baseball. In the spring they'll pack the stands for a college tournament hosted by the Grays. Harvard, Lafayette, and Coppin State will be in town for the DC Grays College Classic.

Next year, by the time the summer Grays are on the field, their RBI brethren will feature nine teams for the in-house league. The board expects more than two hundred children to be signed up.

In Kenosha the long grind of a Northwoods League season finally came to an end on August 14. The Kingfish actually finished fairly well, winning three of their last four games, but their rough start was too much to overcome. Only four of nine teams in each Northwoods division qualify for the playoffs, and Kenosha's 26-46 record wasn't good enough. Home run–derby king Marty Bechina finished as the team's top hitter, closing with a .316 batting average and team bests of six home runs and forty-two RBI.

While the Kingfish missed out on postseason play, their Big Top Baseball brethren made a mark. The Wisconsin Rapids Rafters and Madison Mallards finished as the top two teams in the South Division. The Rafters advanced into the league championship series against the Eau Claire Express and their star Daulton Varsho. Varsho had two hits in the championship series, but the Rafters—the top team in the league all summer—prevailed. They won the opening game of the series 5–4 on a walk-off home run and blasted their way to an 11–4 win in game two.

The championship win happened on the road, but the organization staged a celebration the next day at Witter Field, inviting fans to join in. In the Northwoods League, they always show up.

◆ ◆ ◆

There was no more baseball for the Cotuit Kettleers after their season-finale loss on August 3, but their name was invoked anyway as the 2016 Cape Cod Baseball League playoffs hit a crescendo.

The Yarmouth-Dennis Red Sox were rolling again and bidding to become the first team to win more than two league championships in a row since the Cotuit dynasty of the mid-1970s. The Kettleers won their fourth in a row in 1975. That streak was part of a longer stretch of dominance that included seven championships in thirteen years, something else the Red Sox were within range of. If they could win the 2016 title, it would be their sixth in thirteen years.

The Red Sox entered the postseason as the No. 2 seed from the East Division, behind the pitching-rich Harwich Mariners and ahead of the Orleans Firebirds and Chatham Anglers. They hit the playoffs with three consecutive wins and tacked on two more right out of the gate with a sweep of a best-of-three series against Orleans. Cape Cod native Will Toffey from Vanderbilt homered in the second game, a 2–1 win.

Harwich loomed as the likely East Division finals opponent after bouncing back from a game-one loss to Chatham with a 13–1 win the night the Red Sox swept their series. But in game three, the upset-minded Anglers—who were under .500 in the regular season—pushed through for a 3–1 win.

The Red Sox got their own scare from Chatham in game one of the East Division finals but won a slugfest by a 9–8 score, stranding the bases loaded in the ninth inning to do it. From there it was smoother sailing, as they swept the series with a 4–2 win in game two and punched their ticket to the Cape League championship round.

In the title series Yarmouth-Dennis would face a team that was pretty hot in its own right. The Falmouth Commodores finished the regular season with the best record in the league and dispatched Hyannis and Bourne in sweeps to earn the championship series berth. It would be a rematch of the championship series from two years prior, when a really good Falmouth team couldn't overcome a relentless offense or the pitching of eventual first-round pick Walker Buehler.

This time the rivals staged a thrilling series. Falmouth won the opening game 5–4, as Lipscomb pitcher and league ERA champ Jeffrey Passantino picked up the win. But the Red Sox came back with a vengeance in game two, smacking fourteen hits, including three home runs, in a 9–4 victory. Toffey and Maryland star Kevin Smith—who had been red-hot in the playoffs—both went deep.

That set up a winner-take-all game three for the second year in a row in the championship series. The Red Sox had prevailed over Hyannis in 2015. This time they did it again, riding early offense and dominant pitching to a 3–0 win. Bryan Sammons, a lefty from

Western Carolina University who had pitched mostly out of the bullpen during the summer, delivered a tremendous clutch performance with six shutout innings. Smith led the offense with an RBI as the Red Sox played from the lead throughout. And reliever Calvin Faucher of UC Irvine notched his fourth save of the post-season to finish off the win.

The dynasty rolled on. Y-D had won three championships in four years not long before. Now the Red Sox had three titles in three years. As they posed for post-dog-pile photos, they held a handmade sign from the crowd that read "Y-D 3-PEAT."

Cotuit's record of four titles in a row would be safe for another year, but the way things were going for the Red Sox, maybe just that one year.

◆ ◆ ◆

The summer baseball season of 2016 wrapped up by mid-August with dog piles around the country. School and fall practices began soon after for the players, but the memories surely kept coming, along with the accolades.

Bret Boswell of the Santa Barbara Foresters and the Texas Longhorns added a national honor to his California Collegiate League MVP Award. Perfect Game, which covers college baseball online and runs showcase events for prospects, named Boswell its 2016 Perfect Game/Rawlings Summer Collegiate Player of the Year.

It was an easy choice. Boswell finished the summer hitting .392 with a .470 on-base percentage, a .715 slugging percentage, and a 1.185 on-base plus slugging. His performance in Wichita only helped matters.

In the article announcing the selection, Boswell credited his time in Santa Barbara—and his coach, Bill Pintard—for a lot of his success. "It helped being able to play for Bill and just relax out there," he told Perfect Game. "I just worked on keeping everything simple. That's what Bill preaches, being smooth and comfortable on the field." Like many who have come before, Boswell can count himself among the Pintard disciples.

Perfect Game's awards also included the Team of the Year honor to—who else?—the Yarmouth-Dennis Red Sox of the Cape League. The All-America teams included Northwoods League star Daulton Varsho, named the first-team catcher; pitchers Kyle Johnston and Connor Mayes of the Foresters; and Will Shepherd of the Peninsula Pilots. Quinn Brodey, the Cotuit center fielder who made huge strides under Mike Roberts, also earned a nod.

The top honor in the Cape League's postseason awards went to Ernie Clement of the Harwich Mariners and Virginia Cavaliers, who was named league MVP. Jeffrey Passantino continued Lipscomb's breakout summer with top pitcher honors, and teammate Michael Gigliotti was named the league's top pro prospect.

Brodey was the lone Cotuit Kettleer to earn a spot on the all-league team, but a few others saw their names on different lists, led by Colton Hock. The hard-throwing right-hander was picked as the Cape League's No. 4 prospect by MLB Pipeline. On Perfect Game's list, he ranked seventh.

The annual wrap-up of summer ball also included *Ballpark Digest*'s rankings of summer baseball attendance figures. Once again in 2016, the Madison Mallards of Big Top Baseball and the Northwoods League claimed the top spot, with a per-game average of 6,039 fans and a stunning season total of 205,324. The Kenosha Kingfish ranked sixth overall. For the first time in a long time, the NECBL's top draw was not the Newport Gulls, as the Valley Blue Sox's per-game average edged them out. The Peninsula Pilots ranked fourteenth.

◆ ◆ ◆

While their summer was short on victories, Cotuit's Stanford University trio didn't have the same problem back at school. In the spring of 2017 the Cardinal went 42-16 and earned a national seed in the NCAA Tournament, hosting a regional at Sunken Diamond in Palo Alto. It was their first regional appearance since 2014.

Colton Hock had a hand in more than half of the wins. After his stretched-out summer spent mostly in the starting rotation, Hock settled back into the bullpen for the Cardinal and had a record-breaking spring. He saved sixteen games, which set a new single-season school record. He finished tied for third nationally in saves. He also recorded six wins, giving him a win or a save in twenty-two of the team's forty-two victories. For the season he had a 2.08 earned run average with thirty-five strikeouts in 47.2 innings pitched. Accolades rolled in at the end of the season—selections to All-American Teams by *Collegiate Baseball News* and *Baseball America*, a spot as a finalist for the National Collegiate Baseball Writers Association Stopper of the Year Award, and a place on the all-conference team.

Teammates Quinn Brodey and Jackson Klein helped lead the offense. Brodey continued his summer emergence with a tremendous junior season. He batted .314—best on the team among regulars—and led the squad with eleven home runs and fifty-one runs batted in. Klein hit .293 with three home runs.

A solid summer in Cotuit also sparked spring success for Ross Achter. In his final season at the University of Toledo, Achter saved his best for last. Pitching in the weekend rotation, he led the Rockets in strikeouts with sixty and logged the best earned run average on the team among starting pitchers. He earned All-Mid-American Conference second-team honors for the second year in a row.

Patrick Dorrian knew his lessons learned at the plate in Cotuit would help him down the line, and it didn't take long to see results. Beginning his career at Division II Lynn University in Florida as a junior-college transfer, Dorrian delivered a sensational debut. He batted .372 with nine homers and forty-three runs batted in on his way to second-team all-conference honors.

With confidence gained from his full summer on Cape Cod, David Gerics reached a new career high in strikeouts in his final season with Pomona-Pitzer. He led the team with eighty-six, while also leading in innings pitched with ninety-five as he emerged as a workhorse in the starting rotation. He finished with a 4.17 earned run average.

Fresh off his Most Valuable Player Award in the New England Collegiate Baseball League, Troy Dixon never cooled off in his return to St. John's. He batted .394 with a .473 on-base percentage and swatted three home runs. He earned a spot on the All-Big East Conference first team and was a semifinalist for the Johnny Bench Award, which is given annually to the nation's best catcher. His success helped lead the Red Storm to forty-two wins, one shy of the program record. They earned an at-large bid to the NCAA Tournament and played in the Clemson Regional. Dixon went 2-for-3 in his final collegiate game.

Dixon had some company on the Johnny Bench Award list. Ben Breazeale, who hit .232 with the Gulls, had a breakout senior season at Wake Forest, hitting .333 with eleven homers against some of the nation's top competition in the Atlantic Coast Conference. He was named an All-America selection by three publications.

After his summer with the Gulls, Middletown native Mark Powell made a late move from Bucknell to the College of Saint Rose, a Division II school in the Northeast-10 Conference. He started forty games in his senior season, batting .236 with two home runs and nineteen runs batted in.

The Texas Longhorns were spring beneficiaries of Santa Barbara's national championship run. Summer Player of the Year Bret Boswell cooled down a bit, but still managed to hit .273, good for third on the team. He finished second on the team with seven home runs. Pitcher Kyle Johnston finished his season with a 3.56 earned run average, while teammate Connor Mayes was at 6.00.

Hunter Williams kept mashing in his senior season at Tulane, launching a career-high eleven home runs to go with a team-best .357 batting average. Lex Kaplan chipped in nine home runs and batted .302, though he did not run wild like he was wont to do in Santa Barbara, stealing just three bases.

A part-time Santa Barbara Forester had perhaps the best season of any 2016 alumni. Keston Hiura, who had a cameo with the team before joining Team USA, returned to UC Irvine and won the national batting title with a .442 average. He also led the country with a .567 on-base percentage. The Big West Conference Player of the Year and a Golden Spikes Award semifinalist, Hiura was a consensus All-American and was projected as one of the top collegiate hitters on the board for the 2017 Major League Baseball Draft.

DC Grays alum Marques Inman was in the midst of the breakout he was hoping for when he started his sophomore season at West Virginia with twenty hits—including two home runs—in his first sixteen games. But a leg injury cost him the rest of his season, and he took a medical redshirt, set to return in the spring of 2018. Outfielder Lamar Briggs shone in his return to Jackson State, hitting .356 and stealing fourteen bases. He was set to play another summer with the Grays in 2017.

Peninsula Pilots star Will Shepherd closed out his career at Liberty University with four homers and a .257 average in his senior season. Pitcher Chris Gau struck out nearly a batter an inning in his second year at Jacksonville University and was headed to play for the Harwich Mariners of the Cape Cod Baseball League in the summer of 2017.

While they didn't hit any more home runs into a body of water, Marty Bechina, Griffin Conine, and Daulton Varsho all hit a lot of them in their return to school. After his summer with the Kenosha Kingfish, Bechina launched seven home runs for Michigan State while hitting .263. Conine delivered a breakout season at Duke with thirteen homers. And Varsho just kept hitting, turning in a .362 batting average with eleven home runs in his junior season at Wisconsin-Milwaukee. With rankings projecting him as one of the top available catchers in the draft, his junior year would be his last.

◆ ◆ ◆

The Minnesota Twins selected Royce Lewis, a high school short-stop from California, with the No. 1 pick in the 2017 Major League Baseball First-Year Player Draft. Another high school star, Hunter Greene, went 2nd to the Cincinnati Reds. A third, MacKenzie Gore, was drafted by the San Diego Padres.

Then came the biggest names from the college ranks, many of whom plied their trade on summer-ball diamonds. Louisville two-way star Brendan McKay—a former Bourne Brave in the Cape League and a Team USA standout—went 4th overall to Tampa Bay. Former Harwich Mariner Pavin Smith went 7th to the Arizona Diamondbacks. And Keston Hiura, almost exactly a year after his brief cameo with the Santa Barbara Foresters, was selected 9th overall by the Milwaukee Brewers.

The first Cotuit Kettleer off the board came later in the first round, as Vanderbilt's Jeren Kendall went to the Los Angeles Dodgers with the 23rd pick. After his strong summer in 2015 and his short stay at Lowell Park in 2016, Kendall impressed with Team USA and then hit fifteen home runs and stole twenty bases for Vanderbilt in the spring.

Northwoods League slugger Daulton Varsho was drafted in the supplemental second round, with the 68th overall pick, by the Arizona Diamondbacks. He was the first collegiate catcher to come off the board.

Quinn Brodey's remarkable rise continued when the New York Mets picked him in the second round, making him the highest draft pick among regulars in the 2016 Cotuit lineup. He signed a contract two weeks later.

Colton Hock's name was called soon after. The Miami Marlins chose him in the fourth round, with the 119th overall pick. He shaped up as a potential steal at that point in the draft, with the only question mark a familiar one—would he be a starter or a reliever at the next level?

One pick after Hock, Cape League top-prospect award winner Michael Gigliotti of Lipscomb and the Falmouth Commodores was selected by the Kansas City Royals. League MVP Ernie Clement went a few picks after that, to the Cleveland Indians.

Sixteen more Cotuit alumni were selected over the course of the forty-round draft, including catcher Tim Susnara, pitcher Josh Roberson, Stanford outfielder Jackson Klein, and former temporary players Tanner Nishioka and Ricky Surum. Ross Achter was not drafted, nor was Patrick Dorrian, who would return for his senior year at Lynn University. The Cape League had a total of 253 former players selected, the third consecutive year with at least 250.

NECBL MVP Troy Dixon got his shot to stay hot in pro ball when the Seattle Mariners selected him in the twentieth round. His Gulls teammate Ben Breazeale went in the seventh round to the Baltimore Orioles.

A year after getting selected in the fortieth round and returning to school, Bret Boswell parlayed his big summer in Santa Barbara to move up thirty-two rounds; the Colorado Rockies selected him in the eighth round. His teammate Kyle Johnston went even earlier, going in the sixth round to the Washington Nationals. Connor Mayes was drafted in the twenty-fourth round by the Kansas City Royals. The Tulane duo of Lex Kaplan and Hunter Williams did not hear their names called.

Neither did David Gerics. He had been waiting for a call. The Mets had shown a lot of interest, but forty rounds came and went. Like his time in Cotuit, though, it wasn't over yet. Just over a month after the draft, the Minnesota Twins offered a Gerics a free-agent contract. He was on his way to play in an independent league when the contract offer came in. These things always seemed to happen when he was driving, though he didn't get a ticket this time. Gerics turned around and got ready to hop on a plane.

The contract wouldn't be for much money and the road would be long, but it would be a chance, the one he'd been chasing. He signed on July 20.

◆ ◆ ◆

A year after hinting at his potential, Greyson Jenista returned to the Cotuit Kettleers and batted leadoff in the first game of the 2017 season. He knocked the fourth pitch he saw for a base hit, a fitting way for the page to turn on Cotuit's rough 2016 summer.

Jenista went 2-for-5 at the plate, and the Kettleers won their season opener 5–3 over the Bourne Braves. They followed with a 10–0 blowout of Falmouth and then swept a doubleheader with the Brewster Whitecaps. It was just the kind of start they needed and a reminder that every summer can be vastly different from the one that came before.

Joining Jenista in the Cotuit lineup on opening night was Griffin Conine, the former Northwoods League standout. He also had two hits—including a triple—in the season opener as he began what shaped up as a crucial summer. In nearby Falmouth home run–derby champ Marty Bechina hooked on with the Commodores as a temporary player. He homered in his first game, part of a 3-for-4 night. Former Newport Gull Stephen Scott suited up for the Orleans Firebirds.

Jenista and Conine went on to star all season for the Kettleers, both earning all-star honors. On a late-season afternoon at Lowell Park, Cape League officials pulled into the parking lot with a lot of hardware in tow. Jenista was presented with the league MVP Award, and Conine was honored as the top pro prospect.

Bechina stuck around all season in Falmouth and finished the summer with eight home runs, good for second in the league. Scott led the league in runs batted in. New stars emerged as well, with North Carolina pitcher Tyler Baum leading the league in wins, strikeouts, and earned run average. Jenista's Wichita State teammate Alec Bohm batted .351 with eight home runs for Falmouth, giving the Shockers two likely first-round picks for the 2018 draft.

The Kettleers finished in second place in the West Division behind Falmouth, closing with a 22-21-1 record. Back in the playoffs, they suffered an early exit when the third-seeded Bourne Braves got hot for two straight wins and a sweep of the West semifinals.

The Orleans Firebirds and Yarmouth-Dennis Red Sox led the East with the two best records in the league, but neither made the finals. The upstart Brewster Whitecaps knocked off both of them in thrilling three-game series and then did the same to Bourne in the championship round, winning the franchise's first title since 2000.

The Newport Gulls and Ocean State Waves started new seasons with familiar scripts in the New England Collegiate Baseball League. The Gulls lost their first two games while waiting for reinforcements. The Waves, with most of their team in town at the starting line, won ten of their first eleven games, continuing to establish themselves as a new power in the league's Southern Division. By midseason they would go on to earn a No. 1 national ranking.

This time the early trends persisted. The Gulls never quite found a groove and finished with a sub-.500 record for the first time since their move to Newport. Across the bay the Waves stayed hot all season, winning a franchise-record thirty-one games and advancing to the NECBL championship series. The Valley Blue Sox stopped the ride there, sweeping to the league championship.

The Alaska Goldpanners got off to a strong start in their second go-round as a barnstorming squad, winning nine of their first twelve games in the summer of 2017. But for the first time since 2007, they ended up on the wrong end of the scoreboard in the Midnight Sun Game. The San Diego Waves scored early and held the Goldpanners down in a 4–2 win. On the bright side—the true bright side—the weather was perfect, and a crowd of 3,531 filled Growden Park.

Losses are rare for the Goldpanners in the Midnight Sun Game, and, for this team, losses of any kind were rare. They finished 29-9, one of their best seasons in recent memory, though they did not make the trip to the NBC World Series.

The defending national champion Santa Barbara Foresters christened their new home field on June 9 with a 7–4 victory over the Orange County Riptide. And soon enough Pershing Park in Santa Barbara—a long-toss throw from Santa Barbara Harbor and the deep-blue Pacific—had a signature moment. On June 18, in the eleventh game of the season, the Foresters beat the Academy Barons 3–1 to give manager Bill Pintard his 900th career victory. It was a typical Pintard performance, full of good pitching, good defense, and timely hitting. After the final out the team doused him with water bottles.

Win number 901 came two days later, and the Foresters would get Pintard to 905 before another loss. The team again shaped up as a strong one, and more victories followed, with the Foresters finishing regular-season play at 30-12. The annual trip to Wichita and the NBC World Series began with three more wins. Returning Forester Hank LoForte from Cal State–Fullerton was among the hottest hitters, and a new star, Texas Tech's Joshua Jung, brought the power. The wins advanced the Foresters out of pool play, but for the first time in more than decade, the single-elimination portion of the tournament was unkind to the champs. Santa Barbara lost its quarterfinal game by a 6–3 score to the Everett Merchants. The Foresters' bid for a record seventh NBC World Series championship would have to wait another year. The Kansas Stars—a team of former Major League Baseball players who made their debut in the tournament in 2016—won the 2017 championship.

The Kenosha Kingfish improved on their 2016 record but remained outside the top tier in the 2017 Northwoods League season. The reigning champion Wisconsin Rapids Rafters were again the top team in the league through the regular season, but they were ousted in the playoffs. The St. Cloud Rox of Minnesota beat Michigan's Battle Creek Bombers to win the league championship.

As usual the Madison Mallards led the nation in attendance, seeing a slight uptick from their 2016 numbers and again drawing more than 200,000 fans. The Kingfish ranked sixth nationally and third in the Northwoods League.

The DC Grays struggled in the win-loss column for the second straight year in 2017, dropping their last five games to finish 13-27. It wasn't for lack of trying from returning outfielder Lamar Briggs.

The Jackson State standout batted an even .400 in his second turn with the Grays, ranking second in the league. He was named a first-team all-league selection.

There were no struggles off the field. The RBI program grew as expected, and community clinics remained a hit. In their second foray into the RBI regional tournament, the 15U team went 2-2 and the 18U squad went 1-3.

After their runner-up finish in 2016, the Peninsula Pilots finished the 2017 regular season in first place in the Coastal Plain League's East Division standings. Their pitching staff ranked as the second best in the league by earned run average, though the offense was more middle of the road. Four straight wins to close the regular season vaulted them to the No. 1 seed for the postseason.

The one-game playoff in the East semifinal provided a roadblock. The Edenton Steamers scored three runs in the top of the ninth inning to take a 6–3 lead and held the Pilots to two in the bottom half, stranding the winning run on base for a 6–5 victory. The Wilmington Sharks beat Edenton in the East finals before falling to the Gastonia Grizzlies in the championship series.

The Pilots ranked sixteenth in the nation in attendance, with an average of 1,761 fans a night packing into War Memorial Stadium.

◆ ◆ ◆

Professional careers began quickly for players who were drafted or signed, usually just a month or two after their collegiate careers ended.

Troy Dixon headed west to join the Everett Aqua Sox of the Class A Northwest League. Almost a year to the day after he made his Newport Gulls debut, he got his first professional action and had two hits in each of his first two games. Daulton Varsho was also bound for the Northwest League. He hit a home run in his sixth game with the Hillsboro Hops. Bret Boswell headed there, too, and smacked eleven home runs in fifty-four games with the Boise Hawks.

First-round pick Keston Hiura was dispatched to the rookie-level Arizona League. With at least one hit—and often two or three—in fourteen of his first fifteen games, he was quickly promoted.

Former Cotuit Kettleer Quinn Brodey headed back to the Northeast to join the Brooklyn Cyclones of the Class A New York Penn League. He homered twice and batted .257 in his debut season.

Colton Hock and David Gerics both found themselves in the Gulf Coast League. Hock made his debut on July 10 with a scoreless inning of relief. Gerics opened his pro career a month later, striking out two in an inning of relief.

No word on whether they staged a little Wiffle-ball game before their seasons began.